LUCINDA'S PARTY FOODS

Lucinda's
PARTY FOODS

By Lucinda Christenson Larsen

A Reprint of the Original

Favorite Recipes Press , Inc. ©MCMLXVI

Post Office Box 18324

Louisville, Kentucky 40218

The Caxton Printers , Ltd.
Caldwell , Idaho
MCMLX

Library of Congress Catalog Card Number 58-13074

THEY ARE NEVER TOO YOUNG

Mrs. Larsen and three of her grandchildren, Sherry Marie, Linda Susan, and Cindie Lu.

I dedicate this book
to my fond and patient husband,
Al,
and to my four wonderful sons
and their lovely wives.

Preface

Having had thirty-five years of experience in preparing foods, especially pastries and candies of all kinds, also in teaching classes, giving demonstrations and serving the public in making wedding cakes, I followed the advice of my many friends and wrote this book. I have compiled select recipes in step-by-step sequence so that even the newest cook might follow the instructions given easily and accurately.

The contents of this book on Party Foods consists of cakes of all kinds and frostings, both plain and decorative, for beginners and advanced decorators; every type of candies, both homemade and commercial—hard candies, creams and chocolate dipped; complete instructions on procedures and the art of chocolate dipping. Also included are plain and fancy cookies, rolls, sweet rolls, coffeecakes, doughnuts, pastries, pies, frozen desserts, puddings and Danish pastries. Complete instructions on all types of cake decorating with picture guides. Novelties such as merry-go-round cakes, gingerbread dolls and houses, decorated candy Easter eggs, and sugar lumps. The cake decorating instructions are my original ideas and may be followed easily. The illustrations shown are of my own work.

The recipes are very choice, mostly original; some are gifts, and all have been tested and revised.

I wish to acknowledge my gratitude and thanks to those who have given their recipes to me to be used in this book; I also would like to thank my very good friend Dr. King Hendricks, head of the English Department of the Utah State University, for kindness and advice in the compilation of this book.

LUCINDA C. LARSEN
Logan, Utah

Contents

LUCINDA'S PARTY FOODS

Let's Bake a Cake

Let's give ourselves "that special lift" achieved only through the satisfaction we get in the creation of a lovely homemade cake.

We chuckle at the saying "If I'd a knowed you were comin', I'd a baked a cake." How often we wish we could produce a light, fluffy homemade cake when that unexpected visitor arrives. But no need for such an excuse to have a lovely cake on hand. Nothing can give us that special lift as does the satisfaction of creating a tempting homemade cake.

Too many homemakers are deprived of the glorious feeling of accomplishment in our modern, fast-moving world because they dislike the cleaning up after cake mixing or feel they don't have the time to engage in this most pleasant of culinary arts. Accordingly, they reach for a package of ready-mix cake or rush to the neighborhood store for the completed product. But for that occasional "ego booster" we all need, nothing can surpass the joy of turning out a beautiful, moist, fine-grained cake.

To be an excellent cake baker, you must follow simple mixing, measuring, and baking rules. You may be an amateur cook and quickly become an expert cake baker.

A delicious-tasting cake, delicate in texture, frosted neatly, is a good cook's crowning glory.

Choose the type of cake preferred, assemble the equipment and the ingredients needed, and have your working space in order.

Simply follow a few rules: accurate measurements, proper method of mixing ingredients, using only the best materials available, and properly baking the product.

There are really only two different kinds of cakes, cakes containing shortening and those which rely on the egg whites for leavening as Angel Food and Sponge cakes. We also have cream cakes, both sweet and sour, using cream for shortening.

Within each group of these cakes we have a great many variations. Butter cakes, commonly called plain cakes, are the most common. The most popular cake in the other group is the Angel Food cake. A new but popular variation is the Chiffon cake and this is really a combination of both methods or kinds of cake as it contains shortening and also the egg whites for leavening. The Chocolate, Mahogany Fudge, or Devil Food cakes are all varieties of the cakes containing shortening.

Then we have the ever-loved Fruit cakes, so popular for festive occasions and made in so many varieties—dark and light, boiled method and uncooked style. And there are always the delightful coffeecakes made in so many different textures and types.

It is wise to assemble all equipment necessary before beginning the actual measuring or mixing. Place out all ingredients needed and allow them to become room temperature.

Standard measuring spoons and cups should be used. Cups of graduated sizes are preferred. The aluminum and Pyrex glass baking pans are the favorites and should be greased and lightly floured.

The flour to be used should be sifted and then measured. A convenient way is to sift the flour onto an aluminum or paper plate, bent so as to allow the flour to pour out easily, thus avoiding spilled flour on your working space. This makes it much easier to pour into your mixing bowl without spilling.

When measuring the flour, spoon it carefully into the measuring cup, scraping the top with a spatula. Resift with baking powder, salt, or other leavening agents.

INGREDIENTS AND MIXING

Use only the best material for cake making. The shortening may be butter, margarine or commercial vegetable shortening or oils and should be creamed with sugar to a fluffy, light stage—the texture of whipped cream. If using the conventional method or in the "quick-cake method" the shortening may be added directly to the flour. It is well to have the sugar completely dissolved to make a fine-grained, smooth-textured, and moist cake. Choose fine granulated sugar unless recipe states otherwise. When using brown sugar, pack it firmly into the cup when measuring.

There are various kinds of baking powders, and they

react differently. Choose the one best suited for your recipes. You should also keep in mind that the amount of leavening agents varies with the altitude.

I recommend double-acting baking powders to be used in all recipes calling for baking powder in this book.

Cake flours are best for cakes because they are milled finer and are higher in starches, thus more adapted for cake making.

There are some recipes that call for all-purpose flour, in this case it may be used safely.

In adding the eggs, follow the instructions in the recipe closely. Some recipes require the eggs to be added one at a time; some require eggs to be lightly beaten or added separately; in either case follow instructions given.

For perfect blending of flavorings add them to the creamed mixtures or to the liquids. Most recipes still say to add the flavoring to the finished cake just before pouring it into the pan, which is acceptable.

All dry ingredients should be added alternately with the liquids beginning and ending with the flour mixture. There are exceptions when a one-bowl cake, commonly called quick-method, is made.

If beating cakes with a mixer, start on low speed and do not overbeat.

If beating by hand, always beat in the same direction after each addition of flour and liquid. You will find that this gives a finer texture.

Care should be taken in mixing especially not to overmix. This causes the cake to have a solid texture which is un-desirable, also, undermixing makes a coarse-grained cake having a tendency to dry out quickly.

When adding egg whites, beat them until they hold in peaks but are not too dry. They should be folded carefully into the batter, quickly and lightly to keep the air in the beaten egg whites.

BAKING THE CAKE

Pour the batter lightly into greased and floured pans, avoid filling too full, allow space for rising, spread the batter lightly with a rubber spatula beginning in the center and spreading to the edge of the pan. When baking more than one layer, measure batter evenly so the layers will be uniform in size. Place the pans on the oven rack so they do not touch, allowing air in the oven to reach each layer. Cake may be baked on both racks at the same time.

Preheat the oven before putting cake in to bake, set the timer if you have one and, if not, it is well to place a small clock on the oven to serve as a reminder for the time needed for baking the cake.

Better results will be obtained if oven isn't opened during the baking time; opening of the oven door allows the heat to escape and the cake will bake unevenly on the top and require a longer period to bake. Too slow an oven will cause the cake to rise and then fall, and the results will be a heavy, coarse cake. Too hot an oven causes the cake to cook too fast on the sides and forms a crust. Then, when the heat reaches the center, the moisture expands causing the cake surface to burst and giving a cracked appearance in the center and a bump on the top.

When removing the cake from the oven, allow it to stand on a rack for several minutes in the pan, then turn it over on another rack. This allows the cake to leave the pan freely and will avoid breaking. The layers should be allowed to cool before frosting. Frosting the cake while warm will give a soggy appearance and taste and will allow the layers to slide apart.

All recipes in this book are tested for high elevation and should be adjusted when used in lower elevations.

The abbreviations used in these recipes are as follows:

tbs.—tablespoon

ts.—teaspoon

lbs.—pounds

pkg.—package

c.—cups

and all recipes call for level measurements.

Light Cakes

BANANA CAKE

This is a moist and very tasty cake. It has good keeping qualities and is one you will enjoy making.

1. Cream together until light
    ½ c. shortening
    1⅓ c. sugar
2. Sift together
    2 c. cake flour
    1 ts. baking powder
    1 ts. soda
    ¾ ts. salt
3. Beat lightly
    2 eggs
4. Mash soft, ripe bananas to fill
    1 c.
5. Add beaten eggs to sugar and shortening then add
    1 ts. vanilla
6. Mix alternately with first mixtures
    ½ c. buttermilk
    ¼ c. milk (mix until free of lumps)
7. Add mashed bananas last.
    Bake in two 8-inch layers at 375° until firm.

CAKE FILLING

1. Mix in a pan
    2 c. sugar
    4½ tbs. flour
2. Peel and cut in pieces
    2 oranges and add
    ½ c. crushed pineapple
3. Mix two mixtures together and cook until thick.
4. Add 1 pkg. of coconut and cook 3 min. more.
    When cool spread on cake between layers. Then frost with favorite frosting.

ORANGE BLOSSOM WEDDING CAKE

1. Sift together and place in mixing bowl
     2½ c. sifted cake flour
     1½ c. sugar
     2 ts. baking powder
     1 ts. salt
2. Add in order
     ½ c. cooking oil
     5 egg yolks
     ¾ c. orange juice
     2 tbs. orange rind, grated fine
3. Combine mixtures carefully and beat slowly for 3 minutes.
4. Beat
     5 egg whites and
     ½ ts. cream of tartar until they form very stiff peaks and are partially dry, much stiffer than for angel food cakes.
     Gently fold beaten egg whites into first mixtures, using a wooden paddle or rubber scraper. Pour into ungreased tube pan, large size. Bake at 325° for 65 minutes. Invert until cool. Frost with:

ORANGE FLUFF FROSTING

1. Place in double boiler
     1½ c. sugar
     2 egg whites
     5 tbs. orange juice
     ⅛ ts. salt, stir with beater until sugar is dissolved.
2. Place over boiling water, beating continually and cook for seven minutes, or until frosting stands up in peaks. Remove from heat and add 1 ts. almond flavoring and beat until thick enough to spread on cake. A drop of orange frosting color or paste may be added if desired.

HEARTS AND FLOWERS WEDDING CAKE

Adapted for weddings and announcement parties, etc., this may be increased to larger amounts if desired.

1. Sift once and measure
      2⅔ c. flour then sift with
      3 ts. baking powder
      1 ts. salt
2. Cream until light and fluffy
      ⅔ c. shortening
      1¼ c. sugar
3. Add flour to shortening and sugar alternately with
      1 c. milk
      1 ts. fruit flavoring
      1 ts. finely grated lemon rind
4. Beat until foamy
      3 egg whites and add
      ¼ c. sugar and continue beating until soft peaks are
      formed, then fold carefully into cake batter.
5. Pour into 2 large heart-shaped pans and bake for 30
    minutes or more until cake is firm on top when touched
    with finger. Remove from oven and place on rack to cool.

DECORATING TIP

1. Outline a large heart in the center of cake.
2. With Royal Icing (found in frosting recipes) spread
    evenly over the inside heart.
3. Then with seven minute frosting, cover the rest of the
    top of cake and the sides and sprinkle with soft white
    coconut. Then fill a paper cone with a decorating frost-
    ing of your choice and outline the edges of the center
    heart, also around the outside edge and around the
    bottom of cake with a pretty edging. With a writing
    tube of frosting, write the names desired in the center
    of the heart.
    If you desire a colored cake, the coconut may be tinted
    by adding one or two drops food coloring in a spoonful
    of water, sprinkling over the coconut and lifting lightly
    with a fork until color is well mixed, then sprinkle on
    top and sides of the cake. This cake also may be deco-
    rated with flowers and buds, if desired.

*   *   *   *

This recipe may be made also in a large wedding cake
and decorated with tiny hearts and flowers as shown in
the picture, very appropriate for a Valentine wedding.

SURPRISE CAKE

This cake is especially good for afternoon snacks.

1. Beat until creamy
    ¼ c. shortening
    ½ c. sugar
    3 egg yolks
2. Then sift
    1 c. flour
    1 ts. baking powder
3. Combine above mixtures with
    6 tbs. milk and before baking spread with the follow-
    ing topping.

TOPPING

1. Beat
    4 egg whites and
    1 c. sugar
    Spread on top of cake dough, sprinkle with chopped
    nuts and bake at 350° for 25 minutes. Remove from
    oven and cool.

FILLING

1. Cook in saucepan
    1 egg yolk
    1 c. milk
    ½ c. sugar
    1½ ts. cornstarch
    1 ts. vanilla
    Stirring carefully so it won't stick, cook for 5 min-
    utes. Cool. Then spread between the layers.

LADY BALTIMORE CAKE

This is an old stand-by recipe, but one that will never
grow old. It is a favorite among many cake lovers.

1. Sift together three times
    3 c. cake flour
    ½ ts. salt
    3 ts. baking powder

2. Cream until light
    ½ c. shortening
    1½ c. sugar
3. Add altogether alternately with
    1¼ c. milk
    1 ts. vanilla. Beat until smooth.
4. Add and fold gently
    4 stiffly beaten egg whites
5. Bake in two 9-inch pans at 350° for 25 to 30 minutes.
6. Cool on rack and then spread freely with the following filling:

LADY BALTIMORE FILLING

1. In a double boiler scald
    2 c. milk
    2 tbs. butter
    1 c. sugar
2. Make a thickening by using
    3 tbs. cornstarch or potato flour
    ½ c. milk
3. Slowly pour into the scalded milk and cook for several minutes.
4. Add
    2 beaten egg yolks. Stir well.
5. Add
    1 ts. vanilla and then remove from heat and cool before spreading between the layers of cake.

LADY BALTIMORE FROSTING

1. In the double boiler put
    2 egg whites
    1½ c. sugar
    5 ts. water
    1½ ts. white syrup. Mix well.
2. Continue beating with a beater all the while you are cooking this frosting, this usually takes from 7 to 10 minutes.
3. Remove from hot water and continue beating; add
    ¾ tbs. rose water which may be obtained from the drug store.

4. Spread in fluffy twirls on sides and over the top of cake. Press the spatula deep into the frosting and then quickly pull it upward in an oval motion, raising the frosting in round peaks. This really gives eye appeal to the finished product.

BRIDE'S CAKE

Unusually good for weddings or parties, this recipe may be doubled or tripled.

1. Cream well
    ½ c. shortening
    1 c. sugar
2. Sift three or four times
    2 c. cake flour
    ½ c. cornstarch
    2 ts. baking powder
3. Add
    1 c. milk alternately with the flour and cream mixture. Beat until smooth.
4. Fold in
    7 beaten egg whites and
    1 ts. fruit or almond flavoring
5. Pour into well greased and floured pans. Bake at 350° for 40 minutes. Frost with wedding cake frosting (see chapter on frostings).

FLUFFY WHITE CAKE

1. Sift
    2½ c. cake flour
    ¼ ts. salt
    2 ts. baking powder
2. Cream
    ½ c. shortening
    1¼ c. sugar
    2 tbs. milk
    1 ts. flavoring
3. Beating carefully, add the flour to the creamed mixture alternately with
    ½ c. milk
    ½ c. water beginning and ending with flour

4. Beat
  4 egg whites until stiff. Fold in gently.
5. Bake in a loaf or sheet pan at 350° for 20 minutes or longer.

BONBON CAKE

This cake received its name for its candy-like flavor. It's unusually good and easy to make.

1. Cream until light
  ½ c. butter
  1½ c. sugar
  4 egg yolks
  1 ts. vanilla
2. Melt
  2 squares bitter chocolate in
  5 tbs. boiling water
3. Sift together
  1¾ c. cake flour
  2 ts. baking powder
  ½ ts. salt
4. Beat the flour and creamed mixture together alternately with
  ½ c. milk, then stir in the melted chocolate.
5. Beat until frothy
  4 egg whites and fold into mixture last.
6. Bake in 7-inch layer pans for 30 minutes at 350°. Cool and spread the following filling between the layers:

FILLING

1. Cook over boiling water until it holds in peaks, beating continually,
  1 c. sugar
  6 tbs. water
  1½ ts. corn syrup
  ⅛ ts. salt
  1 egg white
2. Some filling may be saved to dot on top of frosted cake.

FROSTING

1.   Cook slowly, stirring all the time,
         2 c. sugar
         $3/4$ c. cream or canned milk
         2 squares of bitter chocolate
         2 tbs. corn syrup
         $1/4$ ts. salt
2.   Remove from heat and add
         2 tbs. butter
3.   Cool until lukewarm, and add
         1 ts. vanilla
4.   Beat slowly until thick enough to spread on cake. Frost generously and use remaining filling to dot here and there over the top of frosted cake.

PARTY MARBLE CAKE (IN VARIATIONS)

A marble cake is such fun and looks so enticing. It can be made in varied colors and flavors.

Try your skill in arranging the batter so that it has a marble effect. Begin by spooning out the white batter, 1 inch apart, in rows to cover the baking tin. Have the remaining batter colored as desired and drop in between white batter until pan is covered. Use a table knife and cut through the batter in a rolling motion to blend the colors together.

When making large loaf cakes, you may repeat the first process to fill the pan, but reverse the colors, such as chocolate on top of white, pink on chocolate, etc.

Frosting may be blended in colors, also. Colors may extend into three or more shades in one cake, with each color flavored differently.

1.   Sift
         2 c. cake flour
         1 ts. soda
         $1/2$ ts. salt
2.   Combine
         $1/4$ c. vinegar
         $1/2$ c. milk
         1 ts. vanilla

3.   Beat until creamy
        2 eggs and
        1⅓ c. sugar
4.   Melt
        ½ c. shortening
5.   Mix altogether, using only half the liquid, beat for 3
     minutes, then scrape the sides of the bowl. Add the rest
     of the liquid and beat again.
6.   Drop the batter by spoonfuls on the greased, flat baking
     tin.
7.   Stir cooled chocolate into the remaining batter and spoon
     in between the drops of white batter, now cut through
     the batter with a knife to produce the marble effect.
8.   Bake in 350° oven for 25 minutes.

CANDY AND CAKE "CAKE"

You will enjoy this unusual cake. It's so interesting to
make and has such a fine flavor and texture.
1.   Boil to 232° using the candy-making instructions
        1¼ c. sugar
        ½ c. water
2.   Beat until stiff and firm
        6 egg whites with
        ¼ ts. salt
        ½ ts. cream of tartar
3.   Pour candy syrup over the beaten egg whites and con-
     tinue beating carefully until smooth, and then set to one
     side to cool.
4.   Beat egg yolks well and add
        1 ts. of your choice of flavoring and add to the above
        mixture.
5.   Add
        1¼ c. sifted cake flour by folding it in carefully a
        small amount at a time.
6.   Bake in a tube pan 1 hour at 350°.
        Peppermint candy frosting is tempting on this cake.

PEPPERMINT FROSTING

1.   Crush peppermint candy to fill 1 cup, using the hard type
     of candy.

2. Add
    ½ c. top milk or half milk and half cream
    ¼ of a cube of butter or margarine.
3. Add enough powdered sugar to make a smooth paste.
4. Peppermint flavoring may be added if a richer flavor is
   desired.
    The pink and white coloring from the candy makes a
    pretty tint to the frosting.

EVERYDAY WHITE CAKE

1. Sift into mixing bowl
    2 c. flour
    1 c. sugar
    2 ts. baking powder
    ½ ts. salt
2. Cream till smooth
    ½ c. shortening (vegetable preferred)
    ½ c. milk
3. Combine two mixtures and add
    3 unbeaten egg whites
    ½ c. milk. Continue beating on low speed until
    creamy.
4. Add
    1 ts. vanilla
5. Pour into layer pans and bake for 25 minutes at 350°.
    When cool, frost with favorite frosting.

CORNSTARCH CAKE
(A large recipe)

This is an unusual cake; it has a very fine texture and
resembles a poundcake very much.
1. Sift together
    4½ c. all-purpose flour
    2 ts. baking powder
    2 c. cornstarch
    2 c. sugar
2. Melt in a pan
    1 c. margarine and add
    2 c. milk. Cool.
3. Combine the two mixtures and beat until smooth and
   free from lumps.

4. Add
    2 ts. almond flavoring
5. Beat until light
    8 egg whites and fold in carefully.
6. Bake in poundcake tins (loaf) 40 minutes at 350°. Cool
   and frost before serving.

ICE-WATER CAKE

This is my pet recipe. I use it for demonstrations and for
teaching students. It is a never-fail recipe, if followed correctly. The texture is fine, the flavor luscious, and it is perfect for any occasion. It may be made in large amounts by
increasing the recipe, thus making good cakes for weddings,
parties, etc.

Two bowls will be needed for this cake.

1. In first mixing bowl, cream
    ½ c. white shortening (vegetable preferred)
    1 c. sugar
    2 tbs. cold milk
    1 ts. almond flavor
    Beat until the mixture resembles whipped cream.
    This process takes several minutes.
2. Sift together three times
    2 c. cake flour which has been sifted
    2 level ts. baking powder
    ½ ts. salt
3. Have ready
    ¼ c. ice water or very cold water
    ½ c. plus 2 tbs. cold milk
    This makes one full cup of liquid used in recipe.
4. Begin by adding flour mixture alternately with the
   liquid to the creamed sugar and shortening. Beat slowly
   until well blended.
5. In the second mixing bowl, beat until stiff but not dry
    ½ c. egg whites, then gently fold them into the bat-
    ter, folding over and over.
6. Pour into prepared pans and bake at 350° until light
   brown and firm on top. Do not overbake.
    Overbaking has a tendency to toughen the crust. Re-
    move from oven, and let stand on cake rack 5 minutes in
    pan. Then, turn out on rack to cool for 2 or 3 minutes.

Frost when cool with any frosting desired. My favorite frosting for this cake is called, Cherry Dream Frosting, listed with the frosting recipes.

LEMON CREAM CAKE

1. Sift together
   2 c. cake flour
   2 ts. baking powder
   ¾ ts. salt
   1 c. sugar
2. To the flour add
   ½ c. shortening
   ¾ c. milk. Mix well.
3. Beat until stiff
   3 egg whites, add
   ¼ c. sugar and beat until it forms meringue.
4. Fold into flour and sugar very gently beating over and under.
5. Flavor with
   1 ts. lemon extract
6. Bake at 350° for 20 minutes.
7. When cool, cover with Lemon Topping.

LEMON TOPPING

1. In a saucepan mix together
   1 pkg. lemon pudding
   ½ c. sugar
   2 egg yolks
   2 c. water
2. Cook over low heat until thickened. Cool.
3. Then spread a liberal portion between layers of cake. Add some whipped cream to the remaining filling and spread over top and sides of cake.
4. Chill and serve.

LARGE WHITE CAKE (50 servings)

1. Mix for 2 minutes or more
   3 c. sugar
   1½ ts. salt

      1 c. milk
      1 tbs. flavoring
      1¼ c. shortening
2.   Sift
      3 c. flour
      3 ts. baking powder
3.   Beat until very light
      8 egg whites
4.   Mix flour alternately with 1¼ c. milk into creamed mixture, stirring until smooth. Then fold in beaten egg whites.
5.   Bake in sheet cakes or layers at 350° for 15 to 20 minutes according to size of layers. May be frosted and then cut in squares.

TWO-DAY CARMEL CAKE

1.   Melt until brown
      2 c. sugar in fry pan
2.   Then add
      1 c. warm water and cook to a thick syrup then set aside until the following day.
3.   Beat until light yellow
      2 egg yolks and add
      1 c. of the carmel syrup and
      1 c. whipping cream
4.   Fold in
      1½ c. all-purpose flour sifted with
      2 ts. baking powder
5.   Add
      ¾ c. ground nuts
      ½ c. ground raisins
      ¼ c. peanut brittle crumbs
6.   Fold in the stiffly beaten whites of the
      2 eggs
      Bake at 350° for ½ hour or more until firm. Serve with or without frosting.

NUT LAYER CAKE

1.   Beat until light
      3 eggs and add
      1½ c. sugar

2. Add
   1 c. melted butter, slightly cooled
3. Pour in without stirring
   1½ c. milk and
   1 ts. vanilla
4. Sift in and beat until smooth
   3½ c. cake flour
   2 ts. baking powder
5. Add
   1 c. nut pieces
6. Bake in two 9-inch layers or three 8-inch layer pans at 350° for 30 minutes. Cool and frost with favorite frosting, then cover generously with ground nuts over sides and top. If you prefer, you may place walnut halves in pattern on top.

QUEEN'S ORANGE CAKE

1. Combine and mix well
   ⅔ c. shortening
   1 tbs. grated orange peel
   1½ ts. grated lemon peel
2. Add gradually
   1½ c. sugar and beat until creamy
3. Then add
   3 eggs, one at a time, beating after each addition.
4. Sift together
   2½ c. sifted cake flour
   2½ ts. baking powder
   ¾ ts. salt. Add alternately to the creamed mixture with
5. ¾ c. milk and
   2 tbs. lemon juice
   ¼ ts. orange food coloring. Mix lightly.
6. Bake in 9 in. layer pans at 375° for 25 to 30 minutes.

BIRTHDAY CAKE
Three-color cake

This special occasion cake is nice for children's parties.
1. Sift together in a large bowl
   3½ c. flour
   4½ ts. baking powder
   1½ ts. salt

2.   Cream and beat for two minutes
         2 c. sugar
         ¾ c. shortening
3.   Add
         1¾ c. milk and mix it well
4.   Then add
         3 egg whites unbeaten and beat again until smooth.
         Divide in bowls, color pink, yellow or add cooled,
         melted chocolate, enough to color batter. Fill in pan
         as for marble cake recipe.
         Bake either in layers or loaf for 25 or 30 minutes at
         350°.

BURNED SUGAR CAKE

1.   Carmelize
         ½ c. sugar in frying pan and then add
         1 c. water. Stir until dissolved.
2.   Cream
         ½ c. butter
         1 c. sugar
3.   Sift
         2 c. cake flour
         2 ts. baking powder
4.   Beat slightly and add to mixture
         3 eggs
5.   Mix all together and add
         ½ c. nuts, if desired
6.   Bake at 350° for 25 minutes.

ORANGE LOAF CAKE

1.   Sift
         2½ c. cake flour
         1 ts. soda
         1 ts. salt
2.   Cream
         1 c. sugar
         1 c. butter or margarine
         3 egg yolks
3.   Add
         1 c. sour milk and
         grated rind of 2 oranges

4. Add flour mixture and mix well.
5. Add
        1 c. raisins
        1 c. broken nuts
6. Fold in last
        3 beaten egg whites
7. Bake in loaf tin for 45 minutes at 350°.

ORANGE FROSTING

1. Squeeze juice from 1 orange, add a small amount of grated orange rind and enough powdered sugar to make paste.
2. Add
        2 tbs. shortening and a few drops of orange coloring. Beat until creamy and spread evenly over top and sides of cake.

ORANGE CREAM CAKE

1. Cream
        ½ c. shortening
        1 c. sugar
        2 eggs, one at a time
2. Sift
        2 c. cake flour
        2 ts. baking powder
        ½ ts. salt
3. Add ½ c. milk alternately with the flour mixture to creamed ingredients. Beat until smooth and then fold in the following orange mixture.
4. Put through the food chopper
        1 large orange, skin, pulp and juice and
        1 c. seedless raisins
5. You may add if you desire
        1 c. chopped pecan nuts
6. Bake in two 8-inch pans for 30 minutes or more at 350°. Remove from oven and cool. Cover with orange icing.

ORANGE ICING

1. Beat in beater bowl
        1 lb. powdered sugar

1 orange, juice and grated rind
1 egg white

2. Beat for several minutes and add more sugar if necessary.

EGG CUSTARD CAKE

1. Beat for 15 minutes
   6 eggs and
   6 tbs. sugar
2. Add slowly a little at a time and continue beating
   1 c. cake flour
3. Pour into greased and floured, flat loaf tin and bake until light brown. Usually takes 30 minutes or more at 350°.
4. Turn out on rack and cut in 3 pieces. Fill between pieces with jelly and whipped cream and stack in 3 layers.

PINEAPPLE UPSIDE-DOWN CAKE

1. Melt in cake-baking mold
   ½ c. butter
   1½ c. brown sugar, then remove from heat
2. Place large slices of pineapple to cover bottom of mold. Add a maraschino cherry in the center of each slice. Put back on low heat and simmer for 2 or 3 minutes.
3. Beat well
   3 egg yolks and add
   1 c. sugar slowly, then add
   ½ c. pineapple juice
4. Sift together
   1 c. cake flour
   1 ts. baking powder
   ¼ ts. salt and add to the egg yolks and sugar mixture
5. Beat till stiff
   3 egg whites. Fold into batter and pour over the slices of pineapple.
   Bake at 350° for 30 minutes.
   Turn out on large tray and serve with whipped cream, if desired.

CREAM PUFFS

1. In a large frying pan put
   ½ lb. butter
   1 c. boiling water
   2½ c. cake flour or pastry flour
   Gently cook until mixture leaves the sides of the pan and doesn't stick. Turn out into bowl to cool slightly.
2. Add
   8 eggs, one at a time and beat after each addition.
   Beat on medium speed until dough looks soft but firm.
3. Place on greased cookie sheet by dipping dough with tablespoon, allowing at least 2-inch space between each puff. Slide dough from the spoon with the tip of your finger.
4. Bake in the oven, which has been preheated to 400°, for ½ hour. Do not open oven while baking as this causes the puffs to fall. Reduce heat to 300° and allow 10 minutes more baking time to assure perfect baking in the centers.
5. Remove from oven, cool. Then, make a small hole on upper side of puff with a sharp knife. Fill a decorating bag with sweetened and flavored whipped cream. Place end of bag into the hole and squeeze the puff full of cream. Do this just before you are going to serve the puffs. Then sprinkle the top with powdered sugar. Serve immediately.

CHERRY CAKE

This cake is made with dark canned cherries and spices.
1. Sift together
   2½ c. all-purpose flour
   1 ts. baking powder
   ½ ts. salt
   ½ ts. soda
   ½ ts. cloves
   1 ts. nutmeg
2. Cream well
   ¾ c. shortening
   1¼ c. sugar
   3 eggs

3. Combine flour and creamed mixture with
    ¼ c. milk
    ¼ c. cherry juice
4. Stir in
    1 can stoned dark cherries (drained)
    1 c. chopped nuts (preferably almonds)
5. Pour into loaf tins and bake for 35 to 45 minutes at 350°.

CHLOE'S CHERRY CAKE

My lifelong friend, Chloe, said she always wanted to add a cake to my collection. This is one of her favorites.
1. Sift together
    1½ c. cake flour
    ¼ ts. salt
2. Whip 6 egg yolks slightly and add
    1 c. sugar
    Beat for 5 minutes and then combine flour and egg mixtures.
3. Mix carefully with
    1 tbs. vinegar
    25 maraschino cherries and juice
    ½ c. nuts
4. Beat until they are light
    6 egg whites and add
    ½ c. sugar
5. Fold into cake batter and bake in ungreased tube pan for 1 hour and 15 minutes at 325°.

APPLESAUCE CAKE

1. Cream together
    1 c. sugar
    1 tbs. shortening
2. Sift
    2½ c. flour
    1 ts. cinnamon
    ½ ts. cloves
    ½ ts. nutmeg
    3 tbs. cocoa
    2 ts. soda
3. Add altogether with
    1½ c. applesauce
    1 c. raisins—whole or chopped
4. Mix well and bake in loaf tins for ½ hour at 350°.

PUMPKIN CAKE

1. Cream together
   - ½ c. shortening
   - 1¼ c. sugar and add
   - 2 beaten eggs
2. Sift together
   - 2½ c. cake flour
   - 3 ts. baking powder
   - ½ ts. salt
   - ½ ts. cinnamon
   - ½ ts. ginger
   - ½ ts. nutmeg
   - ½ ts. soda
3. Mix
   - 1 c. pumpkin and
   - ¾ c. milk. Add to creamed mixture alternately with the flour.
4. Add
   - ½ c. chopped nuts, if desired.
5. Bake in either loaf pans or layer pans.

FROSTING

1. Cook in double boiler over boiling water, beating constantly, for seven minutes
   - 1½ c. brown sugar
   - 5 tbs. cold water
   - ¼ ts. salt
   - ¼ ts. baking powder
   - 2 egg whites
2. Flavor with
   - 1 ts. black walnut, butterscotch or vanilla.
3. Spread in mounds between the layers and over top and sides of cake.

HOT MILK CAKE

1. Scald
   - ¾ c. milk and add
   - 3 tbs. butter
2. Beat lightly
   - 3 eggs, add

1½ c. sugar
1 ts. vanilla. Beat until creamy.
3. Sift
  1½ c. flour
  1½ ts. baking powder
  ⅛ ts. salt
4. Beat three mixtures together. Pour into well-greased pans and bake 20 minutes at 350°.

SILVER DREAM CAKE

1. Sift in mixing bowl
  2¼ c. flour
  1¼ c. sugar
  3 ts. baking powder
  ½ ts. salt
2. Add and mix for 2 minutes
  ½ c. shortening
  ½ c. milk
  1½ ts. flavoring of choice
3. Add
  3 unbeaten egg whites
  ½ c. milk. Beat slowly until creamy.
4. Pour into prepared pans and bake for 25 minutes at 350°.
5. When cool, frost with Fluffy White Frosting, White Mountain Frosting or Seven Minute, etc.

PLAIN JELLY ROLL

This is a conventional type roll, very easy to make without a failure.
1. Beat until foamy
  5 eggs
2. Add gradually
  1 c. sugar. Continue beating.
3. Stirring carefully, add
  4 tbs. milk and
  4 tbs. water
4. Sift in and stir well
  1 c. flour
  2 ts. baking powder

5. This is a thin batter and may be poured in a well-greased and floured cookie sheet with sides. Bake in a moderate oven 15 minutes at 375°. When done remove from pan onto a damp cloth and roll at once, unroll again and fill with favorite jelly or filling. Reroll and sprinkle with powdered sugar.

SWEDISH JELLY ROLL

Luetta makes wonderful jelly rolls. Will you try her recipe?

1. Sift together
   ⅔ c. flour
   1 ts. baking powder
2. Beat until very light
   3 eggs and slowly add
   ½ c. sugar
3. Mix flour and eggs and sugar together, stirring until smooth
4. Pour into flat pan, lined with buttered waxed paper. Bake in a hot oven 425° for 5 minutes.
5. Turn out on a wax paper. Remove the paper on which it was baked, then spread quickly with jam or applesauce. Roll lengthwise into a large roll. Cover a few moments with a cloth.
6. While still warm spread a thin covering of frosting over the top and sprinkle with nuts.

OLD-FASHIONED JELLY ROLL

The memory of warm jelly rolls in my old Aunt Lena's kitchen is one I will always cherish. The large serving was placed on our tiny palms, and we could smear the rich jelly on our faces and even lick our little fingers so we wouldn't lose a crumb. Many times have I watched with awe how skillfully she would roll the cake and how even and pretty it would look as we peered at it with our hungry eyes. It is still one of my favorites.

1. Arrange two cookie sheets, one inside the other. Grease the upper one freely and flour lightly.

2. Sift together
    ¾ c. cake flour
    ¾ ts. baking powder
    ¼ ts. salt
3. Beat until very light
    4 eggs. Place in top of double boiler over hot water.
4. Beat with rotary beater and add
    ¾ c. sugar gradually. Continue beating until mixture thickens.
5. Remove from hot water and fold in flour mixture very carefully. Add
    1 ts. lemon or vanilla extract
6. Pour out on greased cookie sheet.
    Bake at 375° for 12 to 15 minutes. Remove from oven. Have ready a slightly dampened white cloth. Turn roll out on it and immediately begin rolling from one end. Let stand a few minutes. Then unroll and gently spread with favorite jelly. Reroll and place on waxed paper. Sprinkle top with powdered sugar and serve warm or cold.

BUTTER SPONGE CAKE

You will like the softness and texture of this lovely cake and you will also enjoy making it. It may be made in layers, open pan, or in tiny teacakes to be decorated.

1. Sift together several times
    2 c. cake flour
    2 ts. baking powder
    ½ ts. salt
2. Cream until soft and creamy
    ½ c. butter or shortening
    1 c. sugar
3. Add to the creamed mixture
    2 eggs, one at a time, beating after each, and
    2 egg yolks
4. Add alternately with the flour, beating only until mixture is well blended
    1 c. milk
5. Add
    1 ts. fruit flavoring
6. Bake in 2 9-inch layers at 350° for 25 minutes.

BANANA CREAM FROSTING

1. Mash
    2 ripe bananas
    2 tbs. drained crushed pineapple
    enough powdered sugar to make a paste
    1 tbs. butter or shortening
2. Arrange a layer of Butter Sponge Cake on a plate or tray. Spread the banana paste over the top, then place the other layer of cake on top. Cover the entire cake with sweetened and flavored whipped cream and arrange sliced bananas on top. Serve at once.

BUTTER SPONGE COCONUT CAKE

1. Spread one layer of Butter Sponge Cake with butter cream frosting. (See frosting recipes.) Sprinkle generously with fresh moist coconut. Place the other layer on top. Continue frosting the entire cake and cover top and sides with coconut. Seven minute icing may likewise be used if you prefer.

BUTTER SPONGE TEACAKES

1. Arrange bonbon paper cups in the very small cupcake tins, fill ¾ full of Butter Sponge Cake batter. Bake 10 to 12 minutes at 350°. Cool and decorate as desired.

    Designs:
1. Place a small star tube in a paper cone filled with Butter Cream or Royal frosting, begin by squeezing the frosting through the tube, around the outer edge, gradually filling the space to the center, make a tiny rosebud or rosette in dainty colors and place in the center. A small green leaf may be added to the flower. Many different designs may be made on top of each little cake.
2. The tiny cupcakes may be frosted all over and rolled in ground nuts, or coconut, flavored with different flavors, and tinted differently. Maraschino cherries, nut halves and gumdrops may be used to decorate each little cake. The frostings chosen may be white. Coconut may be tinted pale shades by dropping one or two drops of food coloring in a few drops of water, sprinkle over coconut and stir gently. Cover and use when desired.

CUPCAKES FOR A SHOWER

1. Sift several times
        1 c. cake flour
        1 ts. baking powder
        ¼ ts. salt
2. Beat until thick
        3 eggs and add
        1 c. sugar
        2 ts. lemon juice
3. Add flour to the egg mixture alternately with
        6 ts. hot milk
4. Bake in paper cups 15 minutes at 375°. Cool.
5. Frost with moist frosting and cover with tinted coconut. Place a tiny rosebud and leaf on top of each, using decorating icing in pastry bag and tube.

CRUSHED PINEAPPLE CAKE

1. Cream till fluffy
        ½ c. shortening
        1⅓ c. sugar and add
        1 ts. pineapple flavoring and
        1 c. crushed pineapple
2. Sift together
        2½ c. all-purpose flour
        2 ts. baking powder
        ¼ ts. salt. Add to first mixture alternately with ¼ c. cold water.
3. Beat until stiff
        3 egg whites and gently fold into cake batter.
        Pour into loaf pans and bake 30 to 35 minutes at 375°.
        When cool, frost with pineapple frosting.

PINEAPPLE FROSTING

1. In a bowl place
        1 lb. powdered sugar
        1 small can crushed pineapple
        1 tbs. melted butter
        Stir until completely creamed. Spread over layers, on top and sides. Sprinkle with chopped pecans.

SPONGE CAKE

1. Measure and sift separately
   1½ c. cake flour
   1½ c. sugar
2. Beat until thick
   7 egg yolks. Add gradually to the sifted sugar.
3. Add
   ½ c. pineapple juice
   1 tbs. lemon juice
4. Beat until they hold in peaks
   7 egg whites with
   1 ts. cream of tartar and
   ¼ ts. salt
5. Fold egg yolks into the beaten whites with
   1 tbs. of flour at a time.
6. Pour into ungreased tube pan and put into a slow oven, 250°, for 10 minutes, then raise the heat to 325° and continue baking for 1 hour.
   This cake is good plain or frosted.

ORANGE SPONGE CAKE

This is an old-fashioned method, but makes a lovely cake, a favorite among the elderly ladies.

1. Sift several times and measure
   1 c. flour and also
2. Sift
   1 c. sugar
3. Beat
   7 egg yolks until thick and gradually add
   ½ c. of the sugar slowly
4. Add the juice and grated rind of
   ½ orange
5. Beat egg whites until stiff and add the remaining
   ½ c. sugar
6. Then combine the two mixtures slowly and then carefully add the sifted flour.
7. Pour into ungreased tube pan and bake for 1 hour at 325°. Cool in the pan.

ORANGE FRUIT FROSTING

1. In a bowl mix until creamy
     1 lb. powdered sugar
     1 orange—juice and grated rind
     1 tbs. butter
     1 ts. orange emulsion or extract
2. Spread a liberal amount on top and sides of cake.
3. Small slices of whole orange may be placed on top of the frosted cake, or pieces of orange candy jellies are tasty as a decoration.

PINEAPPLE SPONGE CAKE

This is a little different procedure from the average sponge cake. I hope you like it.
1. Sift
     1½ c. cake flour with
     ½ ts. salt and
     1 ts. baking powder
2. Beat until the soft peak stage
     6 egg whites and
3. Add quite slowly
     ¾ c. sugar
4. Have ready in another bowl
     6 egg yolks beaten thick with
     1 tbs. lemon juice and
     ½ c. of pineapple juice gradually added
5. Fold flour into egg yolks and lastly into the beaten egg whites.
6. Bake in an ungreased tube pan 1 hour at 325°. Remove from oven and cool in pan. Then remove from pan and frost with pineapple frosting.

PINEAPPLE FROSTING

1. Combine
     2½ c. powdered sugar
     1 small can crushed pineapple
     2 egg yolks
     1 tbs. butter
     1 ts. fruit flavoring
2. Beat until smooth—more sugar may be added if necessary.
3. Spread over top and sides of cake.

CHERRY CHIFFON CAKES (ONE-BOWL CAKE)

This cake is very tempting; your family and friends will like it.

1. Sift together in mixing bowl
    2 c. all-purpose flour
    1½ c. sugar
    3 level ts. baking powder
    1 ts. salt
2. In the center of the flour pour and beat in gently until it is a smooth batter
    ⅔ c. cooking oil
    2 egg yolks
    ½ c. cherry juice
    ⅓ c. water
    1 ts. almond flavoring
    1 tbs. lemon juice
3. Add ½ c. finely chopped maraschino cherries
4. Whip until very stiff and almost dry
    1 c. egg whites
    ½ ts. cream of tartar and fold into batter carefully.
    Pour into ungreased tube pan and bake for 1 hour and 15 minutes—until firmly done. Remove from oven and place on rack upside down to cool. Do not remove from pan until real cool. Gently loosen edges with a knife and tap with fingers to force from pan. Choose cherry frosting for sides and top.

PINEAPPLE FLUFF CAKE

1. Beat to firm glossy peaks
    6 egg whites and
    ¼ ts. salt
2. Gradually add
    ¾ c. sugar
3. Beat
    6 egg yolks until thick and add
    ¾ c. sugar slowly
4. Fold over carefully
    ½ ts. lemon juice
    ½ c. pineapple juice
5. Add in small amounts at a time
    1½ c. sifted cake flour and
    1 ts. baking powder
6. Then fold into the beaten egg whites and pour quickly into layer pans and bake for 25 to 30 minutes at 350°.

7. Frost with a fruit frosting and you will be delighted with the compliments received.

ORANGE SUNSHINE CAKE

1. Beat until lemon colored
    8 egg yolks, then add
    ⅓ c. orange juice and
    ¾ c. sugar
    1 ts. vanilla or orange emulsion
2. Beat until stiff
    8 egg whites with
    ½ ts. salt
    ¾ ts. cream of tartar
    ¾ c. sugar
3. Fold whites into the yolks and slowly add
    1½ c. sifted cake flour. Don't overbeat.
4. Pour into ungreased tube pan and bake for 1 hour at 325°.

FAVORITE CHIFFON CAKE

1. In a mixing bowl, sift
    2¼ c. cake flour
    1½ c. sugar
    1 ts. salt
    3 ts. baking powder
2. Make a well in the center of this mixture. Then add
    ½ c. salad oil
    5 unbeaten egg yolks
    ¾ c. pineapple juice
3. Beat egg whites until very stiff and dry with
    ½ ts. cream of tartar
4. Fold egg whites and yolks together gradually.
5. Pour into tube pan and bake for 55 minutes at 325°. Increase heat to 350° and bake 10 minutes more.

MILE-HIGH ANGEL FOOD

1. Sift several times
    1 c. cake flour
    ¾ c. sugar
2. Beat until foamy
    1¼ c. egg whites, then add
    ¼ ts. salt

3. Add
    1¼ ts. cream of tartar and continue beating until stiff but not dry.
4. Fold in one teaspoon at a time, folding carefully
    ¾ c. sugar and then add
    1¼ ts. of favorite flavoring and continue the beating while adding flour and sugar. Do not overbeat.
5. Pour into ungreased tube pan which has been rinsed in cold water and shaken dry. Bake in slow oven at 325° for 60 minutes. Cool in pan at least 1 hour. Frost as desired.

COOKED ANGEL FOOD FROSTING

1. Cook until thick
    4 egg yolks
    1 c. sugar
    1 large orange, juice and grated rind
2. Remove from heat and add
    ½ c. coconut, then set aside to cool.
3. When cool add
    ½ pt. whipped cream.
4. Spread on cake just before serving.

GROUND RAISIN CAKE

This good, choice cake is wholesome for children and choice for all the family.
1. Carmelize in a skillet
    1 c. sugar and add
    ½ c. hot water—cook until sugar is dissolved, then add
    1 c. milk and cool
2. Cream and mix into the liquid
    ½ c. butter or margarine and
    2 eggs
3. Sift
    2½ c. cake flour
    ¼ ts. soda
    2 ts. baking powder
4. Mix altogether and add
    1 c. ground raisins
    1 ts. vanilla
5. Bake in loaf tins at 350° for 25 to 30 minutes.

LAZY DAISY CAKE
(a small recipe)

You will like this cake for its good flavor and aroma. The melted brown topping is ideal for a hurry-up occasion.

1. Sift together
    1 c. cake flour
    1 ts. baking powder
2. Beat until creamy
    2 eggs
    1 c. sugar
3. Scald and cool
    ½ c. milk
    1 tbs. butter
    ¼ ts. salt
4. Mix altogether gradually and pour into a flat baking dish which has been greased and floured. Bake for 20 minutes at 350°.
5. Have ready a frosting made from mixing together
    5 tbs. brown sugar
    2 tbs. cream
    2 tbs. butter
    ½ c. coconut
6. Remove cake from oven and carefully spread the frosting over the top and place in the oven to brown lightly.
7. Remove from oven and serve hot.

DELICATE SYRUP CAKE

1. Sift together 3 times
    2 c. flour
    3 ts. baking powder
    ¼ c. sugar
2. Cream until smooth
    ¼ c. sugar
    ½ c. shortening
    1 c. white syrup
3. Combine two mixtures beating slowly and gradually adding
    ¾ c. milk and
    1 ts. flavoring
4. Then beat in carefully
    2 whole eggs and
    1 egg yolk. Save the one egg white for the frosting.

Beat for 2 minutes and pour into pans and bake at 350° for 25 to 30 minutes.

1.   Variations
     1½ ts. spice may be added to the flour to make a spice cake from this recipe.

2.   Variations
     ½ c. cocoa may be added to flour to make a fudge cake.

SOFT DELICATE FROSTING

My sweet, lifelong friend, Geneva, gave this recipe to me and it is especially good for dainty cakes calling for soft frosting. It may be delicately tinted and flavored and will hold up for several days.

1.   Place in a beater bowl
     1 c. sugar
     ⅓ ts. cream of tartar
     1 egg white
     1 tbs. white syrup

2.   Begin beating adding
     ½ c. boiling water, continue beating until frosting is stiff and firm enough to spread.

3.   Add flavoring to taste and coloring if desired. Quickly spread on cakes.

CENTURY-OLD POUNDCAKE

For those who like an unfrosted cake for tea time or after-meal snacks, the poundcake is the most preferred. It may be wrapped in wax paper and kept for many days.

1.   Cream until soft
     1 lb. butter or margarine
     1 lb. sugar

2.   Continue beating and add one at a time
     10 eggs (beating after each addition)

3.   Fold in
     4 c. cake flour

4.   Flavor with
     1 tbs. rose water or 1 tbs. orange juice if preferred.

5.   Bake in paper-lined loaf tins for 1½ hours at 325°. Cool in pans after removing from the oven.
     Serve in thin slices.

A Tall Wedding Cake

Done in pale blue frosting and decorated with white roses, lilies, bells, and blue forget-me-nots.

BOUQUET CAKE
A three-tiered wedding cake decorated with open roses and buds in pastel pink

OLD-FASHIONED JAM CAKE

This recipe makes a very moist cake that ages well, retains its flavor.
1. Cream together
       ½ c. butter or margarine
       1¼ c. sugar
       3 egg yolks
2. Dissolve
       1 ts. soda in
       1 c. buttermilk
3. Sift together
       2¼ c. all-purpose flour
       ¼ ts. salt
       ½ ts. allspice
       ¼ ts. cloves
       ½ ts. cinnamon. Add to first mixture.
4. Gently mix all together and stir in
       1 c. strawberry or blackberry jam
5. Beat
       3 egg whites stiff and fold in last
       Pour into flat loaf tin, 8x8 inches and bake at 375°
       for 35 to 40 minutes until firm on top. Frost with
       Butter Cream Frosting.

ANGEL FOOD CAKE (Slow-Baked Method)

1. Sift several times and remeasure
       1 c. cake flour
2. Beat with a wire whip until frothy and large peaks are
    formed
       14 egg whites
       ¼ ts. salt
       1 ts. cream of tartar
3. Add 1 tbs. at a time, folding over and over
       1 c. sugar
4. Add
       1 ts. almond flavoring
5. Add flour a little at a time, still folding over and over.
6. Pour into an ungreased tube pan and bake at 275° for 45
    minutes, then 285° for 20 minutes. Turn off oven and
    continue baking 5 minutes more.
7. Remove from oven and place on wire rack to cool. Do
    not remove cake from pan until it is entirely cool.

Dark Cakes

DELIGHT FUDGE CAKE

1. Melt over warm water
   2 squares of bitter chocolate in
   ½ c. milk
2. Cream well
   1¼ c. sugar
   ½ c. shortening and add
   2 eggs. Beat again.
3. Sift together
   2 c. flour
   1 ts. salt
   1 ts. soda
4. Mix altogether with
   ½ c. buttermilk
   1 ts. vanilla
5. Bake in 9-inch layer pans 25 minutes at 350°. Cool on cake rack and frost with the following frosting.

JELLY FROSTING

1. Beat until light
   1 egg white and
   1 large glass of favorite jelly
2. Spread on cake just before serving.

CHOCOLATE MINT ROLL

1. Sift together
   12 tbs. cake flour
   1 ts. baking powder
   ⅛ ts. salt
2. Beat until light and fluffy
   8 egg whites, and gradually add
   1½ c. sugar, then fold in
   8 beaten egg yolks and
   2 ts. vanilla

3. Gradually fold in the flour mixture folding over and over.
4. Add
   4 squares bitter chocolate, which has been melted and cooled.
5. Pour on a flat, greased baking pan and bake for 10 minutes or more at 400°.
6. Remove from oven and turn out on a damp cloth, roll like a jelly roll, unroll and spread with mint frosting or mint ice cream. Reroll and chill or freeze before serving.

LUCKY CHOCOLATE CAKE

A rich, dark-colored cake really catches one's eye when frosted with a mile-high frosting.
1. Cream until smooth
   2 c. sugar
   ½ c. shortening and
   2 egg yolks
2. Sift together
   2 c. cake flour
   ½ ts. salt
   1 ts. soda
   ¼ ts. cloves
3. Begin by adding a little of the flour to the creamed mixture alternately with
   ½ c. buttermilk and
   3 heaping tbs. dark cocoa dissolved in
   1 c. boiling water which has been cooled
4. Beat until very light
   2 egg whites and fold into batter. Quickly pour into 9-inch layer pans.
5. Bake for 25 minutes at 350°.

MILE-HIGH FROSTING

1. Stir in a saucepan until well blended
   ½ c. sugar
   ¼ c. white syrup
   2 tbs. water
2. Boil rapidly without stirring. Put the lid on the kettle for a few moments to steam the sugar particles from the sides. Cook until syrup spins a long thread when poured from a spoon.

3. Have
   2 egg whites beaten stiff
4. Pour hot syrup slowly over the beaten whites. Continue beating until the frosting holds in large peaks.
5. Flavor with your choice of flavoring.
6. Spread generously between the layers, and evenly over sides of cake. Drop remaining frosting in mounds on the top.

SLOW-BAKED CHOCOLATE CAKE

1. Sift together three times
   1¾ c. cake flour
   1¾ ts. baking powder
   ½ ts. salt
2. Cream thoroughly
   ½ c. butter or margarine
   1 c. sugar
   1 beaten egg
3. Melt and cool
   2 squares unsweetened chocolate and add to the creamed mixture
4. Sift flour into the creamed mixture and beat gently with
   ¾ c. milk
   1 ts. vanilla
5. When well mixed pour into a greased, flat pan 8x8x2 inches and bake in a slow oven (325°) for 1 hour.
6. Cool and spread generously with fudge frosting.

CHOCOLATE SPICE CAKE

1. Cream until smooth
   ½ c. shortening
   1½ c. sugar
   2 eggs
2. Sift
   2¼ c. cake flour
   1 ts. baking powder
   ½ ts. salt
   ¾ ts. soda
   ½ ts. cinnamon
   ¼ ts. nutmeg
   ¼ ts. cloves

3. Combine both mixtures with
   1 c. milk
4. Pour
   ½ c. hot water over
   ½ c. dark cocoa, cool slightly and stir into batter.
5. When well mixed, pour into tins and bake for 30 minutes at 350°.
6. Frost with Brown Satin frosting.

CHOCOLATE COCONUT CAKE

You who like coconut in the cake itself, as well as on the top, will like this recipe.

1. Cream
   ½ c. shortening
   3 squares of melted chocolate until well mixed
2. In a mixing bowl place
   1¾ c. cake flour
   1¼ c. sugar
   ¾ ts. salt
   ¼ ts. baking powder
   ¾ ts. soda
3. Add flour mixture to shortening alternately with
   1 c. buttermilk
   1 ts. vanilla
   ¼ ts. powdered cloves. Beat slowly until well creamed.
4. Then add one at a time, beating slowly,
   2 eggs and
   1 c. fine macaroon coconut
5. Pour into prepared baking pans, two 9-inch tins or one large loaf tin.
   Bake at 350° for 30 minutes.
   Use a fluffy, white frosting and dice with moist fresh coconut.

CHOCOLATE ANGEL FOOD

1. Sift together three times
   ¾ c. flour (sifted before measuring)
   1 (scant) c. sugar
   ¼ c. cocoa
2. Beat with a wire whip
   1½ c. egg whites

       1½ ts. cream of tartar
       ¼ ts. salt

3.   Add the flour, sugar and cocoa
       2 tbs. at a time to the egg whites. Fold over and over, being careful not to overbeat.

4.   Add last
       1 ts. vanilla

5.   Pour into ungreased tube pan and bake 30 to 35 minutes in a 375° oven. If the slow method of baking is preferred, bake at 300° for one hour and five minutes.

6.   After baking, cool on cake rack until cold. Frost if desired.

CHOCOLATE CAKE

    This is a family favorite.

1.   Beat well for 3 minutes
       ½ c. shortening
       1 c. sugar, add
       2 eggs, one at a time, beating after each

2.   Dissolve
       ½ c. dark cocoa in enough hot water to make a smooth paste and then set aside to cool.

3.   Sift into mixing bowl
       2 c. cake flour
       1 ts. soda
       ¼ ts. salt
       ¼ ts. cloves

4.   Begin beating by adding
       ½ c. sour cream
       ½ c. milk
       ½ ts. vanilla

5.   When smooth add the cocoa and water and beat for 2 minutes more.

6.   Bake in layers or loaf tins at 350° for 20 to 25 minutes for the layers and 30 to 40 minutes for the loaves.

OUR FAVORITE FROSTING

1.   Mix
       1 lb. powdered sugar
       3 tbs. canned milk
       1 large tbs. vegetable shortening

1 ts. vanilla

⅛ ts. cloves

2. Beat for 5 minutes.
3. Spread between layers, then on top and sides.
4. Melt over warm water

    ¼ lb. sweet chocolate and pour in ribbons over the top of frosted cake.

CHOCOLATE ALMOND TREAT

1. Use the recipe for chocolate cake.
2. Eliminate spice and add

    1 c. finely chopped almonds
3. Sprinkle chopped almonds over the frosted cake.

MY FUDGE CAKE

This was the first cake I learned to make of which I was really proud. It is of a soft texture and has a dark red color.

1. Measure out

    ½ c. butter, remove 1 tbs. and place in a small pan and melt with

    2 squares of baking chocolate.
2. Cream the remaining butter with

    1¼ c. sugar and

    2 eggs. Beat for 2 minutes.
3. Sift together three times

    2 c. cake flour

    1 ts. soda

    ½ ts. salt
4. Beat altogether with

    1 c. milk, beginning and ending with flour. Do not overbeat.
5. Mix in cooled chocolate and

    1 ts. vanilla
6. Pour into prepared pans and bake for 20 to 25 minutes at 350°. Fudge frosting or White Mountain frosting is delightful on this cake.

ONE-BOWL FUDGE CAKE

1. Into a large mixing bowl sift

    1¾ c. cake flour

      1¼ c. sugar
      6 tbs. cocoa
      ½ ts. soda
      1¼ ts. baking powder
      1 ts. salt
2. To the flour add
      ⅔ c. shortening
      2 eggs
      1 c. buttermilk
      1 ts. vanilla
3. Begin beating and scrape the sides of the bowl at intervals. Beat for 3 minutes.
4. Bake in 2 9-inch layer pans for 25 minutes at 350°.

BLACK CHOCOLATE CAKE

1. Cream well
      2 c. sugar
      ½ c. shortening
      2 egg yolks
2. Sift
      3 c. cake flour
      ½ ts. salt
      1 ts. soda
      ¼ ts. ground cloves
3. Dissolve
      3 heaping tbs. cocoa in
      1 c. boiling water and let cool
4. Add to the cocoa
      ½ c. sour milk or buttermilk
5. Beat alternately the flour and liquid into creamed sugar and eggs.
6. Add stiffly beaten egg whites last.
7. Bake in layers at 350° for 30 minutes.

CHOCOLATE SPICE CAKE

1. Cream
      ½ c. shortening
      1½ c. sugar
      1 c. milk
2. Add
      2 eggs, one at a time. Beat well.

3.   Sift
          2¼ c. cake flour
          ½ ts. salt
          1 ts. baking powder
          ¾ ts. soda
          ½ ts. cinnamon
          ¼ ts. nutmeg
          ¼ ts. cloves
4.   Add all together and then add
          ½ c. hot water and
          ½ c. cocoa mixed
          1 ts. vanilla
5.   Bake at 350° for 30 minutes.

CONFECTIONERS' NUT FUDGE CAKE

1.   Dissolve
          2 squares of chocolate in
          5 tbs. boiling water. Let cool.
2.   Cream well
          1 square butter
          1½ c. sugar and add to the chocolate
3.   Add
          4 beaten egg yolks
          1 ts. vanilla
4.   Sift
          1¾ c. cake flour
          3 ts. baking powder
5.   Add alternately with
          ¾ c. milk
6.   Fold in
          4 beaten egg whites and
          ½ c. chopped nuts
7.   Mix carefully and pour into prepared tins. Bake at 350°
     for 25 minutes. When cool frost with:

PEPPERMINT FROSTING

1.   Melt
          1 square chocolate
          2 tbs. butter
          4 tbs. cream

2. Add
    3 drops oil of peppermint
3. Add enough powdered sugar to make a creamy consistency. Spread on layers and sprinkle with nuts.

FUDGE CAKE

1. Cream
    ½ c. butter or margarine
    1 c. sugar
2. Add
    2 egg yolks. Continue beating.
3. Sift
    2 c. cake flour
    2 ts. baking powder
    ½ ts. soda
    ¼ ts. salt
4. Add flour alternately to the egg and butter mixture with
    1¼ c. milk
    3 squares melted and cooled chocolate
    1 ts. vanilla
5. Fold in stiffly beaten whites of
    2 eggs
6. Bake for 25 minutes at 350°.

NUT FUDGE CAKE

1. Cream until light
    ½ c. shortening
    1 c. sugar
    2 ts. vanilla
2. Add
    2 eggs beaten well
3. Melt and cool
    3 squares of bitter chocolate. Add to creamed sugar and eggs.
4. Sift together
    2 c. cake flour
    2 ts. baking powder
    1 ts. salt
5. Alternately add flour mixture and
    1½ c. milk. Beat until smooth.

6. Stir in
     1 c. chopped nuts
7. Bake in pan 10x15x1 inch, in moderate oven 375° for 30 minutes. Frost as desired.

CHOCOLATE MACAROON

Double recipe for parties.
1. Melt over hot water and cool
     5 squares of bitter chocolate
2. Mix well
     1 c. shortening
     2 c. sugar (1 brown and 1 granulated)
3. Add one at a time and beat after each addition
     4 eggs
4. Sift together three times
     4 c. cake flour
     2 ts. soda and
     1 ts. salt
5. Add alternately with
     1 c. sweet milk
     1 c. buttermilk
6. Bake in layers at 375° for 20 or 25 minutes.
7. While cake is baking, cook for 5 minutes the following macaroon
     1 c. glucose
     2 c. sugar
     ½ c. water
8. Remove from stove and add
     3 c. shredded coconut
     1 ts. almond or vanilla flavoring
     1 to 2 c. cake crumbs (white crumbs preferred)
9. Stir well.
10. When cake is partially cooled, cover with macaroon, also between layers if desired. A generous amount improves cake. When cooled, serve with or without whipped cream or marshmallow topping. Cut with a knife dipped in warm water, as macaroon has a tendency to be sticky, but will cut easily. It is luscious for those who like coconut.

DEVIL'S FOOD CAKE

Marie was one of my students, and a darling cook. She gave me this recipe. It's one of her favorites.

1. Fill cup full with
   $\frac{1}{2}$ c. hot water
   $\frac{1}{2}$ c. cocoa, mix and cool
2. Cream
   $\frac{1}{2}$ c. shortening
   $1\frac{1}{2}$ c. sugar
3. Add
   2 large eggs, one at a time
4. Sift dry ingredients
   2 c. cake flour
   $1\frac{1}{2}$ ts. soda
   $\frac{1}{4}$ ts. salt
5. Add dry ingredients alternately with
   1 c. buttermilk, to which add 1 ts. vanilla
6. Add cooled cocoa mixture and beat until smooth.
   This cake makes three 8-inch layers. Bake at 375° for 30 minutes.

FUDGE CAKE—HOT-WATER METHOD

1. Cream well
   $\frac{1}{2}$ c. butter or other shortening
   $1\frac{1}{4}$ c. sugar
2. Add
   2 squares chocolate, melted and cooled
3. Add to the butter and sugar
   2 beaten eggs
   1 ts. vanilla
4. Sift together three times and add to the butter and eggs
   2 c. cake flour
   $\frac{1}{2}$ ts. salt
   $1\frac{1}{2}$ ts. cream of tartar
5. Add
   $\frac{3}{4}$ c. boiling water to
   1 ts. soda. Stir it quickly into the batter and beat well.
6. Pour at once into the greased and floured layer pans. Bake in a preheated oven for 35 minutes at 350°.
7. Cool and cover with chocolate frosting.

MAHOGANY CAKE
(Dark Red in Color)

1. Cook
    ½ c. milk
    2 squares chocolate in a double boiler, stirring until thick.
2. Cream
    1 c. sugar
    ½ c. shortening
3. Add
    2 eggs beaten
4. Sift together three times
    2 c. cake flour
    ¼ ts. salt
    1 ts. soda
5. Add creamed mixture and eggs to the flour with
    ½ c. milk and beat gently
6. Then add cooled chocolate and
    1 ts. vanilla
7. Bake in layers or loaf as desired at 350° for 25 minutes.

RILLA'S CHOCOLATE CAKE

Rilla makes her chocolate cakes, beating them by hand. This is a very moist, tender cake and each one of you will enjoy making it. A beater may be used if you prefer.

1. Mix by hand in large bowl
    2 c. sugar
    1 c. shortening until smooth and creamy
2. Add
    4 egg yolks, one at a time, beating after each addition.
3. Melt
    3 squares baking chocolate and cool. Then add to the eggs.
4. Sift into the first mixtures
    2½ c. flour
    ¼ ts. salt
5. Then add
    1 c. sour milk or buttermilk and the melted chocolate.
6. Pour
    ⅔ c. boiling water over
    2 ts. soda and add to the mixture quickly.

7. Have ready
    4 stiffly beaten egg whites and fold in gently.
8. Pour into layers and bake 20 minutes at 375°. Frost as
    desired.

SPICE MAHOGANY CAKE

This cake is a favorite because of its dark-red color and
very good flavor.
1. Cream softly
    ¼ lb. butter
    1 c. sugar
    1 ts. cinnamon or
    ½ ts. cloves
2. Add
    3 egg yolks and beat again
3. Sift together
    2 c. flour (all-purpose flour may be used)
    1 ts. baking powder
    1 ts. soda
    ¼ ts. salt
4. Melt and cool
    2 squares chocolate
5. Add all together alternately with
    1 c. buttermilk
    1 ts. vanilla
6. Beat
    3 egg whites until stiff. Fold into mixture carefully.
    Pour into two, 9-inch layer pans and bake at 350° for
    35 minutes. Frost with Fluffy White Frosting or a
    tasty Fudge Frosting.

FUDGY CAKE
(By Peggy L.)

This is a candy-textured cake and is very rich and delicious.
1. Begin by beating together
    2 egg yolks
    2 c. sugar
    4 tbs. butter

2. Sift
     1¾ c. cake flour
     3 ts. baking powder
     ½ ts. salt
3. Melt
     4 squares of chocolate (bitter preferred) and cool.
4. Mix and beat several times
     1½ c. milk alternately with flour mixture to eggs,
     sugar, and butter
5. Add chocolate and
     1 ts. vanilla. Beat again.
6. Fold 2 beaten egg whites in last.
7. Bake for 30 minutes in 350° oven. Use layer pans.

CREAM-CHOCOLATE CAKE

This cake requires no shortening because of the thick
cream, and makes a delightfully soft-textured cake, especially for party cakes.
1. Beat until slightly thick
     1 c. thick, sweet cream
2. Add carefully
     1¼ c. brown sugar
     2 eggs, one at a time. Continue beating slowly.
3. Add
     2 c. cake flour sifted with
     ¼ ts. salt
     1 ts. soda. Add alternately with
     ½ c. milk and
     1 ts. vanilla
4. Add and mix in carefully
     2 squares melted and cooled chocolate
5. Bake in layers for 20 minutes or more at 350°. Top with
     whipped cream if desired.

PRIZE-WINNING CHOCOLATE CAKE

When judging a cake contest, I awarded the second place
in the chocolate cake division to the maker of this very
moist, fine-textured cake. It would have placed first if the
frosting had been of a better quality. After judging all
entries by numbers and not names, I was happy to learn

that this cake had been baked by a thirteen-year-old Boy Scout, and that his mother had hurriedly made the frosting. This event really raised quite an ovation from the audience. Will you please try this recipe?

1. Beat well
    1¼ c. brown sugar
    1 c. thick, sweet cream
2. Add
    2 beaten eggs
3. Sift
    2 c. cake flour
    1 ts. soda and add alternately with
    ½ c. milk
    1 ts. vanilla. Beat just until smooth.
4. Add
    ½ c. cocoa made into a paste by adding a little hot milk.
5. Bake in layers for 20 minutes at 350°. Frost as desired.

CHOCOLATE POTATO LOAF

This is a recipe from my dearest friend, Iva.

1. Cook and mash enough potatoes to fill a cup and
2. Cream with
    1 c. shortening
    2 c. sugar
3. Add
    4 eggs, one at a time. Beat after each addition.
4. Add
    2 squares melted and cooled chocolate
5. Sift several times
    2 c. flour
    2 ts. cream of tartar
    2 ts. cinnamon
    ½ ts. salt
    ½ ts. nutmeg
    1 ts. soda
6. Mix altogether alternately with
    ½ c. sour cream and beat until smooth.
7. Bake in 8x4x3-inch loaf tins for 1 hour at 350°. Test by touching the tip of the finger to the center of loaves to make certain the cakes are well baked.
8. Remove from oven and cool. Delicious without frosting.

TABLE SETTING FOR A WEDDING BREAKFAST

The Bride's Cake, decorated tea cakes, sweet rolls, and fruit drink

BIRTHDAY CAKES
Colonial Doll, Storybook Doll, Clown, and Easter Basket

Fruit Cakes

FRUIT CAKES

Fruit cakes are a joy to make when you achieve good results, when flavors blend, cake remains moist, and the keeping quality is maintained. Fruit cakes are usually seasonal and for special occasions such as weddings, Thanksgiving, Christmas Holidays, birthdays, etc. If properly mixed and baked they will have a keeping quality of several months, and are at their best when fully aged.

Fruits used in fruit cakes should be carefully selected and fresh. Raisins used should be soft and meaty. Purchase raisins fresh, the dry ones may be used by washing, draining, and pouring boiling water over them. Let stand for just a few minutes and then drain well. This will help to restore the freshness.

Nearly all fruits should be conditioned prior to using in order to soften and tenderize the skins and to remove the crystalline sugar coating. The soaking will cause the fruit to absorb sufficient moisture, thereby improving the eating quality. Poorly conditioned fruit will draw moisture from the surrounding cake structure and cause crumbling.

Pans for baking the fruit cake should be well-greased with vegetable shortening. Sprinkle with flour to cover entire pan, and then remove excess flour by patting bottom of pans. If paper-lined pans are desired, cut heavy brown paper to fit size of pan. To make corners fit the pan, cut edges of paper with the scissors, then grease and flour lightly. If a moist cake is desired, a pan of tepid water may be placed on lower rack of oven during baking time.

The oven should be preheated to 275° and no higher than 300°. A low, slow baking method is much better for fruit cakes. A burned, hard-crusted fruit cake is not desirable. To prevent this, cover with aluminum foil the last half hour of baking time. Place cakes on racks in center of oven. Do not let pans touch each other. Baking time should be from 1 to 2½ hours, according to size of pans used.

Test fruit cakes, to see if they are sufficiently baked, by touching the middle of layer with tip of finger. If the surface is firm and doesn't leave finger impression, the cake is done. Remove pan to a wire rack and allow to stand in tins for several minutes. Remove from pan, when cool enough to handle. Place on a wire rack to continue cooling.

To store, wrap in plastic bags, waxed paper, or aluminum foil, and place in crocks, jars, or cake savers, etc.

The following are delightful flavorings for fruit cakes. This is a blending of my own creation:

One 2 oz. bottle of banana flavoring
One 2 oz. bottle of orange flavoring
One 2 oz. bottle of cream flavoring such as is used in soda pop
Two ts. almond flavoring

Then mix all together and keep in one large bottle, to be used as desired. Two tbs. are recommended for a large fruit cake. (This is an excellent flavoring for frostings and does not change the color.) Use one ounce bottles if less flavoring is desired.

You may attain a wonderful flavoring also by mixing 2 or 3 different flavors of Bouquet flavoring.

Following are suggestions for glazing the tops of fruit cakes. For a molasses glaze:

2 tbs. molasses
1 egg white
4 tbs. water
2 tbs. sugar

Mix together and brush lightly over top of cakes before baking for a sweet glaze:

2 tbs. pineapple juice
2 ts. white syrup
1 tbs. orange juice
1 tbs. sugar

Mix together and brush over cakes, for a honey glaze:

½ c. melted honey
1 egg white

Glazing makes top of cake shine while baking. It also makes a finished surface when cakes are done so they don't have to be frosted, unless desired.

If you desire to arrange cherries and nuts on top of

cakes, place nuts face up in pattern form, alternately with candied cherries, candied pineapple, or colored gumdrops.

Flour varies in texture. If you find that batter is too moist, add a little additional flour in order to hold fruit and prevent it from sinking to the bottom. To stop large layers from falling in the middle, place a cone in the middle, as from an angel food pan, allowing oven heat to bake evenly in the center.

MY FAVORITE FRUIT CAKE

This recipe is ideal for weddings, holidays or special-occasion cakes. Increase the recipe for larger quantities.

1. Boil for 5 minutes in a large container
    2 c. fruit juice (grape or other juices)
    2 pkgs. seedless raisins
    1 pkg. seeded raisins
    1 pkg. currants
    1½ pkg. brown sugar
    1¾ c. shortening, butter, or margarine
    2 tbs. vinegar
2. Remove from heat and set aside to cool thoroughly before adding other ingredients.
3. Sift together
    8 c. all-purpose flour (approximately)
    2 ts. soda
    4 ts. spices previously mixed (cinnamon, allspice, cloves and ginger)
    1 ts. salt
    2 tbs. dark cocoa
4. Add to the cooled fruit
    8 beaten eggs
    2 tbs. mixed fruit flavoring and then add the flour and spices and stir carefully to protect the fruits from mashing. Batter should be firm, not sticky. Add more flour if necessary.
5. Then add
    1 lb. chopped dates
    1 lb. candied fruit
    1 lb. broken nuts
    1 lb. tiny gumdrops
    1 pt. maraschino cherries

6. Pour into well-greased and floured pans, level the tops with a spatula and brush lightly with a mixture of molasses and cherry juice to make a pretty glazed effect when baked. Melted honey also may be used to glaze the top. Whole nuts and candied cherries may be placed on top for decoration.

7. Bake in a 300° oven for 1 to 3 hours according to size of pans used. A pan of water may be placed on the lower oven rack during baking time to keep the cakes moist.

Test the cakes in the center with the tip of the finger to be sure of sufficient baking. The sides of the cakes will bake much more quickly than the centers, so if the center is moist and isn't firm when touched with the finger tip, continue baking until it is firm.

Cool the cakes on wire racks and then wrap in aluminum foil and place in jars or cake savers for keeping. Fruit cakes are at their best when aged.

MOM CINDA'S DATE CAKE

"It's a dandy" is the comment of all my friends and relatives who have enjoyed this cake for years. It has such a good flavor, cuts in even, nice slices, and keeps well (if you hide it).

Fresh seasonal dates are best for this cake. Remove the stones and leave the dates in halves. They look so full and tempting when the cake is sliced.

1. Cream together to a creamy paste
   2 full c. brown sugar
   1 c. butter (butter is needed for flavor)

2. Add
   4 eggs, one at a time, and continue beating

3. Gradually beat in
   4 c. flour sifted with
   2 ts. soda
   1 ts. salt, alternately with
   1 c. milk and
   2 ts. fruit flavoring
   1 ts. orange emulsion

4. When mixture is well blended add
   3 lbs. stoned dates and
   2 c. nuts (walnuts and pecans)

5. Stir carefully so as not to crush the dates. Bake in buttered and floured pans at 300° for 1 to 2 hours, or until firm to the touch.

AUNT EVELYN'S BOILED FRUIT CAKE

1. Boil for 10 minutes, then cool thoroughly
    1 c. lard or shortening
    2 c. sugar
    2 c. cold water
    1 pkg. seedless raisins
    1 pkg. seeded raisins
    ½ ts. salt
    1 ts. allspice
    1 ts. cloves
    1 ts. cinnamon
2. When cool, add
    Flour enough to make a stiff batter sifted with
    2 ts. baking powder
    1 ts. soda
3. Add
    1 c. walnut pieces
4. Bake in greased and floured loaf tins at 300° for 1 hour or more, until firm.

ALMOND-PASTE WHITE FRUIT CAKE

A cake designed for special occasions and for you who like an almond flavor.

1. Begin by kneading to a smooth paste
    1 lb. almond paste
    1 c. sugar
    2 egg whites
2. Cream and add to the paste
    ¾ lb. butter
    2 c. sugar
3. Then add
    ½ c. apricot nectar and
    2 ts. almond flavoring
4. Sift together
    4 c. flour
    2 ts. baking powder

5.   Beat until stiff
       15 egg whites and add to the creamed mixtures alternately with the flour.
6.   Prepare and sprinkle lightly with flour
       1 lb. dates, chopped
       1 lb. Brazil nut pieces
       2 lbs. white raisins
       2 lbs. candied fruit mix
       2 lbs. coconut
       Stir in carefully and place in prepared pans. Bake at 300° for 2 hours or longer.

PRUNE AND RAISIN CAKE

A very good all-purpose, family cake, one that will keep for several days.

1.   Cream well
       1 c. brown sugar
       1 c. shortening
       4 eggs and add
       1 tbs. milk
2.   Sift into the creamed mixture
       2 c. flour
       1 ts. mace
       1 ts. cinnamon
       ½ ts. soda
3.   Add
       1 lb. prunes that have been soaked and cut into pieces
       1 lb. seedless raisins, soaked and drained
       ½ lb. candied fruit
       1 c. nut pieces
4.   Bake in loaf pans 250° for 3½ hours.

HOLIDAY-TIME FRUIT CAKE

1.   Cream together
       1 lb. brown sugar
       8 eggs
2.   Soak in
       1 c. grape juice or brandy
       2 ts. cinnamon
       1 ts. nutmeg

½ ts. mace
½ ts. cloves
3. Mix
1 ts. soda in
1 c. dark molasses and add to the sugar, spices, and juice
4. Sift in
2 c. flour
1½ ts. baking powder, stir well and add
1 c. bread crumbs
2 c. suet (ground fine)
1 c. lemon juice
5. Add
2 pkgs. raisins
½ lb. maraschino or candied cherries
2 c. pecan nuts
2 lbs. currants
½ lb. candied pineapple
6. When all blended, spoon into prepared pans for baking. Bake at 250° for 3 hours. Cool on racks and store.

PRUNE FRUIT CAKE

Light and fluffy—a good substitute for fruit cake.
1. Cook, or simmer slowly, enough prunes to make
1¼ c., cut fine. Cool.
2. Cream together
½ c. shortening
½ c. butter or margarine
1 c. sugar
3 eggs
3. Add
¾ c. buttermilk
1 ts. lemon extract
4. Add
2¼ c. flour sifted with
2 ts. baking powder
½ ts. soda
½ ts. salt
5. Mix altogether slowly, do not overbeat. Add chopped prunes and pour into pans. Bake 35 to 50 minutes at 350°. Cool and frost.

OLD KENTUCKY BLACK FRUIT CAKE

This cake is dark in color, rich in fruits, and keeps indefinitely.

1. Cream until smooth
    12 eggs
    1 lb. brown sugar
    1½ c. white sugar
    1 lb. butter or margarine

2. Add
    1 c. dark molasses
    1 c. sour milk or buttermilk and continue beating.

3. Gradually add
    8 c. flour sifted with
    2 ts. soda
    2 ts. cinnamon
    1 ts. salt
    2 ts. ginger
    1 ts. allspice

4. Mix well, then add
    1 c. grape juice and
    1 c. flour

5. When batter is thoroughly mixed, add the following:
    2 lbs. black dried figs
    1 lb. white dried figs
    1 lb. dates, cut in pieces
    ½ lb. almonds chopped
    ½ lb. walnuts
    ½ lb. Brazil nuts, cut in pieces
    ½ lb. candied pineapple
    2 lbs. seedless raisins
    1 lb. currants
    1 lb. seeded raisins
    ½ lb. candied orange peel

6. Stir altogether carefully and while mixing add
    2 tbs. rum extract and
    4 squares of melted and cooled bitter chocolate.

7. Spoon into pans prepared for baking. This cake should be baked slowly at 275° for 2½ hours, or more. Test by touching the tops, to be sure they are firm.

8. Dark fruit juice or wine may be poured over layers sparingly to restore softness as they age.

WHITE FRUIT CAKE

1. Cream together
    ¾ lb. butter or margarine and
    1⅔ c. sugar
2. Add
    9 eggs beaten
3. Add and mix well
    3 c. flour
    1 ts. almond extract
4. Add
    1 lb. white figs
    1 lb. white raisins
    1 lb. candied pineapple
    1 lb. candied cherries
    1 c. coconut
    ½ lb. almonds (blanched). Instructions on blanching almonds below.
5. Mix altogether and spoon into loaf pans. Glaze with fruit glaze and arrange nuts on top. Bake at 275° for 2 hours or more.

    TO BLANCH ALMONDS: place whole almonds (as they come from the shell) into rapidly boiling water for just a few minutes or until the skins are soft. Drain and run cold water over them and remove the skins.

HEAVENLY WHITE FRUIT CAKE

This is one of my family's favorites.

1. Cream together
    1 c. sugar
    1 c. shortening
    4 eggs
2. Add
    1 tbs. lemon juice
    ½ c. pineapple jam
    1 tbs. fruit flavoring
3. Sift together
    2 c. flour
    ¼ ts. salt
    1 ts. baking powder. Add to the above mixtures.

4. Then add and mix well
   1 c. diced candied pineapple
   1½ c. candied cherries
   1 c. blanched almonds (chopped)
   1 c. coconut
   1 c. candy orange slices, cut in pieces
5. Place in prepared baking pans and bake in a slow oven 275° for 2 hours or until firm.

WHOLE-WHEAT FRUIT CAKE

Many people prefer whole-wheat flour. This cake will please them.
1. Pour
   1 c. hot water over
   1 pkg. seedless raisins, then cool and add
   1 ts. soda
2. Cream well and add to the raisin mixture
   1 c. shortening
   2 c. sugar
   2 eggs
3. Add, sifted together
   3 c. whole-wheat flour
   1 c. white flour
   1 ts. salt
   1 ts. nutmeg
   1 ts. cinnamon
   1 ts. baking powder
   Mix well.
4. Add
   1 c. nuts (if desired)
5. Place in baking pans, which have been greased and floured and bake at 300° for 1½ hours or until firm.

SPICY FRUIT CAKE

The spices are predominant in the flavor of this cake.
1. Cream together
   1½ c. sugar
   ½ lb. butter or margarine
   6 egg yolks

2. Add
>   1 c. molasses
>   1 c. buttermilk
3. Add enough flour to make a firm dough, sifted with
>   1 ts. soda
>   1 ts. salt
>   1 ts. cinnamon
>   1 ts. cloves
>   1 ts. nutmeg
>   1 ts. allspice
>   1 ts. mace
4. Mix well, and add
>   1 lb. currants
>   1 lb. raisins
>   1 lb. dates, cut in pieces
>   1 lb. gumdrops (small ones preferred)
5 Stir and place in pans to bake. Bake at 275° for 1½ to 2 hours.

XMAS CAKE BY "MAMPS"
(The name we all call Mamma)

This is a simple fruit cake, tasty and economical. One we enjoyed every Christmas at home when we were youngsters.

1. Cream together
>   2 c. sugar
>   1 c. butter
>   3 eggs
2. Add
>   1 c. buttermilk
>   1 c. molasses
>   ½ c. cocoa, softened in a little hot water
3. Add enough all-purpose flour to make a stiff dough, sifted with:
>   1 ts. soda
>   1 ts. allspice
>   1 ts. ginger
>   1 ts. salt
4. Add
>   1 pkg. seedless raisins
>   1 pkg. seeded raisins
>   1 pkg. currants

       1 c. walnuts, broken in pieces
       ½ lb. gumdrops, cut in pieces
       1 c. maraschino cherries

5. Mix together well and spoon into prepared pans for baking. Bake at 275° for 2 hours or until done.

"YULE" XMAS CAKE

1. Cream until light
       ½ lb. butter or margarine
       1½ c. brown sugar
2. Add
       6 well-beaten egg yolks
3. Add
       1 c. light molasses
       1 c. buttermilk
       1 ts. soda, stirred together with
       1 c. grape juice
4. Sift and add
       4 c. flour
       1 ts. cloves
       1 ts. nutmeg
       ½ ts. allspice
       1 ts. salt
5. Mix well and add more flour to make a stiff batter.
6. Stir in the following fruits and nuts
       2 c. raisins
       2 c. dates, cut in pieces
       ½ c. citron peel
       ½ c. orange peel
       1 c. candied pineapple
       1 c. candied cherries
       2 c. currants
       2 c. nut meats
7. Beat until very stiff and fold into mixture carefully
       6 egg whites
8. Fill pans to be used for baking and bake at 250° for 2 hours or longer until tops of cakes are firm.

FIVE-POUND, OLD-FASHIONED DARK CAKE

1. Cream well
      1 c. butter or shortening
      1¼ c. brown sugar
      4 eggs
2. Add
      ¼ c. molasses
      ¼ c. dark fruit juice
      1 tbs. fruit flavoring
3. Add sifted together
      4 c. flour
      ¼ ts. soda
      ¼ ts. salt
      ½ ts. cloves
      ½ ts. mace
      1 ts. cinnamon
4. Mix well and add
      1 lb. seedless raisins
      1 lb. chopped dates
      1 lb. fruit mix
      1 c. walnuts
      1 c. pecans
5. Bake in loaf tins at 275° for 2½ hours or until firm.

SOUTHERN FRUIT CAKE

This cake is especially rich and has wonderful keeping qualities.

1. Cream together
      1 c. sugar
      ¼ lb. butter or margarine
2. Add
      2 beaten eggs and
      1 ts. fruit or rum flavoring
3. Add
      2 c. flour sifted with
      2 ts. baking powder
      ¼ ts. salt
4. Beat until smooth and add
      ½ lb. candied cherries
      ½ lb. candied pineapple

        1 lb. dates, cut in pieces
        1 lb. pecan pieces

5.   Bake in greased and floured loaf pans until firm to the touch, at 300° for 1½ hours or more. Place on racks to cool, store as desired.

IMOGENE'S FRUIT CAKE (My Sister-in-Law)

This is a recipe from the Dakotas and is one used by her family for many years. I baked and decorated one of these cakes for her sister's wedding. It was a large, three-tiered cake which they carefully carried on the train about 1200 miles from Logan, Utah, to North Dakota.

1.   Begin by preparing all of the fruits and nuts. Cut into pieces, then sprinkle with flour.
        2 lbs. citron
        2 lbs. figs (dark and light)
        1 lb. dates
        6 lbs. raisins (chopped)
        4 lbs. currants
        1 lb. almonds (chopped)

2.   Cream well
        6 c. brown sugar
        2½ c. melted butter

3.   Beat until light
        24 eggs and add to the butter and sugar

4.   Stir in
        2 tbs. lemon juice
        1 c. molasses
        1 c. brandy (or fruit juice)
        1 whole nutmeg (grated)

5.   Mix in gradually
        7 c. flour

6.   When all mixed, add the prepared fruits and nuts. Fill prepared pans and bake in a slow 275° oven for several hours until tops are firm. (Note: the eggs are the leavening in this cake.)
Cool on racks, wrap in aluminum foil to store. This cake has good keeping qualities up to 1 year.

BLACK FRUIT CAKE

One look at this luscious, dark cake and you immediately feel hungry. 'T is of old-fashioned origin, easy to mix, and a joy to serve to your family and friends.

1. Cream together
    2 c. brown sugar
    2 c. shortening
    6 eggs
2. Add
    1 c. molasses
    1 c. grape juice or prune juice
3. Add
    8 c. flour sifted with
    2 ts. baking powder
    1 ts. soda
    3 ts. mixed spices
4. Mix well and then fold in
    1 pkg. fruit mix
    1 pkg. dates
    1 lb. chopped nuts
    1 lb. black figs, if desired
    3 squares bitter chocolate, melted and cooled
5. Bake in prepared tins at 300° from 1½ to 2 hours.

WHITE FRUIT CAKE (FESTIVAL)

This all-occasion cake is very "yummy." It keeps well and is attractive when arranged on serving tray.

1. Sift together
    2½ c. flour
    1 ts. baking powder
    ¼ ts. salt
2. Cream together
    1 c. shortening
    1 c. sugar
3. Add
    5 beaten eggs and
    1 tbs. lemon juice
    1 tbs. orange juice
    1 tbs. pineapple juice

4. Add
        1 c. macaroon coconut
        1 c. blanched almonds
        1 c. diced candied pineapple
        ½ c. orange peel
        1½ c. cherries, candied
        ½ c. lemon peel
        1 tbs. mixed flavoring.
5. Mix together and place in tins. Bake from 1 to 3 hours at 300°, according to size of pan.
6. When cool frost with Butter Cream Frosting, if desired.

MABEL'S FRUIT CAKE

My friend Mabel, who lives in the country, always serves delicious fruit cake and she claims she just throws it all together when making it.

1. Cream together in a large bowl
        1½ c. sugar
        1 c. shortening (she uses home-rendered lard)
2. Add
        6 eggs and
        1 c. molasses
        1 c. sour cream
        1 c. grape juice
3. Sift together
        8 c. flour
        2 ts. baking powder
        1 ts. salt
        1 ts. soda
        ½ ts. cloves
4. Add to the other mixtures and stir until well mixed.
5. Add
        2 pkgs. seedless raisins
        1 pkg. seeded raisins
        1 lb. candied fruit mix
6. Mix altogether and bake in large pans in a 275° oven for 2 hours or until firm.

FAMILY FRUIT CAKE

1. Cream together
        1½ c. sugar

BIRTHDAY CAKES AND FESTIVE COOKIES

Basket of Roses, Colonial Doll, Storybook Doll, and Clown Cake. Santa and other Christmas cookies, Cinderella Slipper, a Swan and a Bootee.

GINGERBREAD HOUSE

Complete instructions are given on page 157 for assembling, baking, and decorating

    1 c. shortening
    5 eggs

2. Add and mix well
    1 c. fruit juice (any flavor)
    ½ c. molasses
    1 c. sour cream

3. Sift together, then add
    8 c. flour (all-purpose)
    2 ts. soda
    ¼ ts. cloves
    1 ts. cinnamon
    2 ts. baking powder

4. Add
    2 pkgs. seedless raisins
    1 pkg. seeded raisins
    ½ lb. candied fruits
    2 c. cherries (maraschino or candied)
    1 c. nut pieces

5. Mix together and spoon into pans. Bake at 275° for 2 hours, or more, until firm.

Cake Decorating and Frostings

THE ART OF CAKE DECORATING

Decorating a cake may be fun—why not try it yourself?
The elaborately decorated cakes which you see in bakery windows are not as difficult to make as you might expect— at least, if you have enthusiasm and determination.

Anyone can learn to decorate cakes, if not professionally, at least well enough to bring a lot of pleasure to family and friends. By securing the proper decorating tubes, bags, and parchment paper for cones, by following the instructions given, both in decorating and in recipes for frostings, and by using ingenuity and individual ideas, cake decorating may become a happy pastime and hobby and, perhaps, eventually a business.

Secure a set of decorating tubes and bags and mix a batch of beginner's frosting. I suggest that you make the decorations on waxed paper in the beginning because the frosting may be scraped up and used over and over again.

The frosting may be tinted by using pure food coloring in liquid form. A dropper may be useful in measuring the coloring. The paste coloring may be measured by use of a toothpick. Mixing the colors gives a more attractive effect than using just one primary color. All sugar used should be sifted before being used to avoid lumps forming in the decorating tubes.

Fluffy white frostings and creamy butter frostings are ideal for decorating cakes because they remain soft and cut nicely for special occasions and party cakes.

Ornamental frostings become hard soon after being applied and are recommended for wedding cakes and other cakes that are to be kept for several days or longer. The frosting acts as a shield and protector to preserve the freshness of the cake. The frosting will retain its color for an undetermined length of time. Although it may be hard to cut when serving, it will still be edible.

Teacakes or cupcakes are the easiest for beginners to try.

You need only to frost the top and use the decorating tube to make little twirls around the edges, or a flower in the center. A small amount of decorating transforms a cake from the ordinary to the unusual. Then try simple layer cakes, special-occasion cakes and fancy *petits fours,* and eventually you may try a wedding cake or an anniversary cake.

The preparation of the cake is the first step in cake decoration. Place the cooled cake on a plate or mirror, then make a simple frosting out of powdered sugar, 'a small amount of flavoring, and enough cold water to make a thin paste. Carefully cover top and sides of cake, and between layers, if desired, making sure the cake is covered. The surfaces to be decorated should be smooth and free from crumbs. Allow this coating to dry before applying the finishing frosting, which should be one that will hold its shape, yet be soft enough to pass through the decorating tube.

In making the fluted edging, you will have no difficulty because the frosting will leave the tube when you press gently on the bag of frosting and move the hand in different motions. Pretty patterns will form as you decorate. Move the hand up and down, back and forth, in eyelet form, making rows of e's. Squeeze gently because the size of the decoration pattern will depend on the pressure you give. Practice will prove this. Keep all containers holding frosting covered and airtight while decorating.

STEPS IN DECORATING FOR BEGINNERS

1. Make a beginner's frosting and fill a paper cone or canvas bag using the decorating tube you desire to try. Begin squeezing the frosting onto a large piece of heavy waxed paper. Try making straight lines of 3's, 1's, and m's—now join them together and continue in motion. Then try the letter S, also joining them as you go. Try a pattern moving the hand back and forth, forward and back.
2. Scrape up the frosting and repeat. Use frosting over again.
3. Patterns of different edges will come naturally as you practice these simple rules, using different tubes.
4. As you hold the paper cone or bag in the hand, press only

with the tips of the fingers. The thumb is used just as a guide — pressing with the thumb will force the frosting out of the top of the bag.

When you make the designs well and evenly, try making rosettes and leaves. The directions for rosettes are found in the flower instructions.

FROSTING LEAVES

Leaves are the simplest of cake decorating. They are made with a No. 67 tube, smaller or larger tubes are available.
1. Tint some decorative frosting with one or two drops of green coloring or one spot of green paste coloring. Stir well and place in a paper cone with the tube in the end.
2. Begin pressing gently, one squeeze at a time, releasing each leaf on a waxed paper at first, for practice. The leaf should be wide at the top being pulled to a point at the finish; to attain this, squeeze the tube pressing against the paper and quickly drawing the hand away, pulling the frosting to a point and releasing; this will make a plain leaf. To make a ruffled leaf, move the tube in a pushing back motion two or three times and release. The size of leaves you make depends on how hard you press the bag. With practice you will make the sizes you desire.

TUBE WRITING

To do decorative writing, simply fill a paper cone with ornamental frosting, tinted in color, and use the writing tube No. 1 or the paper cone with a very small opening in the end. Begin squeezing the frosting out, writing in the same manner as with a pen or pencil. If you hold the top of the paper cone firmly in the palm and press gently with the fingers, the frosting will ooze out and the lettering will take form. As in writing, you will, of course, need practice and, in time, will be able to write beautifully with ease and skill. This idea is carried out in many ways in decorating— in making stems for flowers, holly leaves, and in some edging outline work, and also for making the fine lace work shown in the pictures of wedding cakes in this book.

These frostings are designed for first steps in decorating.

"BEGINNER'S" BUTTER-CREAM FROSTING

This recipe may be divided if smaller portion is needed. You will enjoy learning to decorate with it because it is inexpensive and may be reused if desired by scooping up the frosting and rebeating it.

1. Flavor to taste and beat for 20 minutes
    1½ lbs. powdered sugar
    ¾ c. vegetable shortening
    a scant ½ c. evaporated milk (or use a scant ½ cup hot water)
    1 unbeaten egg white and ¼ ts. cream of tartar
2. Tint if desired and add more powdered sugar if heavier frosting is to be used.

"BEGINNER'S" PEARL FROSTING

This frosting may be used for any type of decorating.

1. 1 lb. pkg. powdered sugar
    1 rounded tbs. vegetable shortening
    enough top milk or evaporated milk to make the right consistency.
2. Add 1 ts. uncolored flavoring to
    2 tbs. white syrup
    2 egg whites, which will make the frosting much more fluffy.
3. Beat for several minutes on high speed. You may need more powdered sugar if you desire a thicker frosting.

PEARL FROSTING

1. Beat together until stiff
    2 egg whites
    ⅓ ts. salt
2. Add slowly and beat until very light
    1 c. powdered sugar
    ½ c. white syrup
    ½ ts. fresh lemon juice
    ½ ts. lemon flavoring
3. Additional sugar may be added for heavier frosting.

CORNSTARCH BUTTER-CREAM FROSTING
(Large Recipe)

1. Beat together
    - ½ pt. egg yolks
    - 1½ lbs. powdered sugar
2. Mix together
    - 1¼ lbs. butter
    - 4 ozs. cornstarch
    - 2 ts. vanilla or other flavoring
    - ½ lb. powdered sugar
3. Combine mixtures and beat slowly. Avoid overmixing. This frosting is palatable and therefore is very popular. It may be used for decorating as well as frosting by adding more powdered sugar to the thickness desired.

ROYAL FROSTINGS

Royal Frostings are commonly known, widely used, can be made in a hurry, and are recommended for making birds, flowers, brackets, etc.

Frosting will harden soon after being applied; therefore, it is good for making decorations but not too choice for cakes that must be kept overnight or longer.

ROYAL FROSTING No. 1

This is a small recipe and may be increased to larger amounts.

1. Mix together, then beat on high speed of mixer until it is as thick as desired.
    - 2 tbs. meringue powder
    - 1 lb. powdered sugar
    - ¼ ts. cream of tartar
    - ⅓ c. water
2. Flavor to taste.

ROYAL FROSTING No. 2

1. Beat until frothy
    - 3½ tbs. meringue powder
    - ½ c. powdered sugar
    - ½ c. cold water

2. Add
     1 lb. powdered sugar, then beat again
3. Gradually add
     1 more lb. powdered sugar and beat until fluffy.
     Flavor to taste.

MERINGUE POWDER

This is a product made of albumen, dextrose, starch, vegetable gum, sodium aluminum sulphate, salt, fruit acid, cream of tartar, and vanillin.

It may be used for making topping for meringue pies, and for frostings. It is an important factor in making frostings for the experienced decorator.

BOILED MERINGUE-POWDER ICING

1. In a saucepan place
     2 lbs. sugar and
     1 pt. water. Stir well and bring to a boil.
2. In the beater bowl, beat up
     6 oz. meringue powder and
     1 pt. cold water
     1 lb. sugar and beat until stiff
     add flavor to taste
3. Add the boiled syrup to the beaten meringue and beat on low speed for five minutes or more until frosting stands in peaks.
     Use for frosting as well as decorating cakes.

PLAIN MERINGUE ICING

1. In a large mixing bowl place
     5 heaping ts. meringue powder and
     1 c. cold water. Beat on high speed until foamy and firm.
2. Add slowly
     3 pkgs. sifted powdered sugar and beat until smooth.
3. Add
     2 ts. fruit flavoring.
4.   1 egg white may be added while beating.
     This is optional.

Sifted powdered sugar may be added and beaten after each addition to make a stiff frosting for decorating. Keep bowl of frosting covered while decorating to avoid crust forming on top.

BOILED MERINGUE ICING

1. In beater bowl place
    1 pt. water
    1 lb. sugar
    6 oz. of meringue powder and beat until frothy and will hold in peaks.
2. While beating meringue, cook the following
    2 lbs. sugar
    1 pt. water (stir before cooking and wash the sides of the kettle)
3. Bring to a full rolling boil and pour quickly over the beaten meringue, beat on low speed for 5 minutes. Flavor to taste.

FROSTING SUPREME

By combining a batch of candy syrup and mixing it with a bowl of meringue-powder icing, I created a perfect frosting with a waxed-like finish—ideal for making lilies, birds, etc. The frosting sets quickly and the shiny lustre remains for several weeks. It is ideal in making ornamental decorations, days in advance, to be used on special-occasion cakes.

FROSTING SUPREME

1. Sift 2½ pkgs. powdered sugar in advance
2. In a small utensil place
    ½ c. glucose and warm slowly
3. Dissolve
    1 tbs. marshmallow powder in
    ¼ c. cold water
4. In a large mixing bowl beat
    5 full tsp. meringue powder and
    ¼ c. cold water until stiff
5. Add sifted powdered sugar slowly and beat well

6. Pour

> ¼ c. boiling water over soaked marshmallow powder.
> Stir well and add to the hot glucose.
> Then stir it slowly into the sugar mixture, beating
> constantly.

7. Flavor with fruit flavoring and thicken with sifted pow-
    dered sugar for thicker frosting.

PLAIN BOILED ICING

Some decorators prefer a boiled icing. This one is a
favorite. It may be used for coating, and it spreads smoothly. It also may be used for decorating by adding more
powdered sugar according to the thickness desired. It sets
quite quickly so you will have to work fast. Keep frosting
covered while decorating.

1. In a large mixing bowl place and beat until it comes to a
    peak

> 1 c. cold water
> 7 tbs. of meringue powder

2. Add

> 1 lb. powdered sugar
> Beat at high speed for 2 minutes. Turn to 2nd speed
> for 2 minutes, then back to high speed.

3. In a saucepan boil to 242° (in high altitudes, 240°)

> 2 c. white sugar
> ¼ ts. cream of tartar
> ½ c. water

4. Then add slowly to meringue mixture and beat for 3
    minutes.

5. Fold in sifted powdered sugar to make the consistency
    desired. In climates where humidity and temperature
    are different, you will have to add more powdered sugar
    accordingly.

GLUCOSE ICING

This frosting is designed for decorating. It is beautifully
white, spreads evenly, holds its shape, and is easy to handle.
It is recommended for cakes that are to be kept for any
length of time.

1. In a large mixing bowl place

> ¾ c. cold water

     4 tbs. meringue powder
     2½ lbs. powdered sugar
     ½ c. warmed glucose
     ½ ts. cream of tartar
     ¼ ts. salt

2. Begin by beating slowly, then increase the speed and beat until it is very light and ready to use.
3. Add

     2½ ts. glycerine and beat again.
     Keep in covered bowl while decorating.

ADVANCED FROSTINGS FOR THE DECORATOR

For those who are decorators and advanced enough to handle different frostings, this chapter will prove invaluable. The frostings are tested and are accurate in measurements as well as perfect in results. The recipes call for many products used by bakers and professional decorators. These will have to be purchased through the bakeries or bakery supply house. Because these products are obtainable and sold only in large amounts, it is not practical for those who do decorating in small amounts and only occasionally to purchase these supplies.

For beginners, the same results may be obtained by using the more simple frostings. But to give the professional touch and appearance these frostings are recommended. Listed below are some of the products used for professional decorating:

Whip Powders
Invert Sugars
Dryvert Sugars
Meringue Powders
Marshmallow Powders
Glucose
Stayice
Fondants

WHIP POWDER

This product is similar to meringue powder. It makes a very light frosting suitable for birthday cakes and teacakes, also for topping sweet rolls.

1. In a large bowl put
   1 c. boiling water
   2 c. sugar
   5 ts. whip powder
   1½ tbs. white syrup
   1 ts. pure glycerine
   Mix together and beat until sugar is thoroughly dissolved.
2. Then add enough powdered sugar to make the frosting the thickness desired.
   Flavor to taste.
   Keep frosting covered when not in use to keep it soft and moist.

MARSHMALLOW POWDER

This is also a baker's product and may be obtained from bakeries or supply houses. It is valuable in making marshmallow frostings, dressings, candies, and cake toppings.

MARSHMALLOW POWDER FROSTING

This is a soft, smooth frosting and tastes like candy marshmallows.
1. In a mixer bowl place
   1⅔ c. boiling water
   3 tbs. marshmallow powder. Mix on slow speed until dissolved.
2. Add to this
   1½ pkgs. powdered sugar
   1 c. invert sugar (Invert sugar is a paste sugar product)
3. Use flavoring and coloring desired. May be used for marshmallow rolls, fillings between cakes, toppings, and icings.

GLOSSY FROSTING

This frosting may be used to frost and decorate as it is easy to apply and stays soft.
1. Combine in saucepan and stir until dissolved
   1 c. sugar
   ½ c. light syrup

½ c. water
½ ts. cream of tartar

2. Place over low heat and boil, washing the sides of kettle while boiling, until it spins a thread or reaches 234°.

3. Beat until stiff
   2 egg whites

4. Gradually pour hot syrup over the egg whites and beat until it is thick enough to spread. Flavor to taste. Cover top and sides of cake, then add enough sifted powdered sugar to make the frosting stiff enough to use for decorating. Tint as desired.

FONDANT ICING

Fondant icing is a product made for bakers and those who frost and decorate cakes in large quantities. It is a time-saving product and produces wonderful results. It is especially good for dipping *petits fours* and small party teacakes. A variety of frosting may be made from this base by addition of egg whites, shortenings, sugar, fruits, flavoring, etc.

A very nice fondant may be made from dryvert sugar and water, flavored to taste, by beating.

1. 2½ c. water to
   10 lbs. of dryvert sugar
   Beat until creamy and the consistency desired; more sugar may be added if thicker frosting is desired. This mixture may be kept for days and melted over warm water when ready to use. Simply add flavoring and coloring as desired.
   For a richer fondant icing, use "Butter-Cream Fondant Frosting."

BUTTER-CREAM FONDANT ICING

1. Cream until light
   8 lbs. fondant icing
   2 lbs. shortening
   1 lb. butter
   2 lbs. powdered sugar
   8 ozs. powdered milk
   1 oz. vanilla

2. Beat until light
   12 ozs. whole eggs

3. Gradually add to the first mixture and beat until fluffy. Frost cakes as desired.

For frosted teacakes:

1. Melt the amount of fondant icing needed over a pan of warm water.
2. Place the small cakes to be used on a wire rack or use a wire whip spoon and dip the cakes in the melted fondant and slip them on a rack to cool and harden. For large quantities melt the fondant in a pan large enough to cover a rack full of cakes at a time. The cakes may be left on the rack to cool. The remaining icing may be rewarmed for more cakes.

COFFEECAKE ICING

1. Make a simple syrup by bringing to a boil
   3 lbs. sugar
   1 qt. water
2. Add enough fondant icing to make a thin frosting and while hot spread on cakes.

STAYICE

This is a professional product made especially for frostings. It is rich in flavor, gives the base a smooth texture, and spreads evenly. It has very good keeping qualities and will stay soft for days. It is preferred for its butterlike flavor.

SWEET ROLL ICING (Large Recipe)

1. In a large beater bowl, mix until free from lumps
   10 c. powdered sugar
   1½ c. water
   8 ozs. stayice
2. Gradually add
   ½ c. water. Continue beating, scraping the sides and bottom of the bowl, until frosting is smooth.
3. Use water 80° to 90° in hot weather and hot water in cold weather.
4. Have baked goods cool before frosting and allow ½ hour

for the frosting to dry. Goods frosted with this frosting may be wrapped in waxed paper if necessary. Coloring may be added if desired.

MILK-CHOCOLATE FUDGE ICING (Large Recipe)

1. Mix together until free from lumps
   5 lbs. powdered sugar
   ½ lb. shortening (sweet)
   ¾ lb. stayice
   ½ c. water
   2 tbs. glucose
   ¾ lb. cocoa
2. Then add
   3 tbs. water
   ½ ts. salt
   and vanilla to taste
3. When creamy, frost cakes as desired. (Cocoa may be omitted for plain vanilla frosting.)

CREAM ICING (Large Recipe)

1. Cream until light
   3 lbs. powdered sugar
   1½ lbs. shortening
   8 ozs. egg whites
2. Beat slowly with beater
   6 lbs. fondant icing
   8 ozs. condensed milk
3. Add two mixtures together and beat until light.
4. Flavor with fruit flavors to taste.

ROYAL ICING FOR DECORATING (Large Recipe)

To be used for wedding, birthday, and other special cakes.
1. Work on low speed until smooth, or use wire whip
   4 lbs. of fondant icing
   10 ozs. egg whites
   ⅛ oz. cream of tartar
2. Then turn on high speed and beat until light and fluffy.
3. Flavor to taste.

ROYAL ICING

1. Place in a saucepan
    2 c. sugar
    ¾ c. water
    1 tbs. light syrup
    ⅛ ts. salt
2. Stir well and bring to a boil. Wash the sides of the kettle to avoid graining. Then, boil to 232° without stirring. Remove from heat.
3. Have ready
    2 egg whites, beaten stiff but not dry
4. Pour boiling syrup slowly over the beaten egg whites, beating constantly.
5. Blend in
    1 ts. fruit flavoring, so as not to color the frosting. Continue beating until frosting stands in peaks. Quickly spread on sides and top of cake.

DECORATIVE FLOWERS

Frosting flowers may be made from several types of frosting—Butter-Creams, Meringue Icing, Royal Icings, etc. In the list of frosting recipes you will find many types of decorative frostings. Beginners have better luck with the butter-cream type because of its smooth texture, thus making it easier to push through the decorating tube. Others find the Royal and Pearl frostings easy to manage. Trial practices will help you decide which frosting you prefer.

ROSES

To make a perfect frosting rose is the dream of every decorator. It requires practice and you will enjoy every minute of it. I suggest you use clean bottle caps on which to make the roses, if you do not have rose nails; large jar lids may be used for the larger roses.

Roses are best when made in advance and allowed to dry before using on special cakes. Applying them directly to the cake will not give them the firm natural look that drying will.

Trays of roses, plain and tinted, may be made to be used when needed. But for the cakes that are to be eaten when decorated, it is advisable to make them from softer frosting so the roses will cut easily. To try your luck making frosting roses, begin by:

1. Make a batch of butter-cream or meringue frosting and add more sifted powdered sugar, stir well to make the frosting stiff enough to hold the petals firm and in shape.
2. Place a rose tube in the bag using the size of the one you prefer to make. Use a

    No. 101 tube for very small roses
    No. 104 tube for small roses
    No. 126 tube for larger roses

There are many sizes of rose tubes available. Use only white frosting at first until you acquire the art, then try tinting the frosting in pastel colors to represent the natural color of the roses.

To make tinted roses with deeper colored edges, color a small portion of frosting a darker shade. With a slender spatula spread this frosting evenly over the inside of the decorating bag above the small end of the tube, then finish filling the bag with the other remaining colored frosting and proceed to make the rose.

1. Begin by holding the cap or nail in the one hand and holding a bag of frosting in the other, with the tip of the rose tube small side up. Squeeze a small portion of frosting on the flat side of the caps to make a foundation for the rose. Begin in the center of the mound of frosting and squeeze a tiny center for the rose by turning the hand around; then press one petal at a time all around the center; repeat, forcing more frosting to make larger petals to complete the rose. One squeeze on the bag is ample to force enough frosting for one petal. The pressure applied by squeezing the bag of frosting determines the size of decoration you make. For instance, a little squeeze will force a small amount of frosting to leave the tube, thus making a small petal or decoration; a strong squeeze will force a large amount of frosting to ooze out, making a larger one. Practice will prove the pressure needed in squeezing.

Be sure to hold the decorating tube away from the foundation of the rose at the top of the petal to allow each petal to stand away from the center. Holding the tube too close will force the petals together and take away the natural look of the rose. Turning the hand slightly as each petal is

FROSTING ROSES, PLACED ON BOTTLE CAPS

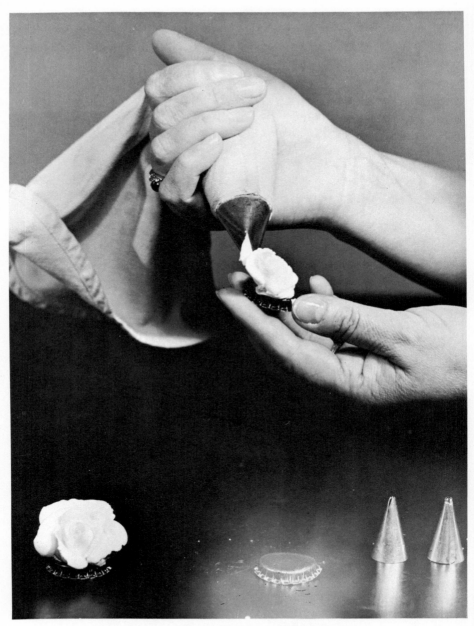

Frosting Roses, Placed on Bottle Caps

applied will give a rounded, full look with the edges curled just as in the natural rose.

Practically all frosting flowers may be made with the small, medium, and large rose tube such as:
Sweet Peas
Wild Flowers
Jonquils
Daisies
Poinsettias
The leaf tubes are used to make:
Lilies
Orchids
Lily of the Valley
Calla Lily

PANSIES

Frosting pansies are a pretty flower for birthday and party cakes. They are made with the small rose tube, No. 104, and the frosting should be tinted and shaded to represent the natural flower. There are five petals—two small ones at the top, one on each side, and a large petal at the bottom. To obtain the lavender and purple shades of some pansies, mix the frosting with red and blue coloring or paste color until you get the color desired. You may also use the prepared lavender coloring for the lighter petals and make a deeper color for the large petals. You will need three cones of frosting for pansies.

1. Make a small mound of frosting on a cap or lid for the base and begin by squeezing two small petals at the top and one small one on each side.
2. With the darker color frosting make one large petal at the bottom, having all petals join together at the center.
3. Then with a cone containing the writing tube No. 1 and the darker shaded frosting, outline the very center of the flower with a line of frosting, following the inside edge of the petals, and finish with several little straight-line darts leading up from the large petal.
   When you have mastered the art of making the pansy, you may try making yellow centers by using yellow frosting as a mound, also line the one side of the cone with shaded yellow frosting before adding the colored.

This will produce the natural effect of having a yellow-centered flower with shaded petals.

For yellow pansies, reverse the shading by making purple centers and yellow petals with purple stripes around the center.

4. Allow the finished flower to dry before placing on the cake.

ROSETTES

Rosettes are the simplest of frosting flowers to make. They serve in place of frosting roses. They may be tinted and flavored to taste and applied directly to the cakes decorated in any size, large or small.

1. Place a rosette tube, called a large star tube No. 30 or a flower tube No. 217 in the decorating bag or cone, fill it with prepared frosting and begin pressing the frosting out. One squeeze is usually enough to make an average rosette; larger flowers will need firmer squeezing. Press the tip of the tube close to the cake, squeeze gently and release, pulling the bag away. Releasing the frosting quickly makes the rosette hold its shape; if this is not done the flower will have a long pointed appearance.

2. Tiny spots of yellow frosting may complete the centers. Large rosettes are pretty when using candles on birthday cakes, as a candle may be placed in the center of each rosette.

ORANGE BLOSSOMS

The orange blossom is a very important flower to know how to make if you intend decorating a wedding, announcement, or bride's cake. It gives such a pretty effect and is easily made.

1. You will need a cone filled with medium, stiff, white frosting, meringue or butter-cream, using the small rose tube No. 104.

2. Begin by making a small mound of frosting on the cap, then gently squeeze six tiny petals, joining in the center.

3. While the frosting is still moist, sprinkle a few yellow

cake decors in the center, giving the natural look of the stamens in the flower.

They may be applied to the cake when firm enough to lift from the cap.

APPLE BLOSSOMS

Apple blossoms may be made by following the same instructions given for orange blossoms. Tint the frosting pale pink, using a portion of white frosting in the cone to give a shaded effect, as is natural in apple blossoms.

CAMELLIA

A pretty frosting flower to adorn special-occasion cakes. They are made on the same order as a rose, with the exception of the mound of frosting. The camellia is a large, flat flower with large, open petals. When you are able to make a full rose, the camellia will be easy to make.

1. Begin by using the large rose tube in a pastry bag or cone of white frosting. This frosting will not have to be as firm as for roses because the petals on a camellia are not so prominent. Make a small mound of frosting on a large jar cap.

2. Make a sharp, round twirl in the center and begin the round, flat petals, around the twirl. Seven or more petals are all this flower requires. The petals are made in the same fashion as are the rose petals.

   Allow camellias to dry partially before placing them on the cakes.

CHRYSANTHEMUMS

To make these flowers you will need a No. 79 tube. The frosting may be tinted yellow, rose-pink, talisman (a combination of red and yellow) or lavender and white.

1. Begin by squeezing a round, flat mound of frosting in the center of the cap.

2. Holding the paper cone full of frosting with the half-circle part of the tube pointing down, squeeze gently and release one tiny part of the flower at a time. It will appear rounded in shape and you may continue

making them, all around the outer edge of the mound, then in rows one after another; complete the entire flower, ending in the center.

3. Allow these flowers to set up before using them. They are attractive in sprays, on top of birthday cakes for the men folk, in place of roses.
4. With the writing tube and green frosting, you may outline the stems of the flowers and fill in with ruffled green leaves with the leaf tube, No. 67.

WHITE LILIES

Lily nails will be needed to make this flower and they should be oiled well with mineral or vegetable oil before applying the frosting.

You will need a stand to hold the nails while lilies are drying. I suggest you use a cardboard box with nail holes pierced in it, 2 inches apart. When flower is completed place the nail in the hole and allow to stand until flower is dry. Drying time will require from 12 to 24 hours.

It is wise to keep the bowl of frosting covered while decorating, either with a dampened cloth or lid.

1. Begin by making a batch of Supreme frosting.
   (Refer to frosting recipes.)
2. In a small bowl place
      3 tbs. frosting and tint a pale green by using
      1 drop of green coloring and
      1 drop of yellow coloring, mix well
3. Place a No. 2 writing tube in a paper cone and fill with the green frosting; gently cover the bottom of the lily nail by squeezing the frosting round and round to cover the cup of the nail halfway up with a thin coating. Leave the center open.
4. Then using a large leaf tube No. 70 in a paper cone filled with white frosting, begin squeezing at the edge of the green frosting by pressing gently and pulling directly to the edge; release, leaving the point of the lily petal; arrange six petals in each lily.
5. While the frosting is still moist sprinkle a few yellow cake decors in the center of the bottom of the lily to represent the stamens or, if you prefer long stamens, use a small piece of yellow thread dipped in yellow frosting on one end and allowed to dry on waxed paper. Place the

unfrosted end in the moist frosting of the finished lily, thus giving the natural look of the flower.

FORGET-ME-NOTS

This is a tiny flower, appropriate for all types of cake decorating; they may be made of white frosting or tinted pastel blue and pink, with a yellow center.

1. Begin by placing a forget-me-not tube, No. 92, or for smaller flowers a No. 225, in a paper cone filled with frosting.
2. Press lightly, forcing the frosting on a waxed paper or directly on the cake being decorated, and release, pulling the cone away quickly. Practice will be needed to make the flowers even in size, and to know the exact pressure needed in forcing the frosting from the tube.
3. Make tiny yellow stamens by applying little drops of yellow-tinted frosting, using the writing tube or a cone folded to a small opening on the end.
   Forget-me-nots may be made in advance and arranged on trays for keeping.

LOVEBIRDS

(Use meringue or other frostings that will harden.)

To make attractive lovebirds is an accomplishment for any decorator.

1. First line a tray with waxed paper. Then begin by making the tail first using a No. 98 shell tube. Have the frosting firm enough to hold its shape well. Press the cone of frosting firmly, give one squeeze, and release. Practicing straight lines with this tube will give you the knowledge of how hard to press and when to release the frosting. Squeeze each bird's tail on the slant— some in one direction and some in the other, then when the finished birds are placed together with their beaks touching, they will appear as pairs, characteristic of lovebirds.
   In making several birds at a time, you may make a row of tails first and then finish the bodies in the same manner.
2. Use a No. 2 writing tube in a cone of softer frosting.

Begin by joining to the edge of the tail, in a tapping motion, making a small round, smooth body; now move the tube to one side, hesitate, and gently squeeze a small round head, then quickly release the frosting pulling it to a point making the tiny beaks.

3. Now add the wings by touching the tube of frosting to the sides of the body, press the cone and draw the frosting to make a pointed wing.

Wings may also be made with a small star tube (No. 13).

BLUEBIRDS

After considerable practice, try making the bluebird. They will be difficult at first.

1. Color a small bowl of meringue frosting a pretty blue, proceed as for lovebirds, making the tails first.

2. For the bodies, color some frosting a light shade of talisman, using a small amount of red and yellow coloring mixed. Prepare a paper cone with the small writing tube and with a spatula carefully spread a coating of the colored frosting on one side of the cone. Fill the remaining side with the blue frosting. Now begin squeezing the small bodies holding the cone with the talisman colored part of the frosting down and the blue on top. This will make the pinkish colored breast of the birds and the blue backs and heads with the pinkish colored throats and beaks. The wings are made of the blue frosting using the small star tube.

With practice you will be able to make very tiny bluebirds using the small writing tube for the whole procedure. Make the tails in three small lines using blue frosting. Begin in the center and add one line on each side. Using another cone with the two shades of frosting, make the bodies and heads.

Tiny bluebirds may be used in decorating sugar lumps, small teacakes and cakes for little tots.

Make trays of all types of birds and allow them to harden if you are doing decorating. When the birds are firm, make eyes of blue and color the beaks red by using coloring on picks, or colored pencils, to give the finishing touch.

LARGE DOVES

These are made freehand. Make the tail on the slant, curving the body and applying the wings in a flying position. They may be made with one tube or the combination of two as in lovebirds. Patterns may be followed if you prefer.

Birds which appear to be flying may be made by placing a finished bird in a trough made of wax paper to hold the wings outward; allow them to dry before removing.

SWANS

Swans may be made in the same way as large doves, planning the pattern or using a copied form.

BUTTERFLIES

These add a pretty touch to the elaborate cakes.

1. Cut the pattern of a small butterfly from a picture. Use silk net for a background; place the net on a small piece of waxed paper.
2. Prepare a cone of frosting with the small writing tube No. 1.
3. Follow the edge of the net in a fine fluted line making the butterfly look as natural as possible by filling in the small body and antennae or feelers, also add a decorative touch in the centers of the wings.
4. Quickly place the paper, holding the butterfly, in a small glass, leaning it against the side of the glass. This will give the wings a flying appearance when dry.

   Allow them to harden before placing them on the cake and stick them on by adding a drop of frosting on a flower or bracket.

DECORATIVE BORDERS

There are so many decorative borders to choose from: garlands, scrolls, scallops, shell, ribbon, vines, and others.

Different patterns will form as you practice decorating. You may have many original ideas.

Use pictures as guides when you are a beginner decorator, later depend on your ingenuity.

The borders are the first steps in decorating and are placed on the cakes directly after applying the first frosting. All other decorations are added later.

DECORATED SUGAR LUMPS

These clever little creations give a finishing touch to teas, luncheons and special parties, served as favors, used at place settings and for decorations. Sugar lumps may be had in different shapes—squares (large and small), oblong and flat pieces.

To decorate you may choose one of two methods:

1st Method

> Prepare in advance all flowers, birds, and trimmings needed and allow them to dry. Then when decorating, place them on the sugar lumps with a drop of white frosting.

2nd Method

> Arrange your frostings, colored in different shades, in several paper cones, using the very smallest tubes available, or just a small opening in the paper cone itself. After practice, this method will be preferred because smaller patterns may be made.

> > Begin by arranging patterns—originals or copies.
> > Decorate the smallest, tinted rosebuds with pale green stems and leaves
> > Nests with tiny bluebirds in them
> > Forget-me-nots in wreaths
> > Holly and berries for holiday favors
> > Little lilies for Easter
> > Small red hearts for Valentine's Day
> > Red, white, and blue flags for patriotic affairs
> > Red hatchets for February

There are so many pretty ideas for this pastime for all seasons of the year.

Always keep the tips of the cone of frosting covered with a damp cloth while waiting to be used in decorating to prevent the frosting from drying in the tube.

SUGAR LUMP HOUSES

Small decorative houses may be made with sugar lumps,

each lump representing a brick. Begin at the bottom arranging the lumps in brick fashion on a paper doily or cardboard, using red colored frosting as mortar. Leave spaces for windows and doors; sheets of baked cookie dough covered with red or green frosting may be used as the roof. Add the chimney on the roof and all other trimmings you may think of. The children will delight in helping you make one.

LACE WORK

To be able to do lace work fine, even, and lacy requires a steady hand and determination. It is applied in the same manner as writing except it is made to hang from the outer edges of the frosted layers in rows and rows of fine lace. Different patterns may be made in single, double, and triple lacing.

It is very fragile and will break easily if touched. Do not be discouraged if you break it and are forced to start all over.

I do not recommend that beginners try lacing at first because of its breaking so easily. After decorating for some time, then you may attempt lacy work.

1. You begin by using the following mixture:
    1 egg white
    ¼ ts. cream of tartar
    Enough sifted powdered sugar to make a firm paste.
    Beat well. (Keep covered.)
2. Put a small amount in a paper cone with a very small opening in the end.
3. To do the lattice work applied on the cake edges, begin squeezing the lacing by attaching each thread to a small rosette, looping it from one rosette to the other in even rows, as many as you have patience to add.
4. In doing the lacing in pattern, refer to the pictures and copy the designs shown here.

BRACKETS OR LATTICE WORK

These decorations are used only in decorating wedding or special-occasion cakes. They must be made a day in advance to be firm enough to hold their shape when applied to the cake, also they should be laid over forms while frosting is moist.

1. Make a bowl of meringue or ornamental frosting.
2. Cut the shapes of the brackets needed from white silk, nylon, or rayon net. Place each one on a piece of waxed paper and with a cone or bag filled with frosting, using a small star or writing tube No. 1 or 13, press the frosting out gently, outlining the entire pattern, then make imaginative patterns in the center in the same manner.
3. Carefully raise the waxed paper with the pattern and place it over a form. Cans, rolling pins, or bottle may serve as forms if you haven't a long wooden one made to order.
4. Some lattice work may be made flat on waxed paper and used to join elevated tiers.
5. Other lattice work is made of all frosting, lacing back and forth in braided style, joining the edges in pretty swirling rows of decorating. They also are placed on forms to harden.
6. When being applied to the frosted cake they must first be removed from the waxed paper and handled carefully to prevent breaking. Refer to pictures for hints in placing them on the cake. The designs shown in the pictures are simple to make and are first steps in decorating.

CRYSTAL EGGS

These may be used for favors and decorations.
1. These are made with crystal sugar by adding enough egg whites to hold together. Press gently into shape in the palm, by rolling a round first, then flatten lengthwise to look like an egg and place on waxed paper.
2. Molds, the shape of eggs, are very nice to use. Simply press the sugar egg into the mold. Gently tap mold on the table and the egg will come out in shape. Allow to harden before moving. The mold must be rinsed and dried after each sugar egg is made to prevent sticking. Decorate them in beautiful style.

SUGAR BELLS

Designed for the decorator to use exclusively on wedding cakes. They are very easily made and will hold their shape for weeks. They are easily broken and should be handled carefully and stored in a paper-lined box.

1. Begin by using

    1 egg white

    Stir in slowly enough granulated sugar to absorb all of the egg white. It requires between 2 and 3 cups of sugar, according to the size of the egg.

    The frosting may be delicately tinted, pastel pale pink, yellow, or blue, and will add a beautiful touch to cakes that are decorated in color.

2. Secure, as a mold, a bell the shape you wish to use (it may be of plastic, glass, or tin). Use bells that have a good shape and do not have an edge inside to interfere with the mixture. Have the bell mold clean and dry.

3. Gently press the sugar and egg mixture into the mold, press down firmly from the bottom with a small spatula or knife, even the edge by rubbing your finger around the outer edge to remove sugar particles, thus making a smooth fine edge. Gently tap the edge of the mold on the table and bell will leave the mold. Continue, making several. After a bell has become firm enough to handle, hold it gently in one hand and with a sharp-pointed knife, cut out the inside of the bell until the entire center has been scooped out. Then allow the bell to dry. The sugar you have cut out may be reused to make more bells.

4. When bell is dry, fill a small paper cone with white decorative frosting, such as Royal, Meringue, etc., and make a small line from the center of the inside of the bell to the edge. Squeeze a drop of frosting at the edge to represent the gong. This is effective and gives a natural appearance to the bell.

    Molds are available to form swans, slippers, angels, and many other decorative figures. Refer to page 314.

BASKET OF ROSES CAKE

This cake is made by using a large angel-food or sponge cake and frosting and decorating it in a weaving pattern to represent a basket. The tube to be used is a No. 46. The frosting should be firm, to give the effect.

1. Begin at the top edge of the cake and press the lines down the sides 1 inch apart all around the cake; then

weave around the cake in a circle using lines the same distance apart. There are many patterns you may try for weaving.
2. A florist's wire, covered with parafilm, may be bent and stuck into the cake to represent the handle. Cover it neatly with an edging of frosting; a ribbon bow of frosting placed in the center of the handle is effective.
3. The entire top of the cake should be an array of different colored roses and other flowers with green leaves neatly arranged. The colors should blend.
   Small bluebirds add a pretty touch.
   Another style of rose cake is to design a lid the size of the top of the cake. Make the pattern out of silk net and place it on waxed paper. Decorate a beautiful design on the net and allow it to dry.
   In place of the handle, put a row of roses on one side of the top of the cake, resting the lid in a partly opened position on the roses. Then cover the top of the cake with a garland of flowers to represent a full basket of blooms.

STORYBOOK DOLL CAKE

Every little girl's dream is to have a Storybook Doll Cake.
1. Bake a large angel-food or sponge cake. When cool, frost it with a light sugar and water frosting to seal the crumbs.
2. Apply a neat coating of decorative frosting, placing a waxed paper cup in the opening at the top of the cake. Stand the storybook doll in this to protect her dress from touching the frosting. The skirt will cover the cup from view.
3. Decorate the cake with small colored rosebuds and dainty edgings in colors to match the doll's dress.
4. When the decorating is completed, stand the doll in the paper cup.

DOLL CAKE

Secure a small doll with just the head and shoulders (like the bust forms used in pincushions).
1. Frost a small sponge or angel-food cake in the usual

manner. When applying the finishing frosting, smooth it on evenly.

2. Place the doll on the center of the cake and begin decorating from the top down, doing the cake in the shape of the doll's dress. A pretty colonial pattern is very effective, doing fancy edges to form the lines of the dress. A laced or lattice work overskirt adds beauty to this doll.

3. Place very small rosebuds and leaves down the sides where the dress meets in front, also place them all around the bottom of the overskirt. A real lacy bodice with puff sleeves completes the effect.

PUMPKIN CAKE (For Halloween)

1. Frost a large sponge cake with orange colored and flavored frosting.

2. Make a thick chocolate frosting and fill a cone using the No. 2 writing tube. Squeeze on this frosting, outlining eyes, nose, mouth, and ears on the one side of the cake. The eyes may be made to look natural by filling in the pupil and making lashes and brows. The mouth may be decorated in shape of lips using red frosting. Make a decorative hat of frosting and tilt it on one side.

    This cake may be made and decorated to look like a large jack-o'-lantern, made from a pumpkin. It makes an effective centerpiece for a Halloween table.

FROSTING ANIMALS

The children will delight in a cake decorated with animals.

1. In making merry-go-round, circus, or special cakes for little tots, you will need frosting animals. They are best when made with the meringue frosting. This will assure the animal being placed on the cake without being broken. They should be made hours before needed. The patterns of clever animals may be cut from books, pictures, cards, etc., and traced on cardboard cut neatly around the outer edge, then place the pattern under waxed paper. With a cone of frosting using a writing tube or just the opening in the cone, squeeze the

frosting in form with the pattern. Repeat a twirl of frosting over the parts to designate the legs, mane, and other features.

2. The eyes may be applied in blue frosting when animal is dry. The bridles, saddles, and other decorations may be made of colored frosting.

3. To make the animals stay in standing position on the cake, use small stick candies and place them down into the frosted cake, leaving a portion of the candy on which to rest the animal. Use a spot of frosting on the candy and while it is still moist, stick each animal in place by pressing its back against the candy. Do not allow the stick to show over the top. When the frosting spot becomes dry, the animals will hold in place indefinitely.

MERRY-GO-ROUND CAKE

1. Bake a cake of your choice in a large, round pan. (An old-fashioned milk pan is ideal.)

2. Frost the cake with a coating of powdered sugar, water, and flavoring to seal the crumbs.

3. Then cover with a finishing frosting.

4. Mark the center of the cake and place a large, peppermint stick candy down in the cake to represent the post in the merry-go-round. Decorate with frosting in pattern around the post.

5. Measure space for sticking 8 small, Society stick candies evenly around the outer edge of the cake 1½ inches from the edge. Then divide a stick candy into small pieces and place a piece in the cake directly in front of the tall stick and one directly in back; place a small drop of frosting on each small piece and place a candy horse on each in standing position.

6. Decorate a pretty edging around the outside of the cake in pink and white frosting, using the small star tube No. 14; also make a larger decoration with the large star tube No. 30 all around the bottom of the cake.

7. Put a drop of frosting on top of each candy stick and place a large, lacy, paper doily on top to represent the canopy on top of the merry-go-round. The name of the child for whom the cake is intended may be written in

frosting on top of the doily. Also, a small flag may be stuck in a mound of frosting in the center.

The entire cake may be prepared and decorated before you add the frosting horses, in case you have trouble making them stay in place.

Frosting horses may be substituted with animal crackers.

CIRCUS CAKE

This may be made in the same manner using frosting animals of all types and colors.

CLOWN CAKE

A birthday cake for boys.

1. You will need a cone, the type used for ice-cream cones and several bright colored gumdrops, for this cake.
2. Frost a large sponge or angel-food cake with a first frosting.
3. Make a fluffy, white frosting for the base coating.
4. Place a frosted cupcake on the top to represent the head of the clown. With frosting, stick the cone on top of the cupcake to make his hat.
5. Cut the gumdrops in shapes to represent the eyes, nose, ears, and mouth and stick them in the frosting while it is moist.
6. Decorate the cone hat with rows of frosting to represent the hats worn by clowns.
7. With frosting make the large collar around the clown's neck, also make large pompon buttons down the front of his costume.

This cake when displayed on a musical cake plate will win the admiration of everyone.

LAMB CAKE

There are pans available in the shape of a lamb. They must be greased and floured well. Fill with your favorite white cake, and bake. Cool slightly before removing from the pan.

1. Make a bowl of fluffy white frosting such as 7-minute or mile-high and frost the cake, sprinkle fresh shredded coconut over the entire surface.
2. Color some of the frosting pink and place it in a decorating cone with the writing tube. Make the eyes and mouth; also, a large pink ribbon and bow around the neck.

BOOK CAKE

This is a decorated cake, appropriate for book-club parties and graduation gifts.

You must bake a cake in a long dripper or baking pan; when cool, place the cake on a long mirror or tray. Cut the cake through the center to represent the center fold of a book. Then using a sharp saw knife, carefully cut the cake from the middle of each half, slanting to the outer edge to give the appearance of the open pages. (Pans for this cake are available.)

1. Make a thin frosting of powdered sugar, water, and flavoring and carefully frost over cake, guarding the parts that have been cut as the open crumbs may cause a breakage. Allow this frosting to become firm and set before continuing.
2. Make the finish frosting of a fluffy white icing such as white-mountain or 7-minute. Apply this frosting neatly and smoothly.
3. Arrange a group of frosting flowers and leaves in each outer top corner.
4. With the writing tube No. 1 in a cone of colored frosting, write the lettering appropriate for the occasion.

   If you wish, the book cake can be tilted upward in the reading position. To do this, place some large, hard frosting roses along the back; this will support the cake and also give a pretty appearance.

GUM PASTE

This frosting is used primarily for making decorative lilies, cupids, molded birds, flowers, etc. Each decoration is formed with the finger tips much on the order of shaping ceramics. It may be made days ahead and kept in the refrigerator until needed. It is a real pleasure to form your

HAND-DIPPED CHOCOLATE CREAMS

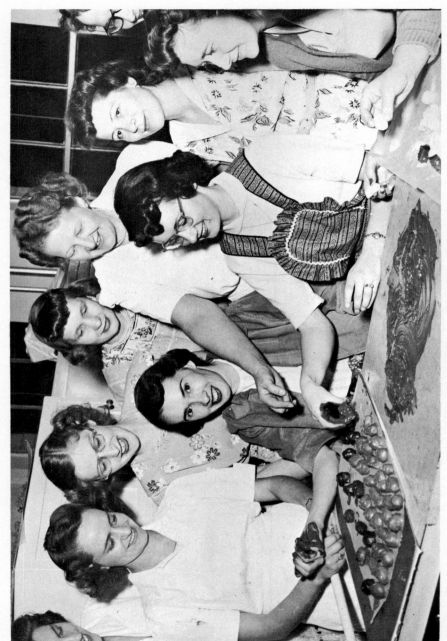

DIPPING CHOCOLATES

Students in one of my Party Foods classes

own individual designs. They may be used for any occasion —for decorating wedding cakes, especially around the bottom of the plate, for making place cards, dinner-table arrangements, or meat-plate trimmings, for molding animals for children's cakes, and so many wonderful ideas. You will of course need practice to make as perfect a specimen as you desire; but you will be able to remold the frosting over and over until you are pleased with the results.

1. Dissolve
     $\frac{3}{4}$ oz. gelatin in
     1 c. cold water. When dissolved strain through a fine strainer or cheesecloth
2. Mix with
     3 lbs. sifted powdered sugar and
     2 oz. cornstarch ($6\frac{1}{4}$ ts.). Mix gently in mixer.
3. Remove to a marble slab or platter and knead with your hands, if frosting sticks, sprinkle platter with a little powdered sugar. Knead until very smooth and white. Place in a bowl, cover with a damp cloth, and store in refrigerator.
4. Chill well. Work paste with fingers and proceed to mold into desired shapes.

INSTRUCTIONS FOR USING GUM PASTE

FLOWER DIVISION

Lilies

Flatten paste in the palm of the hand or on board, cut with sharp-edged knife the shape of a lily petal. The Easter lily has 5 or 6 petals. You should cut all pieces the same size. Mold each piece in the shape of a petal and bend carefully to give a natural look. Tint some of the paste pale yellow and mold like stamen for the centers.

The calla lily is one large petal with the large yellow pistil or pistulate in the center. This may be made by coloring some of the paste yellow and rolling a small piece of paste in a long, thin roll. Cut off the amount needed. Cut a piece of paste the shape of the lily petal and gently bend the edges; place the yellow pistil in the center of the inside. Fold the back edges of the lily over it and pinch gently. The paste will stay in shape. Put the flower on waxed paper until it is needed.

Roses

Roses are made in the same fashion, except that they have many petals which, each in turn, are placed around the others to form the flower. Any color may be obtained by tinting and mixing. Masterpieces will result after practicing.

Orange Blossoms

Orange blossoms are much smaller, but look almost real when made of gum paste. You may use commercial stamens in these if you prefer not to make them of gum paste. They can be made easily by cutting yellow thread in very small pieces and dipping one end of each thread in yellow frosting made of Royal Icing. Place on waxed paper to harden. Then insert in the flower with a tweezer or finger tips.

HOT-WATER GUM PASTE

1. Dissolve
    ⅝ oz. gelatin in
    ½ pt. cold water. Heat to boiling.
2. Pour hot mixture into a big mixing bowl
    Beat in
    3½ lbs. powdered sugar
    ½ lb. cornstarch
    ¼ oz. cream of tartar
3. If a stiffer paste is desired, add more sugar; for a thinner paste, add a little more water.
    Gum paste should be soft and pliable and may be mixed, kneaded, and rolled like pie crust.
4. Roll out paste to about ⅛ inch thickness on a slab, dusted with cornstarch. Cut in shapes, patterns, etc., as desired.
5. To cover trays, bowls, etc., dust the article to be molded with cornstarch and then add the gum paste to conform with the mold; trim the edges with a sharp knife and put the paste in a dry place for 1 to 2 days. Then remove from molds and decorate in pretty designs with frosting flowers, birds, leaves, or other patterns.

BIRD DIVISION

Birds of distinction may be made of gum paste by molding it into shapes or placing it on molds. Design the wings, tails, etc., by pressing into form. Use a sharp wire clip or hairpin to simulate the feather effect.

Swans

Mold the paste with fingers and form 5 sections—the body, neck, head, bill, and wings. Follow a picture design or mold, if you hesitate to use imaginative patterns, allow each piece to dry and then place them together with ornamental frosting.

Love Birds

These are small and require more patience, but use the same method as for swans.

FROSTINGS FOR LAYER CAKES, TEACAKES, AND COOKIES

BROWN-SATIN SEVEN-MINUTE ICING
(Known as Brown-Satin Frosting.)

1. In top of double boiler put
   $\frac{1}{2}$ ts. salt
   1 c. sugar
   $\frac{1}{2}$ c. brown sugar
   $\frac{1}{4}$ ts. cream of tartar
   2 tbs. dark syrup
   4 tbs. water
2. Mix altogether and stir until dissolved over the boiling water.
3. When sugar is all dissolved add
   2 egg whites and beat with a beater continually until frosting becomes thick and will stand up in peaks.
4. Cooking time usually takes 7 minutes, but on moist, stormy days it may vary up to 10 minutes.
5. Remove from hot water and add
   1 ts. vanilla and beat again.
   Spread between layers and on sides and top of cake. Fluff the top with the tip of the spatula to resemble peaks.

BUTTERSCOTCH ICING

You will be well pleased with this frosting for a spice, ground raisin, or mocha cake. Its rich butterscotch flavor is so yummy.

1. Mix well in a saucepan
    2 c. brown sugar, firmly packed
    1 c. white sugar
    2 tbs. white syrup (dark syrup may be used)
    ¾ c. top milk
    ¼ c. shortening
    ¼ c. butter or margarine
    ¼ ts. salt
2. Bring slowly to a boil, stirring constantly. Boil for 2 or 3 minutes according to thickness desired.
3. Remove from heat and cool.
4. Add
    1 ts. vanilla
    1 ts. butterscotch flavoring. Beat slowly in a back and forth motion until thick enough to spread.

MARSHMALLOW SEVEN-MINUTE FROSTING

1. Place in top of double boiler and mix well
    2 egg whites
    1½ c. sugar
    5 tbs. cold water
    1 ts. white syrup
    ⅛ ts. salt
2. Set over rapidly boiling water and beat constantly for 7 minutes or until frosting holds a peak.
3. Remove from water and add
    ½ ts. orange extract
    ½ ts. almond extract
    ½ c. marshmallow cream
4. Beat until spreading consistency.
    This frosting is ideal for chiffon cakes, sponge cakes, or chocolate cakes, as preferred.

UNCOOKED WHITE ICING

If you tire of seven-minute frostings, will you try this quick, fluffy one?

1. Beat in mixing bowl until stiff
        2 egg whites
        1/8 ts. salt
        1/4 ts. cream of tartar
2. Add slowly and beat again
        1 c. powdered sugar
3. Add and continue beating until frosting stands up in peaks
            1/2 c. white corn syrup
4. Add
        1/2 ts. fresh lemon juice
        1/2 ts. fruit flavoring

SHINING ICING

Adapted for cookies, rolls, etc.
1. Cook to 226° (a thin syrup)
        2 c. sugar
        1/8 ts. cream of tartar
        1 c. hot water. Wash the sides of the kettle with a small brush dipped in water.
2. Cool to lukewarm and add
        1/2 ts. vanilla or other flavoring.
        Add enough powdered sugar to make a nice consistency either to pour over cookies or to spread evenly. Will completely glaze 3 dozen small cookies or 12 large ones.

HAPPY MARSHMALLOW FROSTING

1. In a bowl place
        1 lb. powdered sugar
2. Melt
        5 tbs. butter in a pan and add to the sugar
3. Add
        1 c. marshmallow cream
        a small amount of evaporated milk
4. Stir well and add flavoring of choice.

ISLAND DREAM FROSTING

1. Mix thoroughly in top of double boiler
        2 unbeaten egg whites

1½ c. sugar
5 tbs. canned pineapple syrup
1 ts. corn syrup
⅛ ts. salt

2. Place over rapidly boiling water and beat continually with a beater until mixture holds in peaks—about 7 minutes.
3. Remove from hot water and add
   ½ ts. fruit flavoring
   ½ ts. orange extract. Beat until thick.
4. When thick, fold in
   ½ c. drained, crushed pineapple. Mix gently. Spread on cake in fluffy peaks.

COCONUT CAKE TOPPING

1. Mix together, and stir until sugar is dissolved,
   2 c. sugar
   ½ c. glucose
   ⅔ c. water
2. Boil to 242° then add
   ¼ lb. coconut butter
   1 ts. vanilla or almond flavoring. Color pale pink.
3. Add
   ½ lb. of small shredded coconut and stir until the topping forms a grain. Put through a coarse sieve if desired. If a two-tone effect is desired, make one batch white and one colored, then mix them together. This topping keeps well and may be stored in a glass jar.

CHERRY DREAM FROSTING

1. In a bowl place and beat altogether until well mixed
   1½ lb. powdered sugar
   ¼ c. melted butter
   1 egg yolk
   1 ts. lemon extract
   ½ ts. vanilla
   1 tbs. cherry juice from maraschino cherries
   If more powdered sugar is needed to make it a firm base, add more,
   1 tbs. at a time.

2.   Cut into small pieces
        $\frac{1}{2}$ c. maraschino cherries (drained before using)
        $\frac{1}{2}$ c. pecan nuts
        $\frac{1}{2}$ c. crushed pineapple, drained
        Add to frosting and immediately frost the cake.
        This frosting may become a little moist according to
        the care used in draining the pineapple and cherries.
        More sugar added won't change the niceness of the
        frosting.
        Very appropriate for valentine parties.

CARAMEL ICING

   This icing is designed for cookies and small cakes. It may
also be used for glazing fry cakes and doughnuts.
1.   Place in a fry pan
        1 c. sugar and caramelize over low heat until light
        brown by shaking the pan.
2.   Add
        $\frac{1}{2}$ c. cream or canned milk and cook for 2 or 3
        minutes.
3.   Remove from heat and add
        1 tbs. butter and enough powdered sugar to make the
        thickness desired.
        Stir well.
        Frost cookies or cakes in manner desired.

LIGHT, CREAMY BUTTER FROSTING

1.   Cream well
        $\frac{1}{2}$ c. butter or shortening
        2 unbeaten egg whites
2.   Add slowly
        $3\frac{1}{2}$ c. powdered sugar and blend well.
3.   Add
        $\frac{1}{4}$ ts. salt
        $1\frac{1}{2}$ ts. flavoring. Beat until fluffy (about 10 minutes
        or more).

BUTTERSCOTCH FROSTING

1.   Boil slowly to 232°
        $1\frac{1}{2}$ c. brown sugar

¾ tbs. butter
½ c. sugar
½ c. sour cream

2. Remove from heat and cool. Beat until smooth and creamy. Flavor with 1 ts. butterscotch flavoring.
3. If frosting becomes too thick, add a drop or two of hot water.
   Spread on cake as desired.

WHIPPED-CREAM FROSTING (Leora's)

This recipe was given to me by one of the dearest people I have ever known. When she laughs, it thrills your soul.

1. Put in a bowl and mix
      1 c. cream
      1 c. powdered sugar
      3 tbs. cocoa. Put in the refrigerator for ½ hour.
2. Remove from refrigerator and beat on fast speed until thick.
3. Add
      1 ts. vanilla or mint flavoring
4. Spread in mounds on top and sides of cake.

WHITE PEAK MARSHMALLOW FROSTING

I recommend this for chocolate cakes.

1. Mix in top of double boiler
      2 egg whites
      1½ c. sugar
      3 tbs. white syrup
      4 tbs. water
      ¼ ts. cream of tartar
      ⅛ ts. salt
2. Place over rapidly boiling water and beat constantly for 7 full minutes.
3. Remove from water and add
      1 ts. vanilla
4. When slightly cool fold in
      1 c. finely cut marshmallows
      Spread over cake as desired.

GOOD OLD CARAMEL FROSTING

1. Melt in a heavy pan and caramelize until light brown by just shaking the pan, not stirring
    ½ c. sugar
2. Then add
    ½ c. water and boil until sugar is dissolved
3. Add
    2 c. sugar
    1 c. evaporated milk
    1 tbs. white syrup
    Stir lightly over heat until it comes to a boil, cook with the lid on for 3 or 4 minutes. Remove lid and cook to a soft-ball stage at 235°.
4. Remove and let cool. Then beat until caramelized. Let stand several minutes, then add enough cream to make it spread nicely.
    Frost cakes as desired

ORANGE FLUFF FROSTING

A delightful frosting for special cakes such as wedding and party cakes, etc., especially nice for the Orange Blossom Wedding Cake. The recipe may be found in the cake division.

PENUCHE ICING

1. Mix together in a pan
    1½ c. brown sugar (packed)
    6 tbs. milk or cream
    6 tbs. shortening—margarine or butter preferred
    ¼ ts. salt
    Bring to a boil and stir constantly for 1 minute.
2. Remove from heat and beat until lukewarm then add
    ¾ ts. vanilla. Beat until ready to spread.
    If icing should become too hard add 1 more spoonful of cream and rebeat.

COOKED WHITE ICING

1. Place in pan
    1½ c. sugar
    ⅓ c. water. Boil for 3 minutes. Wash the sides of pan to avoid graining.

2. Beat until frothy
    2 egg whites
    Add boiled mixture and beat for 5 minutes.
3. Add
    1 c. of drained, crushed pineapple, if desired, or other candied fruit
    1 ts. of vanilla or fruit flavoring last. Spread on cooled cake immediately.

BOILED ONE-MINUTE CHOCOLATE FROSTING

When you desire a speedy frosting and one that will cut nicely immediately after it is spread, this one will please you.
1. Melt in a saucepan
    4 squares chocolate
    2 tbs. shortening
2. In another pan place
    ⅔ c. milk
    ¼ ts. salt
    3 well-beaten egg yolks
    2 c. sugar
    Bring to a boil and cook just 1 minute while stirring.
3. Then add chocolate and shortening and beat until creamy and thick. Spread over sides and top of cake and decorate with nuts or fruits if desired.

EASY-TO-MAKE CHOCOLATE FROSTING

1. Let boil for 3 minutes, stirring all the while,
    1 c. and 2 tbs. sugar
    6 tbs. cream
    4 tbs. butter
2. Remove from heat and add
    ½ c. chocolate chips
    1 ts. vanilla. Stir until thick enough to spread.
3. If you prefer a predominant chocolate flavor, add
    1 full c. chocolate chips. Spread over tops of teacakes, cookies, or doughnuts.

EGG-WHITE CHOCOLATE FROSTING

1. Beat until stiff
    2 egg whites and gradually add
    1 lb. powdered sugar

1½ ts. top milk
1 ts. vanilla and a few drops of oil of peppermint (the last may be omitted)
1 sq. melted and cooled bitter chocolate
1 tbs. soft butter
2.   Beat until smooth. Frost cakes as desired.

ORANGE-LEMON CREAM ICING

For you who like a natural fruit flavor a little on the tart side, this frosting will meet approval. It is recommended for orange-sponge and chiffon cakes.
1.   In a mixing bowl blend
2 tbs. shortening
1 tbs. butter or margarine
⅛ ts. salt
¼ ts. grated orange rind
1 tbs. lemon juice squeezed from the oil of the lemon peeling. This is the natural lemon oil and is very rich in flavor.
2.   Beat in
½ c. powdered sugar
3.   Add alternately
5 tbs. scalded cream (while hot) and
2½ c. powdered sugar. Beat briskly after each addition.
4.   Tint with a few drops of yellow frosting color. Spread in folds over top and sides of cake and place a pecan half here and there over the top.
Especially tasty served with fruit desserts.

MAPLE SATIN FROSTING

This has a luscious brown tone and a distinct flavor.
1.   Mix thoroughly in top of a double boiler
2 egg whites
1 c. brown sugar
4 tbs. water
3 tbs. dark syrup or maple syrup
¼ ts. cream of tartar
⅛ ts. salt
2.   Set over boiling water and beat continually until mixture will hold a peak. Cook seven minutes or more.

3. Remove from hot water and add
    1 ts. maple flavoring. Butterscotch may be added if desired. Beat gently and spread over cake in the twirling motion.

SPEEDY FUDGE FROSTING

1. Melt slowly
    2 squares of bitter chocolate
2. Scald
    ⅓ c. cream with
    2 tbs. butter
3. Add
    2 c. sifted powdered sugar
    ⅛ ts. salt
4. Beat until creamy then add the melted chocolate and
    1 ts. vanilla
5. Spread in pretty twirls over and around the cake.

MY FAVORITE CHOCOLATE FROSTING

This recipe is an old stand-by, one of my own creations, and one on which I always rely when I wish to serve a cake frosted to please my family and friends.

1. In a mixing bowl place
    1½ lbs. powdered sugar
    3 tbs. vegetable shortening
    1 tbs. butter
    ¼ ts. salt
2. Bring to a boil on low heat
    4 tbs. cream or milk
    3 sq. bitter chocolate
3. Gently stir until chocolate is completely melted.
4. Mix into the sugar gradually, adding a few more drops of cream if necessary, and add
    1 ts. vanilla, then beat on high for several minutes until frosting stands in peaks. This frosting has a shine and will spread so evenly and may be thickened to use for decorating if chocolate icing is desired.
5. You may also add
    6 marshmallows cut into pieces or
    ½ c. marshmallow cream and streak the chocolate frosting with lines of marshmallow.

BOILED FUDGE ICING

1. Chip fine 2 oz. of bitter chocolate
2. Add

    1½ c. sugar

    7 tbs. cream or milk

    2 tbs. shortening

    2 tbs. butter for flavor

    1 tbs. corn syrup

    ¼ ts. salt

    1 ts. vanilla. Mix altogether and bring to a boil for one full minute. Cool to lukewarm and beat until thick enough to spread on cake.

FUDGE FROSTING

If you prefer a cooked frosting, this will be your favorite.

1. Combine in a saucepan

    3 oz. bitter chocolate cut fine

    2¼ c. sugar

    6 tbs. butter or margarine

    3 tbs. shortening

    1½ tbs. syrup

    ¼ ts. salt

    ¾ c. milk

2. Bring slowly to a boil, stirring constantly, and boil at a full rolling boil for 3 minutes.
3. Remove from heat and cool, then add

    1 ts. vanilla. Beat until creamy enough to spread on a cake.

QUICK CHOCOLATE FROSTING

Very nice for topping cookies as well as cakes.

1. In top of double boiler place

    1 pkg. semi-sweet chocolate tidbits. Place over hot water until melted. Remove from heat

2. Add

    3 to 4 tbs. hot milk

    1 c. powdered sugar

    1 tbs. butter or margarine

    1 ts. vanilla

3. Mix well and add a little more powdered sugar if necessary to spread well.

CROWN FUDGE FROSTING

1. Mix together
   - ¼ c. hot water (boiling)
   - 1 tbs. shortening
   - 2 tbs. butter
   - 2 squares of bitter chocolate (melted)
   - 1 ts. vanilla
   - ¼ ts. salt
   - 2 full cups powdered sugar
2. Mix altogether until well blended and stir in
   - 1 c. finely chopped nuts
   - 1 c. finely cut raisins or dates
   This frosting won't spread evenly so it is very effective when just dropped on by spoonfuls and swirled with a spatula.

WHOLE-EGG CHOCOLATE FROSTING

1. In a saucepan place
   - 2 c. sugar
   - 4 tbs. milk and stir well
2. Add
   - 4 tbs. butter or margarine (melted)
   - 3 sq. of chocolate
   - 2 eggs
3. Bring to a boil, stirring all the while. Boil for 1 minute.
4. Remove from heat and beat until thick and ready to spread.

Cookies

A Filled Cookie Jar Is a Must in Every Home

In this chapter you will find cookies of all descriptions, plain, filled, decorated, for all occasions.

OLD ENGLISH SHORTBREADS

A cookie that is a delight to anyone, young or old. It is so easy to make and can be made in so many variations for every festive occasion. Has a wonderful keeping quality. May be made weeks in advance.

1. Cream in beater bowl for several minutes
   1 lb. butter and
   1½ c. powdered sugar
2. Slowly add
   4 c. flour (cake or all-purpose flour)
3. Add choice of flavoring (mine is
   1 ts. almond extract)
4. Stir until well mixed. This is a firm dough, but may be squeezed through a cookie bag or press, if desired.

   Variations to be added to the above mixture:
1. Add
   1 ts. maple flavoring, mix and mold by hand into balls. Cut in small pieces and place one inch apart. Bake on cookie sheet. Remove from oven and while still warm, roll in powdered sugar.
2. Melt and cool
   2 squares of chocolate and add to cookie batter with
   1 ts. vanilla
   ¼ ts. cloves
   Press through cookie press in fancy shapes.
3. Add
   ½ c. finely chopped nuts
   1 ts. rum flavoring. Roll into balls and press with the back of a fork.

4. To one batch of cookie dough add
    ½ c. drained maraschino cherries
    ½ c. chopped pecans
    1 ts. almond flavoring
5. Add
    1 c. coconut
    1 ts. vanilla
6. Chocolate chips and vanilla flavoring may be added.
7. Orange flavoring and color may be added. Also, lemon flavoring and color may be added.
8. Margarine may be used in place of butter, but the cookie won't have the same flavor, not the same good keeping quality either, and will have a drier texture.
9. Dough may be tinted any color desired, with a few drops of food coloring.
10. Nuts and coconut may be added and the dough dropped by spoonfuls onto a baking sheet.
    Bake without opening oven door for 20 minutes at 350°.

EVERYDAY SOUR-CREAM COOKIES (Large Recipe)

1. Mix like pie dough
    1 lb. lard
    6 c. flour
2. Add
    1 c. sour cream with
    1 ts. soda added
    ½ ts. salt
    1 ts. lemon flavoring
    2 beaten eggs
    2 c. sugar
3. Mix altogether and knead slightly, then roll out on floured board and cut with cookie cutter. Bake on cookie sheet for 12 minutes at 350°.
4. When cool cover with lemon frosting and sprinkle with nuts or cookie candies.

MINCEMEAT COOKIES

1. Cream until smooth
    2 c. brown sugar
    1 c. shortening

2. Add
        1 c. mincemeat
        2 beaten eggs
3. Then add and mix till well blended
        4 c. flour sifted with
        1 ts. salt
        1 ts. soda
4. Fold in
        1 c. nuts
5. Bake for 12 to 15 minutes at 375°.

DANISH ALMOND COFFEE COOKIES

1. Cream well
        1 lb. butter
        1 c. sugar
2. Add
        2 beaten eggs
3. Sift into the creamed mixture
        4½ c. all-purpose flour
        1 ts. soda
        ½ ts. salt. Mix until smooth.
4. Add
        1½ ts. almond flavoring
        1 c. finely chopped almonds
        ½ c. broken pieces of almond paste
5. Press into a pan lined with wax paper and chill over-
    night.
6. Remove from pan, cut in strips, then in thin slices. Place
    on buttered pan and bake for 12 minutes at 375°. Makes
    150 cookies.

BUSY DAY COCONUT DROPS

1. Mix together
        1 c. shortening
        2 c. brown sugar
        2 eggs
2. Sift in
        3½ c. flour
        1 ts. soda
        1 ts. salt

3.   Mix altogether with
     ½ c. buttermilk and add
     1 c. coconut and
     ¼ c. molasses
4.   Drop by spoonfuls onto greased cookie sheet and bake in moderately hot oven (375°) for 10 minutes.

ALMOND SPRITZ

A Spritz cookie is known and liked the world over and can be made easily by young and old.

1.   Cream
     1 c. shortening
     ¾ c. sugar then add
     1 egg or 3 egg yolks
2.   Sift in
     2¼ c. flour
     ½ ts. baking powder
     ¼ ts. salt
3.   Add and mix well
     1 ts. grated lemon rind
     1 ts. almond extract
4.   Put through a cookie press onto a greased baking sheet and bake 12 minutes at 400°. Makes 5 dozen cookies.

FANCY CREAM ALMOND SPRITZ

1.   Prepare one batch of almond Spritz, then
2.   Roll out thin and cut with fancy cutter and place on greased cookie sheet.
3.   Make a topping by mixing well the following:
     1 c. almond paste
     1 large egg white
     ¼ c. sugar
4.   Squeeze the almond topping over half of each cookie, then in the center spoon a drop of red jelly, or a tiny, red gumdrop.
5.   Bake for 15 minutes or until light brown. Serve on any occasion.

BROWN-SUGAR SPRITZ

1.   Cream altogether
     ½ c. shortening

       1 c. brown sugar
       1 egg
       1 ts. vanilla
2. Fold in gradually
       1½ c. flour
       ¼ ts. salt
3. Press through cookie press in shapes desired. Bake at 400° for 8 minutes or 375° for 10 minutes.

SOFT SUGAR COOKIES

1. In beater bowl mix
       1 c. shortening
       1½ c. sugar
2. Add
       4 c. sifted flour
       2 ts. baking powder
       1 ts. nutmeg
       1 ts. vanilla
       ½ ts. salt
3. Beat
       2 eggs and add to other mixtures with
       3 or 4 tbs. cream or canned milk
4. Roll out on floured board to a medium-thin thickness. Cut with cookie cutter into different shapes, sprinkle with sugar, and bake for 12 minutes at 375°.

BROWN-SUGAR ICEBOX COOKIES

1. Cream until light
       1 c. brown sugar
       1 c. white sugar
       1 full c. shortening
2. Add
       2 beaten eggs
3. Add
       3½ c. flour sifted with
       ¼ ts. salt
       1 ts. soda
4. Stir in
       2 c. raisins
       1 c. chopped walnuts

½ c. tiny gumdrops cut in very small pieces (Maraschino cherries may be used in place of gumdrops,)
5. Roll in a wax paper and chill in refrigerator until baking
time.
6. Cut in slices and bake on greased cookie sheet for 15
minutes at 350°.

AUNT EVELYN'S RAISIN-FILLED COOKIES

Aunt Evelyn is a dear, little old lady, whom our family
loves very much. She would tend our children when they
were youngsters while my husband and I went on our vaca-
tions. During those times she would always bake raisin-
filled cookies.

1. Bring to a boil
    2 pkgs. seedless raisins
    1½ c. sugar
    1½ c. boiling water and then thicken with
    2 tbs. cornstarch, moistened in water
2. Cream together
    2 c. shortening
    4 c. sugar
    4 eggs
    2 ts. maple flavoring
3. Sift
    4 c. flour
    3 ts. baking powder
    1 ts. soda
4. Add flour to creamed mixture with
    1 c. milk
    More flour may be added if dough is too soft, but do
    not knead the dough.
5. Roll out on floured board to ¼-inch thickness, cut with
    round cookie cutter. Place 1 inch apart on greased
    cookie sheet and fill, using a spoonful of raisin filling
    in the center of each cookie. Take another cookie and
    put on top of the first one. Press gently with the tips
    of your fingers, around the outside, to seal the two
    cookies together, so the filling will not ooze out while
    baking.
6. Bake at 350° for 25 minutes.

HAWAIIAN DATE BARS

1. Place in frying pan and melt
    ½ c. butter or margarine and then add
    1 c. brown sugar and simmer for a few moments and
    then cool
2. When cool, add and stir until blended
    1 c. whole-wheat flour and
    1 ts. baking powder, sifted together.
3. Add
    ½ c. chopped nuts and
    1 c. fresh dates, cut in pieces.
4. Place in flat—shallow—pan and bake at 350° for 30
    minutes. Cut in bars.
    While warm roll in powdered sugar.

PEANUT-BUTTER COOKIES

Children and grown-ups love this cookie.
1. Sift together
    1½ c. flour
    1½ ts. baking powder
    ¼ ts. salt
    ¾ ts. soda
2. Cream together lightly
    ½ c. shortening
    ½ c. sugar
    ½ c. brown sugar
    1 egg
    ½ c. peanut butter
3. When well mixed, roll into little balls. Place on cookie
    sheet and press on top with the back of a fork, which
    has been dipped in hot water, to make line indentations.
4. Bake for 10 minutes at 375°.

COCONUT BARS

1. Sift together
    2 c. flour
    2 ts. baking powder
2. Cream well
    ¼ c. shortening
    1 c. sugar
    1 egg

3. Add while mixing altogether
    ½ c. orange juice
    ¼ c. milk
    1 orange peel grated fine
4. When all blended together add
    1 c. coconut
5. Pour into a shallow, greased, and floured pan and cover
    with the following meringue:

MERINGUE

1. Beat until stiff
    2 egg whites
2. Add slowly
    4 tbs. sugar
    3 drops orange flavoring
3. Pour over cookie batter and quickly put in moderate oven
    at 350° for 25 to 30 minutes.

HONEY-MADE RAISIN BARS

If you prefer honey in place of sugar, try this very good
recipe. Molasses may be used in place of honey.
1. Sift together
    1⅓ c. flour
    ½ ts. salt
    1 ts. baking powder
2. Beat lightly
    3 eggs and add
    1 c. honey
3. Stir in
    1 c. broken or chopped walnuts
    1 c. chopped raisins
4. Mix together well and spread on a greased baking pan.
    Bake at 350° for 35 minutes. When partially cool cut
    into squares.

OLD-CUSTOM COCONUT COOKIES

1. In a large bowl place
    ½ pt. thick cream
    1 ts. soda
    1 c. sugar

      ¼ lb. melted butter
      1 tbs. melted shortening
      1 ts. vanilla or almond flavoring
      3 c. flour
      1 ts. baking powder
      2 beaten eggs

2. When all mixed, add
      1 large c. coconut
3. Roll out on floured board and cut with cookie cutter. Place on greased baking sheet and bake for 15 minutes at 375°.

BROWN-SUGAR COOKIES

1. Beat until creamy
      3 c. brown sugar
      3 eggs
      1 c. shortening
2. Add
      3 c. sifted flour
      3 ts. baking powder
3. Add
      1½ ts. vanilla
      1 c. broken nuts
4. Drop in mounds on greased cookie sheet and bake for 15 min. at 375°.

PINEAPPLE COOKIES

These are real tasty cookies—fine for the kiddies.
1. Cream till smooth
      ½ c. butter or margarine
      1½ c. sugar
      2 eggs
2. Add
      1 c. crushed pineapple (drained)
3. Sift
      3 c. flour (1 cup cake flour and 2 cups all-purpose)
      1 ts. soda
      ½ ts. salt
4. Mix together and add
      1 c. coconut

5. Drop by spoonfuls onto a greased cookie sheet, 1 inch apart.
6. Bake at 350° for 15 minutes.

APPLE TART

1. Pare and cut in slices
    4 c. apples and place them in a shallow baking dish. Sprinkle them with lemon juice and sugar.
2. Sift together
    ⅓ c. flour
    ½ ts. salt
    1 ts. cinnamon
3. Add to the flour and spices
    ⅓ c. melted butter or margarine and mix like pie dough until mixture is crumbly.
4. Spread the dry mixture over the sliced apples and bake for 30 minutes at 350°.
5. Serve hot or cold with whipped cream.

OATMEAL CHOCOLATE CHIPS

1. In a large bowl beat until creamy
    1 c. brown sugar
    ¾ c. shortening
2. Sift in
    1 c. flour
    1 ts. baking powder
    ¾ ts. salt
    1 ts. cinnamon
    ¼ ts. nutmeg
3. Mix well with
    ½ c. milk and add
    1 c. oatmeal and
    1 pkg. chocolate chips
4. Bake in drops on a cookie sheet for 10 or 15 minutes at 375°.

CHOCOLATE SWEDISH COOKIES

1. Cream until light
    1 c. butter
    ¼ c. sugar

2. Add and mix thoroughly
       2½ c. sifted flour
       2 ts. vanilla
3. Divide dough in two portions.
4. To one portion add
       2 tbs. cocoa and mix well
5. Thus you have dough divided in two parts, one chocolate
    and one plain. Arrange the two doughs together in a
    long roll, in pattern form if you desire.
6. Roll in wax paper and chill in refrigerator until firm.
7. Slice crosswise in slices and place on greased cookie
    sheet. Bake for 10 minutes at 350°. Makes 4 dozen
    cookies.

OLD GRANDMA GINGER COOKIE

1. Mix in a bowl
       ⅔ c. shortening
       ¾ c. molasses
       3 c. flour
       1 ts. ginger
       1 ts. salt
       1½ ts. soda
2. Mix to a soft dough and chill for several hours.
3. Roll out quite thin on cookie cloth. Cut into shapes de-
    sired and bake for 15 minutes at 375°.

GINGERBREAD RINGS

1. Melt in pan on low heat
       ½ c. shortening
2. Add
       1¼ c. molasses
       1 egg
3. Sift together and add
       2½ c. flour
       1½ ts. soda
       ½ ts. salt
       1 ts. cinnamon
       1½ ts. ginger
4. After mixing well add
       ¾ c. hot water, stirring carefully.

5. Pour into small ring molds and bake for 30 minutes at 350°.
6. Remove from tins and fill the centers with scoops of ice cream.

WALNUT WAFERS

1. Mix in mixing bowl
       1½ c. brown sugar
       1 egg
       2 tbs. butter
       4 tbs. flour
       2 tbs. water
2. When smooth add
       1½ c. finely chopped walnuts
3. Space 2 inches apart on greased cookie sheet. Bake for 10 minutes at 375°.

PECAN MELTAWAYS

1. Cream until soft
       ½ c. butter
       2 tbs. sugar
       1 ts. vanilla
2. Add
       1 c. cake flour
       1 c. chopped pecans
3. Mold until dough holds together firmly.
4. Form into small balls and place on a greased baking sheet. Flatten each ball with the bottom of a glass tumbler. Bake 15 minutes at 375°.
5. Roll in powdered sugar immediately after removing from the oven. Place on rack to cool.

BANANA OATMEAL COOKIES

1. Spread on cookie sheet and brown in hot oven
       ¾ c. oatmeal
2. Cream until fluffy
       ¾ c. shortening
       ¾ c. sugar
       1 egg

3. Add
    2 mashed bananas
4. Sift in, and stir well
    1½ c. flour
    ½ ts. salt
    1 ts. cinnamon
    1 ts. nutmeg
    1 ts. baking soda
5. Add the cooled oatmeal, and nuts, if desired.
6. Drop by spoonfuls on greased cookie sheet one inch apart.
7. Bake for 15 minutes in a hot oven (400°). Makes 4 dozen.

LEMON PRALINE COOKIES

1. Cream together
    ¾ c. margarine
    2 c. brown sugar
    2 eggs (beaten)
    2 tbs. lemon juice
    2 tbs. grated lemon rind
2. Add
    2 c. flour and mix well
3. Add
    1 c. chopped pecans
4. Shape into small balls and place on greased cookie sheet and flatten with a glass or press, to ⅛-inch thickness. Bake for 10 minutes in a 375° oven. Makes 5½ dozen.

HUMPTY DUMPTY'S

This is a muffin light and fluffy, spicy, and very good.
1. Sift
    2 c. flour
    3 ts. baking powder
    1 ts. salt
    ¼ c. sugar
2. Add
    2 eggs
    ¾ c. milk
    ¼ c. shortening
    1 c. coconut

3. Stir mixture until it is dampened. Put into paper muffin cups.
4. Bake in a hot oven (425°) for 15 minutes. Remove from cups, brush with melted butter or margarine, and quickly roll in cinnamon and sugar.
   ½ c. sugar
   1 ts. cinnamon
5. Keep warm in the oven until served.
6. One tbs. of grated orange rind may be used in place of coconut.

RUSSINA TEACAKES

1. Cream until smooth
   1 c. butter
   ½ c. powdered sugar
   1 ts. vanilla
2. Sift in and cream well
   2¼ c. cake flour
   ¼ ts. salt
3. Add
   ¾ c. chopped nuts
4. Put through a cookie press and bake quickly at 375° for 10 minutes or until light brown.

HOLIDAY COOKIES

1. Cream until light
   1 c. shortening
   1 c. brown sugar
   1 ts. vanilla
   2 eggs
2. Sift in
   4 c. flour
   2 tbs. baking powder
   ¼ ts. soda
   1 ts. salt
   ½ ts. cloves
3. Mix until smooth with
   ½ c. milk
4. Add
   2 lbs. tiny gumdrops

5. This batter may be baked in a flat baking tin and cut in squares, or it may be dropped by spoonfuls onto a prepared cookie sheet and baked.
6. In a flat pan, bake at 350° for 20 to 25 minutes. In spoonfuls, bake at 350° for 10 to 15 minutes.

MACAROONS

1. Beat until quite stiff
   3 egg whites and then fold in
   1 c. sugar slowly
2. Add and mix carefully
   1 c. coconut
   3 c. corn flakes
   1 c. nuts
3. Drop by teaspoonfuls on a greased cookie sheet and bake at 325° for 20 minutes without opening the oven door. Cool before removing from pan.
4. If a colored macaroon is desired, drop 3 or 4 drops of food coloring in the egg whites after the sugar has been added.

CHOCOLATE ECLAIRS

1. In a fry pan place
   ½ c. butter
   1 c. boiling water
2. Add and cool slightly
   1 c. flour and stir very fast until mixture is thick and smooth.
3. Add
   4 unbeaten eggs, one at a time and beat vigorously.
4. Drop dough from a pastry bag onto a greased baking sheet in eclairs 2 inches long leaving some room between them for baking space.
5. Bake in a 400° oven for 25 or 30 minutes without opening oven door. Remove from oven and, when cool, cut through center, fill with whipped cream or vanilla filling. Frost in pretty twirls with chocolate frosting.

HERMITS

This nice, rich cookie may be kept in a jar for several days.

1. Cream well
      2 c. brown sugar
      1 c. butter or margarine
      2 eggs
2. To the creamed mixture add
      1 c. flour
      1 ts. soda
      ¼ c. hot water. Stir well and fold in
      2 more c. flour
3. Add
      1 c. chopped raisins
      ½ c. nuts
4. Drop by spoonfuls on greased cookie sheet and bake at
   375° for 15 minutes.

CHOCOLATE RAISIN-NUT CLUSTERS

This recipe makes a sweet, chewy cookie.
1. Cream until fluffy
      ½ c. butter or margarine
      1 c. sugar
      1 ts. vanilla
2. Add
      2 unbeaten eggs
      3 squares melted chocolate
3. Sift in and beat until smooth
      1 c. flour
      ¾ ts. baking powder
      ¾ ts. salt
4. Stir in
      1 c. seedless raisins
      1 c. chopped nuts
5. Drop in small mounds on a greased cookie sheet and
   bake in a preheated 350° oven for 10 minutes. Place on
   a rack to cool. Makes 3 dozen cookies.
   Chocolate may be omitted if desired.

GWEN'S HEALTH COOKIES

This is a prize recipe from a food carnival that I judged.
It is a "must" in every home. Fill your cookie jar with them.

1. Boil
      2 c. raisins and
      3 c. water until you have 1½ c. liquid, then add to the liquid
      2 ts. soda
2. Cream well
      1 c. shortening
      2 c. raw sugar (unrefined)
      2 eggs and mix well
3. Add
      1½ c. whole-wheat flour
      1½ c. white flour
      2 ts. cinnamon
      1 ts. vanilla
4. Bake on a flat sheet pan 15 minutes at 350°.
5. When cool frost with warm honey and cut in squares.

MY FAVORITE BROWNIES

I hope you enjoy this recipe as I have through the years. It will delight your family, friends, and guests.

1. Butter a shallow baking pan in readiness.
2. Melt together and cool
      2 squares of bitter chocolate
      ½ c. butter
3. Beat until creamy and then add to the cooled chocolate
      2 eggs
      1 c. sugar
4. Sift together
      ½ c. flour
      ⅛ ts. salt. Add very carefully to the creamed mixtures.
5. Fold in
      1 ts. vanilla
      1 c. nut pieces
6. Spread into the baking pan and bake for 20 minutes at 350°. Please do not open oven door while baking. The eggs are the only leavening and the brownies will fall if exposed to the air before baking time is finished. Remove from oven, cool slightly, and cut in generous squares.

JELLY MARGUERITES

1. Cream together
   - ½ c. butter
   - ¾ c. powdered sugar
   - 3 beaten egg yolks
2. Stir in and mix well
   - 1¾ c. cake flour
   - ¼ ts. salt
   - ½ ts. nutmeg
   - ¼ ts. rose extract
3. Form into shapes and place on greased baking sheet. Bake for 5 minutes at 400°.
4. Decorate with meringue and jelly.

CARAMELIZED DUMPLINGS

1. Place in fry pan and let dissolve
   - 2 c. brown sugar
   - ½ c. water
   - 1 tbs. butter
   - 1 caramel pecan roll
   - 1 ts. vanilla
2. Sift together and mix well
   - 2 c. flour
   - ¼ ts. salt
   - 1 c. sugar
   - 2 ts. baking powder
   - ½ c. milk
3. Cut in pieces and add to the batter
   - ½ lb. dates
   - 2 c. pecans
4. Pour caramelized syrup in a baking pan.
5. Dip batter by spoonfuls and drop into the syrup.
6. Bake at 350° for 30 minutes or until pretty brown. Serve hot.

BROWN-EYED SUSANS

1. Cream altogether until smooth
   - 1 c. shortening
   - 3 tbs. sugar

  1 ts. almond extract
  2 c. flour
  ½ ts. salt
2. Roll into small balls and place on greased cookie sheet. Press out flat. Bake at 400° for 10 to 12 minutes. When baked frost with:
1. Mix until smooth
  1 c. powdered sugar
  2 tbs. cocoa
  2 tbs. hot water
  ½ ts. vanilla
2. Place a small nut in each center.

LORNA DOONS

This is a perfect cookie recipe for a cookie press or to be squeezed through a pastry bag. The dough may be tinted and flavored, as desired.
1. Cream
  1½ c. shortening
  1 c. sugar
2. Beat
  5 eggs until light and add to the shortening and sugar
3. Sift in and mix
  4 c. cake flour
  ½ ts. salt
  1 ts. baking powder
4. Color and flavor as desired.
5. Press through cookie press or bake on a greased cookie sheet allowing room between cookies.
6. A small gumdrop or a nut may be placed on top of each cookie before baking.
7. Bake at 350° for 15 to 20 minutes.

VARIATIONS

Chocolate morsels, nuts, coconut, or cherries may be added to this dough. Drop by spoonfuls onto cookie sheet. Bake as above.

PERFECTED BROWNIES

These are wonderful for parties and picnics.

1. Cream together until fluffy
    ½ c. butter or margarine
    1 c. sugar
    1 ts. vanilla
    ¼ ts. salt
2. Beat well
    2 large eggs
    2 squares of melted and cooled chocolate
3. Add
    ½ c. enriched flour
    ½ c. chopped nuts
4. Mix well and then pour into shallow 9x9-inch pan. Bake
    at 325° for 25 minutes without peeking in the oven. The
    eggs are the only leavening and the batter will fall if the
    oven door is opened. Cut into squares when cool.

MOLASSES NUT BARS

1. In a large bowl place
    ½ c. shortening and add
    ¼ c. boiling water, stir and add
    1 c. brown sugar
    ½ c. molasses. Set aside to cool
2. Sift together and stir into first mixture
    3 c. flour
    ½ ts. nutmeg
    ⅛ ts. salt
    1 ts. cinnamon
    1 ts. ginger
3. Shape into a long roll, then wrap in waxed paper and
    chill.
4. Cut in strips and sprinkle with nuts.
5. Bake for 15 minutes at 325°.

DECORATED COOKIES

These nice little cookies are just right for decorating.
1. Cream until light
    1¼ c. sugar
    1½ c. shortening
2. Add one at a time and beat well
    5 eggs

3. Fold in
    4 c. cake flour
    ½ ts. salt
    1 ts. baking powder, then add
    1 ts. banana flavoring
4. Press through a pastry bag onto a greased cookie sheet.
   Bake for 15 min. at 350°.

BITTERSWEET CHOCOLATE COOKIES

1. Cream well
    ½ c. shortening
    ½ c. brown sugar
    ¼ c. white sugar
    1 egg
    1 ts. vanilla
2. Sift
    1 c. flour
    1 ts. baking powder
    ⅛ ts. salt
3. Mix well and add
    1 pkg. of chocolate morsels
4. Drop by spoonfuls onto a greased cookie sheet. Bake
   for 10 minutes at 350°. Makes 50 cookies.

CRUNCHY CHOCOLATE COOKIES

1. Cream
    ½ c. butter or margarine
    6 tbs. white sugar
    6 tbs. brown sugar
    1 egg
2. Sift into butter and sugar
    1¼ c. flour
    ½ ts. soda
3. Add a few drops of hot water just before adding
    1 c. chopped nuts
    1 pkg. chocolate tidbits
    ½ ts. vanilla
4. Drop by spoonfuls onto greased cookie sheet. Bake at
   375° for 12 minutes.

ROLLED SUGAR COOKIES

1. Cream well
   - ½ c. shortening
   - ¾ c. sugar
   - 1 egg
2. Add
   - 1 ts. vanilla
   - ½ ts. grated orange peel
3. Sift in
   - 2 c. flour
   - ¼ ts. salt
   - ½ ts. baking powder
4. Soften dough with
   - 2 to 3 tbs. milk
5. Roll ⅛-inch thick, cut with cookie cutter, sprinkle with decorative cookie candy.
6. Bake in 350° oven for 12 minutes.

ORANGE COCONUT COOKIES

This is a delightful cookie for your children's in-between-meal treats.

1. Cream well
   - 2 c. shortening
   - 1⅓ c. sugar
   - 1 ts. vanilla
2. Add
   - 4 beaten eggs and
   - 1 ts. grated orange peel
3. Add and mix just enough to hold together
   - 1 c. sifted flour
   - 2 c. rolled oats
4. Drop by spoonfuls onto greased cookie sheet two inches apart. Flatten with a fork and sprinkle with coconut. Bake at 375° for 12 minutes.

PECAN KISSES

These are good for parties.

1. Beat until light
   - 2 eggs and gradually add and beat until mixed
   - ½ lb. powdered sugar

2.   Sift in and mix
     1½ tbs. flour and add
     ½ lb. ground pecans
3.   Bake 15 minutes at 375°.

BOHEMIAN COOKIES

1.   Cream
     1 c. shortening
     1¼ c. powdered sugar
2.   Add to the sugar and shortening
     6 oz. grated sweet milk chocolate
     ¼ ts. salt
     1¼ c. all-purpose flour
     1 ts. vanilla
     1 c. ground walnuts
3.   Drop in small mounds onto greased cookie sheet and bake at 275° for 30 minutes.

BUTTER PRETZELS

1.   Cream together
     1 c. butter
     1 c. sugar
     2 egg yolks
2.   Add
     2 egg whites
     ½ ts. almond extract
3.   Gradually add and finish mixing
     2½ c. sifted flour. Prepare cookie sheet and
4.   Press dough through the star tube of cookie press. This forms the pretzel.
5.   Bake at 400° for 12 minutes.

RAISIN-OATMEAL COOKIES

1.   Cream
     ½ c. shortening
     1 c. sugar
     2 eggs and add
     ¼ c. milk
2.   Add
     1½ c. flour sifted with
     1 ts. soda

½ ts. salt
1 ts. cinnamon. Mix well.
3.   Add and continue mixing
1 c. seedless raisins
⅔ c. oatmeal
4.   Drop by spoonfuls onto greased cookie pan and bake 12 minutes at 350°.

OLD-FASHIONED SUGAR COOKIES

1.   Cream for 3 minutes
½ c. margarine
½ c. sugar
1 egg
¾ ts. vanilla
2.   Add and mix until blended
2 c. flour sifted with
½ ts. baking powder
¼ ts. salt
3.   Chill dough in refrigerator for ½ hour or more.
4.   Roll thin on a cookie cloth or floured board. Cut with cookie cutter.
5.   Brush top of each cookie with a small amount of beaten egg. Sprinkle with sugar.
6.   Bake 10 minutes in a 375° oven. Makes 4 dozen small cookies.

BUTTER-RUM COOKIES

These are a treat at holiday time.
1.   Cream
1 c. shortening
½ c. powdered sugar
½ ts. almond flavoring
2.   Mix in
2 c. flour
2 ts. rum flavoring
¼ c. finely chopped almonds
3.   Put through a cookie press onto ungreased cookie sheet. Bake 10 minutes at 400°.

JUMBO RAISIN COOKIES

1. Boil for 10 minutes, then cool
    1½ c. water
    2 c. raisins
2. Cream together
    2 c. sugar
    1 full c. shortening
    4 eggs
3. Sift into sugar, shortening, and eggs and mix well
    4 c. flour
    1 ts. baking powder
    1 ts. soda
    2 ts. salt
    1½ ts. cinnamon
    ¼ ts. nutmeg
    ¼ ts. allspice
4. Add the boiled raisins and
    1 c. nut meats
    1 ts. vanilla
5. Drop in mounds onto greased cookie sheet and bake for 15 minutes at 375°. Serve on any occasion.

ALMOND MACAROONS

1. Pat with a wooden spoon until soft
    1 lb. almond paste and add
    1 egg white. Mix well.
2. Add
    ½ c. sugar and continue beating
3. Add
    1 more egg white and
    ½ c. sugar and beat again
4. Add
    3 egg whites and
    ½ lb. powdered sugar. Beat hard until the mixture is firm.
5. Place a piece of brown paper on cookie sheet. Then drop dough by spoonfuls onto paper. Bake for 15 to 20 minutes at 325°. Please do not open the oven door while baking or the macaroons will fall.

SWEDISH COOKIES

These delicate, dainty, and so delicious cookies are just the right, light touch when friends drop in.

1. Cook
   6 eggs (separate yolks from whites, drop yolks one at a time into hot, salted water). Simmer until hard cooked.
2. Sift together
   2 c. sifted flour
   ½ ts. salt
3. Cream
   ¾ c. shortening and add gradually
   ¾ c. sugar, beating until very light and fluffy
4. Add
   cooked egg yolks which have been put through a wire sieve
   ½ ts. lemon extract
5. Blend into creamed mixture
   3 tbs. cream and the dry ingredients, alternately beating well after each addition.
6. Roll dough to a ⅛-inch thickness and cut into cookie shapes. Place on greased baking sheet. Decorate with colored sugar, candied fruit, nuts, or coconut. If desired, this dough may be used in a cookie press. Cookies may also be shaped into knots by gently rolling a rounded teaspoon of dough on a lightly floured canvas or board until about 6 inches in length and tying in a loose knot.
7. Bake in moderate oven at 375° until edges become delicately browned. Time required for pressed or rolled cookies is 6 to 8 minutes, or 12 minutes for knots.

OLD-TIME RAISIN COOKIES

1. Boil together for 20 minutes, and cool
   1½ c. raisins
   2½ c. water
2. Cream well
   1½ c. sugar
   ⅔ c. shortening
   3 eggs
   1 ts. vanilla. Add the juice from the raisins.

3. Sift in and mix together
     4 c. flour
     4 ts. baking powder
     1/3 ts. soda
4. Add the boiled raisins.
5. Bake in a greased flat pan for 20 minutes or more in a
     350° oven. When cool cut in squares and serve.

DROP COOKIES

1. Cream until light
     1 c. butter
     1½ c. brown sugar
2. Add one at a time, beating after each
     4 eggs and
     1 ts. lemon extract
3. Sift in and mix
     3¼ c. flour
     ½ ts. salt
     1 ts. soda
4. Then stir in
     1½ ts. water
     2 c. soft raisins
     1 c. broken nuts
5. Drop in spoonfuls onto greased sheet and bake 15 min-
     utes at 350°.

NEAPOLITANS

Use this for little heart-shaped cookies or other special,
shaped cut cookies. This is a very good recipe. It is a whip
pastry made by a different method than is used for the
conventional-type cookie.
1. In a bowl put
     ¾ c. vegetable shortening
     3 tbs. boiling water
     1 tbs. milk
     1 tbs. lemon juice
2. Begin beating with a large fork or whip and with rapid
     motion beat this until all the liquid is absorbed and the
     mixture is firm.
3. Beat in
     2 egg yolks

4.   Sift into the shortening mixture
         2 c. all-purpose flour
         ⅓ c. sugar
         1 ts. salt
5.   Beat until the dough is well mixed and leaves the sides
     of the bowl. Knead the dough a little to prepare it for
     rolling.
6.   Roll on wax paper or pastry cloth to ½-inch thickness.
     Cut in desired shapes and bake on ungreased baking
     sheet at 375° for 15 minutes.
7.   The cookies may be filled and stacked or decorated as
     you choose.

GINGER CUT-OUT COOKIES

This is excellent for gingerbread houses, little men, and
cut-out cookies. This recipe is priceless. The dough is easy
to handle, rolls out smoothly, holds its shape, and is "yummy" to eat.
1.   Bring to a boil and cool
         ½ c. shortening
         ½ c. molasses
         ½ c. sugar
         1 tbs. vinegar
2.   Beat slightly
         1 egg and add to the above mixture
3.   Sift together
         3 c. flour
         ½ ts. salt
         ½ ts. soda
         ½ ts. cinnamon
         ½ ts. ginger
4.   Mix together and chill in refrigerator.
5.   Roll out on board and cut in desired shapes. Board may
     be floured lightly if necessary. Bake in 375° oven for
     12 to 15 minutes.

GINGER COOKIES FOR GINGERBREAD HOUSES

This is one of my favorite recipes, one which has brought
so much happiness in our home, catering to the grandchildren.
The texture of the dough is misleading but, if handled

correctly, it brings perfect results. Begin by doing the
following:

1.   Bring to a boil, stir well, and set aside to cool
        ½ c. shortening
        ½ c. molasses
        ½ c. sugar
        1 tbs.vinegar
2.   Sift together
        3 c. flour
        ½ ts. salt
        ½ ts. soda
        ½ ts. cinnamon
        ½ ts. ginger
3.   Beat lightly
        1 egg
4.   Mix altogether, pat into a ball, and chill in the refriger-
     ator.
5.   Roll out on a lightly floured board and cut in desired
     shapes. Bake on greased cookie sheets at 375° for 10
     to 12 minutes.
        In making a gingerbread house, you must have a
     frame for the house, something on which to stick the
     baked cookies. This frame may be made from cardboard,
     beaverboard, or any light wood. Measure and cut ma-
     terial to be used in the shape of the house desired, mak-
     ing cut-out spaces for doors and windows.
        My husband, Al, makes the frames for the houses
     from com-board and fastens the sides, roof, bottom,
     etc., with small screws. This makes the little house
     strong enough to be used for a doll house after the gin-
     gerbread coating has been removed. A flat board is
     fastened to the bottom, large enough to make the
     floor of the house and space around it to represent the
     yard around the house.
        When the frame is completed, trace a paper pattern
     to fit each part—sides, front, back, roof, etc. Now we are
     ready to roll the cookie dough.
1.   Roll large sheets of dough; lay on each pattern and cut
     carefully through the dough with a small, sharp knife;
     gently pick up each piece with a spatula and place on a
     greased cookie sheet. Make a few impressions with a
     fork to allow perfect raising, while baking. Bake at
     375° for 10 to 12 minutes. Remove from the oven and

allow to cool on the pan until you are ready to put them on the frame.

2. Make a large batch of decorating frosting. Ornamental Royal, Glossy, or Meringue may be used. Begin by spreading a thin coat of frosting over the sides of the frame. Put the pieces of gingerbread in place with bottom side next to the frame. Press carefully to force the cookie to adhere to the frosted frame. When the entire house has been covered with gingerbread, thicken the frosting. With a decorating bag and small star tube, full of frosting, join the sides, front, etc., with a pretty fluting, gently squeezing the frosting through the tube in even fancy lines.

3. Fasten a piece of white rayon net over each window with frosting, then decorate around the outer edges, this gives an appearance of curtains at the windows. The roof is frosted to represent shingles, the chimney like bricks. The ground space to be done according to the season, snow-covered for winter scenes, green grass for summer, etc.

For winter season:

1. Frost the house as directed.

2. Cover the space around the house with smooth, white frosting representing the snow, with a spatula make a path to the front door.

3. Make little bushes around the house by using green gumdrops and green-colored frosting. Tip with white frosting to make them appear snow-covered.

4. The evergreen trees can be made by inserting a small green candle in a gumdrop. Using green frosting in a decorating bag with the leaf tube, squeeze the frosting to make the branches of the tree. The gumdrop base may be placed in the moist frosting of the yard around the gingerbread house. A snow man made of frosting, with hat, face, etc., adds to the scene. Gingerbread men and women in frosting attire can be placed around the snow man, or use frosting animals, such as a dog or a cat, around the door or on the porch. The gingerbread children dressed with frosting mittens, boots, caps, coats, etc., will meet with approval. Also make little faces on them using blue frosting for eyes, chocolate or yellow

for hair, pink on their cheeks. Make clothing any color desired.

5. A Santa Claus in red coloring with white cap, whiskers, etc., may be placed near the chimney on the roof. The children will love this idea.

Summer scenes:

1. Proceed as for the winter scene, sprinkle green-tinted coconut over the white frosting in the yard to resemble the lawn. Make green-colored frosting shrubs and trees, bright little colored flowers in the yard and around the house, a swing, a teeter-totter, etc., in back. With the leftover gingerbread make cut-outs of children or animals, a birdhouse, with tiny frosting birds, or a lamp-post by the walk.

2. There are so many suggestions to follow; perhaps you have ideas you may employ to make the job a pleasure. It's a question as to who will have the most fun, the one making the gingerbread house or the little guests who will enjoy it.

There are forms for gingerbread houses on the market. They are made of aluminum and can be put together easily, covered with baked gingerbread, and then decorated.

CHRISTMAS BELLS (Cookies)

1. Obtain some little bell-shaped pans and grease them well.
2. Beat until light and fluffy
    $\frac{1}{2}$ c. shortening
    $1\frac{1}{4}$ c. sugar
3. Sift together
    $2\frac{1}{2}$ c. cake flour
    3 ts. baking powder
    1 ts. salt
4. Add flour and creamed shortening alternately with
    $\frac{2}{3}$ c. milk and
    1 ts. vanilla. Mix until smooth.
5. Beat until stiff
    3 egg whites and fold into the batter with
    $\frac{1}{3}$ c. milk and
    1 c. coconut

6. Fill bell pans ¾ full of the batter and bake at 375° for
    about 18 minutes. Remove from oven and cool for a few
    minutes. Then remove cookies from the pans to a rack
    and cover with frosting. Choose one of the fluffy, white-
    frosting recipes and decorate in Christmas motif.
    Suggestions for Decorating:
       After covering cookies with white frosting, you may
    place cinnamon candies around the edges of each bell.
    "Noel" may be written in red-colored frosting in the
    center. Place each bell on a tiny, white paper doily and
    add a sprig of holly on one side.
       A centerpiece may be made by placing the frosted and
    decorated bells around the edge of a large plate with
    sprigs of holly between and an array of Christmas
    goodies in the center. A scarlet ribbon will also add
    beauty.
       Merry Christmas or names of guests may be written
    with red frosting on the tops and small silver dragees
    placed around the edges of the bells. Small ribbon bows,
    also made from the frosting and placed at the tops, may
    be used.
       Tiny flowers, rosettes, and leaves add to the beauty
    of these little bells.
       Coconut may be tinted green and sprinkled around the
    edges of each bell.

For wedding parties:

   The bells should be decorated either in white or pastel
shades of pink, yellow, or blue. Coconut or finely chopped
nuts may be used around the edges. Put tiny ribbon bows
of frosting on the tops of the bells. Sprays of little rosebuds
and orange blossoms, made previously, may decorate the
bells. When finished, they may be placed on a crystal plate
or paper-lace doily.

   These are especially nice for announcement parties. Refer
to instructions on decorating for hints on making the paper
cones for writing the names, etc., on the tops.

   The initials or names of the bridal couple may be made
on separate bells and the two placed together on a plate with
a touch of greenery.

   For a silver wedding, use all-white frosting and decorations with silver dragees and pale-green frosting leaves for
trim. Add a small, silver-paper leaf on one side.

For a golden wedding, use yellow frosting with deep-yellow trim and gold-colored ribbon, also a small, gold-paper leaf on the edge.

For New Year's parties, these small bells may be decorated in white or pastel shades and a clock made from frosting, with the hands indicating the new year, decorated on the top of each bell. Frosting for the clock may be made of chocolate or colored frosting, placed on with a decorating paper cone.

All kinds of tiny decorative colored candies may also be used to decorate these little bell cookies for other occasions.

Gelatin salads also may be made in these small bell pans for the holiday parties.

Patriotic parties:

For Washington's birthday, little hatchets may be cut from plain cookie dough. When baked, frost and decorate them in white and red frosting.

Flags cut in the same manner and decorated in red, white, and blue frosting in the pattern of our flag are fitting for patriotic dates throughout the year.

ALL-OCCASION PARTY COOKIES

This cookie recipe may be used for all types of cut-out cookies, such as faces and cookies where the features and shapes must be pronounced. Many happy hours will be spent in baking and decorating these cookies.
1. Sift together
    2¾ c. all-purpose flour
    1 ts. baking powder
    ½ ts. salt
2. Cream well
    ⅔ c. shortening
    ⅔ c. sugar
    2 eggs
    1 ts. flavoring
3. Mix all together and pat into ball. Place in refrigerator to chill.
4. Roll small portions of chilled dough at a time to ⅛-inch thickness, using a pastry cloth. Cut into shapes, using special molds or cutters.
5. Bake at 350° for 12 to 15 minutes.

SANTA CLAUS FACES

There are available plastic cutters with pronounced features of Santa's face.

Cut chilled rolled dough with cutter. Gently pat with the fingers, pushing the dough away from the edge of the cutter and pressing the dough down into features, leaving the nose until last. Then gently tap the cutter to release the dough and the features of the face will be clear. Place carefully on a greased cookie sheet. Decorate before baking by using the following:

1. Divide 1 egg white into 2 cups; add 1 drop of red coloring to one portion and 1 drop of blue coloring to the other.

2. With a very small brush tint the circles in the eyes blue and the cheeks and nose red.

3. Place a large silver dragee in the center of the eye to represent the eyeball. A small raisin or currant may be used if preferred.

4. Then bake until light brown and remove from oven. Complete the cookie with frosting, using red frosting or painting the red egg white over the cap and sprinkling with red sugar or red candy decors.

5. Use white frosting in a decorating tube or paint it on with a brush to make the whiskers and mustache and fur on the cap. Sprinkle shredded coconut on beard. Children will be delighted with this cookie at Christmas time.

Other cutters available are:

Clowns
Angels
Jack-o-lanterns
Indian Heads
Cowboys
Frosty The Snow Man
Bunnies
Stars
Trees
Christmas Stockings

Decorate each cookie using your imaginative ideas. Use colored frostings, colored decors, etc.

HOW TO COLOR SUGAR

Place some granulated sugar on a piece of stiff, white paper; sprinkle over it a few drops of the desired food coloring and rub with a wooden spoon or between the fingers until evenly distributed. Dry in a moderate oven (350°), occasionally separating the grains by rubbing them between the fingers. Store in an airtight container.

Rolls

Members in homes where there has never been the wonderful aroma of homemade breads and rolls, have never really lived. Give your family this pleasure by making some luscious rolls.

ORANGE TEA ROLLS (Roses)

These are dainty sweet rolls, frosted before baking, which are lovely to serve for afternoon lunches or teas, especially nice to serve with fruit salads.

1. Soak
      1 yeast cake in ¼ c. warm water
2. Sift into mixing bowl
      2 c. flour
      1 ts. salt
      ⅓ c. sugar
3. Slightly beat
      2 eggs and add with the yeast to the flour
4. Add
      1¼ c. lukewarm water
      ⅓ c. melted butter (slightly cooled)
5. Mix well to a sponge. Cover and let rise until bubbly and then add
      2 more cups of flour and mix well. Let rise again until light.
6. Roll out to ½-inch thickness; cut in strips 3-inches long and 1-inch wide. With the point of a knife cut halfway through the strips, ½-inch apart. Begin rolling at one end, rolling like a jelly roll, place with the uncut side down in a buttered gem tin. The cut pieces will separate like petals of a rose. Handle the dough cautiously so as not to squeeze the petals together. With a small pastry brush, butter over the tops and frost with the following frosting:

ORANGE FROSTING

1. Mix together
   juice and grated rind from 1 orange
   enough powdered sugar to make a smooth, medium-thin paste.
2. Gently pour a spoonful of frosting over the top of each roll. Then place them in a warm place and let rise until light.
3. Bake in a 375° oven for 20 minutes until golden brown. Remove from baking tins quickly after taking from the oven to prevent the frosted roll from sticking to the pan.
4. Serve hot or cold or rewarmed if desired.
   Takes two hours from mixing time to the finished product.

TWO-HOUR BUTTER ROLLS

This light, fluffy roll is made from a never-fail recipe.
1. Sift into mixing bowl
   4 c. flour
   1 ts. salt
   4 tbs. sugar
2. Soak
   2 yeast cakes in ¼ c. warm water
3. Beat slightly
   2 eggs
4. Scald and cool
   1½ c. milk
5. Add altogether and beat until smooth. Set in warm place and let rise until double.
6. Roll on floured board, and spread carefully with a layer of warm, creamed butter. Then begin folding the dough by picking up one end and folding over the buttered surface to the center, then fold the other half and carefully roll out to ½-inch thickness. Cut with a round cutter. Fold like Parker House by buttering ½ of each roll, then fold over and press the edges gently with the finger tips. Place in a buttered roll tin ½ inch apart, and let rise until light. Bake at 375° to 400° for 20 minutes.

CRESCENT ROLLS
(Refrigerator Style)

These appetizing rolls are nice for any occasion.
1. Mix like pie dough
    4 c. flour
    3 tbs. sugar
    1 ts. salt
    ½ lb. butter
2. Dissolve in ½ c. warm water
    2 yeast cakes, or 2 pkgs. dry yeast
3. Add
    3 beaten eggs and
    ½ c. warm milk
4. Mix all ingredients together until smooth. Place in a greased bowl and store in refrigerator overnight.
5. Roll out on floured board; cut into crescents, shaped like a cut of pie; sprinkle with brown sugar and dot with butter and nuts. Roll up, beginning with the wide end. Place on greased baking pan and let rise until light. Bake for 20 minutes at 350°.

POTATO ROLLS
By My Very Dear Friend, Clarise

Clarise taught me to prepare the clover-leaf rolls by gently squeezing the dough in the palm of my hand through the index finger and thumb in a circle causing the dough to ooze out in the neatest little balls. This method will form balls of dough equal in size and smooth. It is so much fun. Won't you try it for a special dinner treat.
1. Begin by mixing together
    1½ c. cooked mashed potatoes
    1½ c. warm water
    ⅔ c. sugar
    2½ ts. salt
    2 yeast cakes
2. Let this form a sponge for 1½ hours and then add
    4 beaten eggs
    ⅔ c. butter and lard mixed and
    enough sifted flour to make a firm but soft dough.
    Mix and knead well. Let rise until light. Form into clover-leaf rolls. To do this dip the fingers lightly

into melted shortening or butter, pick up a portion of the dough in the palm of your left hand, place the forefinger and thumb together and squeeze a portion of the dough through the opening. With the other hand, take each little ball of dough. Place three in each cup in buttered muffin or gem tins and let rise until light. Bake for 20 to 25 minutes at 375.°

LOVE-KNOT ROLLS

1. Soak
     2 yeast cakes in
     $\frac{1}{2}$ c. warm water
2. Sift together
     4 c. flour
     4 tbs. sugar
     $\frac{3}{4}$ ts. salt
3. Scald and cool
     $1\frac{1}{3}$ c. milk
4. Beat lightly
     2 eggs
5. Mix altogether and beat to a smooth dough. Let rise for 1 hour.
6. Roll out on a floured board and spread with a thin layer of soft butter. Fold over three times and roll again. Cut into long strips, (1-inch wide by 3-inches long) and tie in knots. Do not pull or stretch the dough while tying the knot. Place in greased muffin tins. Butter over the top and let rise until light. Bake at 375° for 15 to 20 minutes. Poppy seeds may be sprinkled on tops, if desired.

ENGLISH BATH BUNS

This is June's prize-winning recipe, revised a little to make it a sweeter bun, and flavored to taste.
1. Dissolve
     2 yeast cakes in
     1 c. lukewarm milk
2. Add
     $\frac{1}{2}$ c. melted and cooled butter
     5 slightly beaten eggs
     2 ts. cardamon flavoring or 4 washed cardamon seeds

3. Sift in
4 c. sifted flour
3 tbs. sugar
½ ts. salt. Mix well, cover, and let rise in warm place
1½ hours until light.
4. Sprinkle over the top of dough
2 tbs. sugar and
½ c. finely chopped walnuts
5. Dip carefully with a tablespoon enough dough to fill a buttered gem tin ¾ full. When you dip out the first portion of the dough, you may resugar the balance and sprinkle with nuts.
6. Butter over each gem lightly with a little melted butter, then sprinkle a little sugar over the top and a few more nuts.
7. Let rise until double, then bake at 375° for 15 to 20 minutes.
8. Remove from oven and arrange with the luscious shining tops peeping out of a roll basket. Serve this to your special friends.

WHOLE-WHEAT FRUIT BREAD

1. Sift together in a large bowl
2 c. whole-wheat flour
1 ts. baking powder
½ ts. salt
2. Prepare
1 c. chopped dates
1 c. raisins
½ c. chopped nuts
3. Beat together
½ c. brown sugar and
1 egg. Add
1 c. water
1 ts. vanilla
1 ts. melted butter
4. Mix altogether and pour into a large loaf pan and let stand for 5 minutes. Bake at 375° for 1 hour.

CINNAMON GEMS (By Grace)

This excellent roll was a prize-winner at a food carnival where I acted as judge.

1. Soak
    > 3 yeast cakes in
    > ¾ c. warm water, then add them to
    > 1 pint of scalded and cooled milk
2. Stir in and mix well
    > 1 c. sugar
    > 6 c. flour
    > 1 ts. salt
3. Cover and let rise until double.
4. Pour out on well-floured board and roll gently. Spread evenly with 2 squares of warm, soft butter. Fold three times and roll again. Sprinkle with a generous amount of cinnamon, sugar, raisins, and chopped nuts. Then roll like a jelly roll and cut in 1-inch slices; place in buttered muffin pans, let rise until very light. Bake 10 minutes at 450°.

SUGAR NUT ROLLS

1. Warm
    > 1 c. milk and add
    > ½ c. shortening
    > ½ c. sugar
    > ½ ts. salt
2. When lukewarm, add
    > 1 yeast cake or pkg. dry yeast and let stand for 20 minutes.
3. Then add
    > 3 beaten eggs
    > 4½ c. flour
    > Beat until smooth. Let rise until double in size (about one hour).
4. Butter muffin tins and place
    > 1 ts. of brown sugar in each cup. Cover with chopped pecans.
5. Roll dough out on floured board and spread with soft butter. Sprinkle with brown sugar. Then roll like a jelly roll, cut in slices, and place in the muffin tins. Let rise until double.
6. Just before baking pour maple syrup over each roll. Bake 25 minutes at 400°.

WATER METHOD REFRIGERATOR ROLLS

1. Mix together
        2 c. boiling water
        ½ c. sugar
        3 tbs. shortening
        2 ts. salt
2. When cool, add
        2 beaten eggs
        2 yeast cakes and let stand until dissolved.
3. Sift in
        4 c. flour and beat thoroughly with a wooden spoon.
        Place in refrigerator to chill, or you may prepare them
        when light if desired.
4. Roll out and form into your favorite shape. Let rise and
    bake at 375° for 15 minutes.

SOFT, DELICATE LUNCHEON ROLL (By Mabel)

1. Mix altogether
        1 c. scalded milk
        3 tbs. lard
        1 tbs. salt
        2 tbs. sugar
2. Dissolve
        1 yeast cake in
        ¾ c. warm water
3. Add to the yeast
        1 beaten egg
4. Then add all ingredients together with enough flour to
    make a soft but medium-firm dough. Let rise in a warm
    place for 20 minutes, then punch the dough down and
    let it rise again, until light. Roll out on a floured board
    and cut with a round cutter; butter and fold over and
    place on a greased pan. Let rise until light. Bake at 375°
    for 20 minutes or until a light brown.

LAZY DAISY ROLLS (A Sweet Roll)

1. Combine and then let stand for 5 minutes
        1 c. scalded and cooled milk
        2 yeast cakes
        ⅓ c. sugar

2. Add and let stand until bubbly
       3 beaten eggs
       ¼ c. melted butter
       1 ts. grated orange rind
3. Sift in
       4 c. flour, then beat until smooth, cover, and let rise
       until double in bulk.
4. Prepare gem tins by placing in the bottoms
       1 ts. butter
       ½ ts. brown sugar
       3 or 4 pecan halves, face down
5. Spoon out into each cup
       1 tbs. of dough and let rise until light.
6. Bake at 375° for 20 minutes. Serve warm.

REFRIGERATOR ROLLS

This is an unusually good recipe. It may be made the day before needed and stored in refrigerator.
1. Mix together and let stand 10 minutes
       ½ c. warm water
       2 yeast cakes
       1 tbs. sugar
2. Scald
       1 c. milk and add
       ⅓ c. shortening
3. Cool and add
       2 beaten eggs
4. Mix all ingredients together with
       4 or 5 c. flour according to the texture of the flour.
       Mix until smooth. Cover and put in refrigerator over-
       night.
5. About two hours before you are ready to serve them,
       knead dough well, roll out on a floured board, and spread
       with soft butter. Roll like a jelly roll and cut in thin
       slices. Place in greased muffin tins and let rise for 1½
       to 2 hours.
6. Bake at 425° for 15 minutes. Makes 24 rolls.

SWEET DOUGH FOR ROLLS

This recipe may be used for many types of rolls in variations.

The following method is ideal for a pan of fruit and nut rolls for a lunch or snack.

1. Scald
    1 c. milk and add
    ¼ c. shortening
    ½ c. sugar
    2 ts. salt
2. When slightly cool add
    2 c. flour
    2 yeast cakes dissolved in ¼ c. warm water
    2 beaten eggs
    1 ts. grated lemon rind
    Beat very hard until well mixed and then fold in
    2¾ c. flour and mix well to a soft, smooth dough. Cover and let rise until double. Knead down and let rise again. Then cut dough into pieces and roll into balls, dip each ball in melted butter, and roll in a mixture of
    ¾ c. sugar
    1 ts. cinnamon
    ⅓ c. finely chopped nuts
3. Then place balls in layers in a well-buttered baking dish, sprinkle with currants, candied fruits, and chopped nuts, if desired. Repeat with another layer on top. Let rise 45 minutes and bake 30 to 40 minutes at 375°.

SWISS BRAIDED HOLIDAY BREAD (By Martha)

This braided roll was a prize winner in a cooking contest.

1. Scald
    1 qt. milk and add
    1 lb. butter
2. When cool, mix with
    12 c. flour
    6 beaten eggs
    2 yeast cakes, softened in ¼ c. warm water
    1½ tbs. salt
    1½ tbs. sugar
3. Cover and place in warm place to rise until double in bulk.
4. Knead on floured board and cut into six strips, then roll them gently with the palms and braid two strips together. Pinch the ends to make them hold and place each

braid on a greased baking sheet. Let rise until light.
Brush over the tops with beaten egg whites. Bake at
350° for 1 hour.

ICE-BOX PASTRY

This is an unusual pastry, but it is delicious. You will be
thrilled when you see the finished product, and you will be
proud to offer it to anyone as an outstanding treat. It must
be made the day before you expect to serve it.

1. Cream together
   - ½ lb. butter
   - 2 tbs. sugar
   - 3 egg yolks
2. Dissolve
   - 1 yeast cake in
   - ½ c. lukewarm milk and add slowly to the first mixture.
3. Then sift and add alternately
   - 2 c. flour
   - ½ ts. salt. Mix until smooth and free from lumps.
4. Place in a buttered bowl, cover, and store in refrigerator overnight.
5. Cut the dough into pieces and roll on a wax paper to ½-inch thickness.
6. Beat
   - 3 egg whites until stiff and add
   - ¾ c. sugar gradually, beating all the while, until it is meringue. Spread this quickly over each piece of dough and add a layer of cooked crushed pineapple and finely crushed nuts on top. Immediately roll like jelly roll and slide from the wax paper with a large spatula onto a buttered cookie sheet. Bake in a preheated oven 350° for ½ hour. Serve while hot. Raspberry jam may be used in place of pineapple if you prefer.

APPLE DUMPLINGS (Baked Method)

1. Melt in pan
   - 1 c. sugar
   - 2 c. water
   - 4 tbs. butter

2.   Sift together
         2 c. flour
         ½ ts. salt
         2 ts. baking powder
3.   Mix into the flour mixture
         4 tbs. shortening and add to the first mixture.
4.   Stir in enough milk to make a soft dough.
5.   Roll out on floured board and cut in squares. Put a
     spoonful of applesauce in the center of each, and also a
     small piece of butter. Sprinkle with nutmeg. Fold over
     the edges of dough and press with finger tips. Place on
     greased baking pan and bake at 350° for 20 minutes.
     Serve hot.

APPLE DUMPLING (Syrup Method)

1.   Pare and core
         6 large apples
2.   Sift
         2 c. flour
         ½ ts. salt and cut in as for pastry
         ⅔ c. shortening
3.   Add just enough cold water to hold pastry together.
     Turn out on floured board and roll. Cut into 6 squares.
     Then chill them in refrigerator.
4.   Place an apple in each square of pastry. Fold the sides
     around the apple. Fill each core cavity with sugar and
     cinnamon and a piece of butter.
5.   Wet the edges of pastry with a little water and press
     them snugly to the apple. Place dumplings 2 inches
     apart in a baking dish and pour the following hot syrup
     around them:
1.   Boil for 3 minutes
         1 c. sugar
         ½ ts. cinnamon
         2 c. water
         ¼ c. butter
     Bake for 10 minutes in a 375° oven, then reduce heat
     to 350° and bake for 30 minutes. Spoon the sauce in
     the bottom of the pan over each dumpling. Serve
     with cream if desired.

CANDIED PUFFS

These are inexpensive rolls and may be used in many different ways: in rolls, in loaves, in toasted slices, or fried as scones.
1. Soften
     1 yeast cake in
     ¼ c. lukewarm water
2. Scald
     1 c. milk, and add
     ½ c. shortening
     1 ts. salt
     4 tbs. sugar
3. When cool add
     2 beaten eggs and
     1 c. flour. Beat until smooth.
4. Add
     1 c. currants
     1 ts. vanilla or lemon flavoring
5. Add
     3 more c. flour, and mix to a smooth dough. Cover and let rise until light.
6. Drop by spoonfuls into buttered muffin tins. Cover with the following topping:
1. Make a mixture of cinnamon, sugar, and candied fruit pieces. Sprinkle the topping over each roll and let rise 30 minutes or until light. Bake at 375° for 20 to 25 minutes.

OLD-FASHIONED SHORTCAKE

1. Sift into bowl
     2 c. flour
     3 ts. baking powder
     2 tbs. sugar
     ½ ts. salt
2. Add
     ½ c. shortening and mix like pie dough.
3. Add
     1 beaten egg to
     ½ c. milk
     1 ts. vanilla and blend the dough until it holds together.

4. Put into a greased baking pan, brush over top with melted butter, and bake at 375° for 15 minutes.

MAPLE CRULLERS

1. Beat until thick
   2 eggs and
   ¾ c. sugar, add
   2 tbs. soft butter
   ¼ c. milk
   ½ ts. maple flavoring
2. Sift together
   2½ c. flour
   2½ ts. baking powder
   1 ts. salt
3. Mix to a soft dough. Roll on a floured board to a long roll. Cut in strips 4 or 5 inches long, pick up carefully, drop in hot fat or cooking oil (400°), and fry until light brown, then dip in maple glaze.

MAPLE GLAZE

1. Moisten enough powdered sugar with cold water to make a thin frosting, add 1 ts. maple flavoring. Dip each cruller first on one side then on the other. Place on rack to partially dry.

GOOD OLD SPUD NUTS

1. Begin by cooking 3 medium potatoes until soft. Drain and save 1 c. liquid. Mash the potatoes until light and creamy and set aside in a warm place. Add the 1 c. liquid.
2. Add and beat until smooth
   ¾ c. sugar
   1 ts. salt
   1 c. flour
3. Add
   1 yeast cake dissolved in ¼ c. warm water
4. Cover and let stand in a warm place for 3 hours.
5. To the warm sponge, add
   ½ c. butter or margarine
   ½ ts. nutmeg or mace

2 beaten eggs

5 or 6 c. flour, enough to make a soft dough. Knead on a floured board for 10 minutes. Place in a buttered bowl, cover, and let rise until double in size. Punch dough down and place in refrigerator until 2 hours before serving time.

6. Roll out on floured board, cut with doughnut cutter, let rise until light.

7. Gently slip each spud nut into hot oil or fat (365°). When brown on bottom side, turn with an open wire whip or spoon and brown on the other side. Remove from fat and place on absorbent paper or rack. Sprinkle with sugar or glaze.

HOT CROSS BUNS

1. Scald and cool
   ⅔ c. milk. Soften
   1 cake yeast in the milk and add
   ⅓ c. sugar
   1 c. flour and beat well.

2. Then add
   ½ c. soft shortening
   ¾ ts. salt
   3 beaten eggs
   2½ c. flour. Beat until smooth and let rise until double in size, about 1 hour.

3. Stir in
   ⅔ c. currants
   ½ ts. cinnamon
   ½ c. candied fruits. Place on a floured board and roll out to ½-inch thickness. Cut with round cutter, place on greased baking sheet, cover, and let rise until light. With the scissors snip the dough to form a cross in the top of each bun. Brush lightly with beaten egg white. Bake at 350° for 12 to 15 minutes. With a pastry tube, filled with white frosting, fill in the cross on each top.

SPICED CAKE DOUGHNUTS

1. Beat well
   ½ c. sugar

       1 egg, then add
       ½ c. molasses
       ½ c. milk stirred with
       1 tbs. vinegar
       2 tbs. melted butter

2. Sift together twice
       5 c. flour
       1 ts. salt
       ¾ ts. soda
       4 ts. baking powder
       1 ts. ginger
       1 ts. cinnamon
       1 ts. nutmeg

3. Add 2 mixtures together and stir just until mixed.

4. Roll out dough a small amount at a time on a floured board, cut with a doughnut cutter, and fry in hot fat (400°). Fry first on one side, then tip doughnut over and fry on the other side.

5. Drain on rack or paper for 1 minute and then roll in a mixture of sugar and cinnamon.

AUNT LIZZY'S CAKE DOUGHNUTS

1. Beat until light
       5 eggs and slowly add
       1¾ c. sugar

2. Stir in carefully
       2½ c. top milk and cream mixed
       2 tbs. melted butter or cooking oil

3. Sift together and fold in
       4 c. flour
       5 ts. baking powder
       ½ ts. nutmeg

4. Mix to a soft, smooth dough. If more flour is needed, add just enough to make the dough easy to handle with floured hands.

5. Roll out on board and cut with doughnut cutter. Fry in deep fat (400°). Brown on both sides being careful not to stick a fork into the doughnut. Roll, while still warm, in either sugar or powdered sugar, or frost with light frosting.

SPUD NUTS

1. Scald
    ½ pt. milk in pan and add
    1½ ts. salt
    1 c. sugar
    4 tbs. shortening
    1 c. mashed potatoes
2. When cool, add
    2 yeast cakes dissolved in
    1 c. warm water and
    3 well-beaten eggs
3. Sift in enough flour to make a soft dough, sprinkle with nutmeg, and mix again. Cover, put in warm place, and let rise until double in bulk. Roll thin and cut with doughnut cutter. Let rise until very light, then drop in hot fat (425°). Brown on both sides, by turning carefully. While still warm glaze with melted honey or glaze.

GLAZE

Mix enough powdered sugar with hot water to make a thin frosting and flavor to taste. Drop each doughnut in just enough to cover it. Place on wax paper or rack to partially dry.

OLD-FASHIONED SPUD NUTS (A Large Recipe)

1. Dissolve
    2 yeast cakes in
    ½ c. lukewarm potato water
2. Mix together
    ½ c. shortening
    ½ c. sugar
    3 eggs
    ½ ts. lemon rind
    2 ts. lemon juice
    ½ ts. nutmeg
    ½ ts. cinnamon
    1 c. mashed potatoes
    1½ c. milk, scalded and cooled
    Add yeast mixture
3. Sift in and mix until smooth

7 c. flour
4. Cover and let rise until double in size. Roll out on floured board and cut with doughnut cutter. Place on floured trays and let rise until light.
5. Fry in deep fat, 375° to 400°, until brown on both sides. Drain on paper or wire rack.
6. Glaze if desired with a thin mixture of fruit juice and powdered sugar.

RAISED DOUGHNUTS

1. Warm
   1¼ c. milk and in it dissolve
   1 yeast cake, add
   1½ c. flour, stir well and let rise until it forms a sponge.
2. Cream and add to sponge
   3 tbs. butter
   1 ts. sugar
   1 egg
3. Sift into sponge and mix until smooth
   1½ c. flour
   1 ts. salt
4. Knead the dough lightly and place in a greased bowl. Cover and let rise about 1½ hours.
5. Roll out on floured board about ½-inch thick and cut with doughnut cutter. Place 2 inches apart on a floured tin or board and let rise until double in size. Then fry in a deep fat (400°) until brown, turn and brown the other side. Roll in sugar while warm.
6. Glaze if you desire in
   1 lb. powdered sugar mixed with enough hot water to make a soft paste.
   Add 2 tbs. butter and
   1 ts. vanilla

SOUR-MILK DOUGHNUTS

1. Cream until smooth
   4 tbs. butter
   1 c. sugar
   2 eggs

2. Sift and add alternately with
       1 c. buttermilk and
       1 ts. vanilla
       3 c. flour
       ½ ts. salt
       1 ts. soda
       ½ ts. nutmeg
3. Add more flour if needed to make a soft dough.
4. Roll on floured board to ½-inch thickness, cut with doughnut cutter. Fry in deep fat or cooking oil at 400°.

SCONES

This choice fried cake is in demand at our summer home in the canyon, on every occasion; a party or gathering isn't complete without them, served piping hot with fresh honey.

1. Cook and mash
       1 c. potatoes, then add
       1 ts. salt
       3 tbs. sugar
       2 c. scalded and cooled milk
       1 square butter
       2 beaten eggs
       2 yeast cakes which have been soaked in a little warm water
       2 c. flour
       Mix altogether into a sponge and let rise 1 hour.
2. Mix in enough flour to make a soft, firm dough and knead for several minutes. Good old-fashioned kneading improves this recipe. Cover and let rise in a warm place for 1 hour or until light.
3. Pour out on floured board and roll carefully, cut in strips or squares the size desired, and let them rise until light.
4. Fry at 375° in deep fat (peanut oil preferred) until golden brown on both sides. Serve hot with honey.

GRAPE NUT BREAD

1. Mix together and let stand for several minutes
       2 c. sour milk or buttermilk
       1 c. Grape Nuts

2. Cream well and add to the milk and Grape Nuts
    1 c. sugar
    3 tbs. shortening
3. Sift in and beat
    4 c. flour
    1 ts. soda
    2 ts. baking powder
    ½ ts. salt
4. Stir in
    1 c. raisins
    1 c. chopped nuts
5. Bake in two greased loaf pans for 45 minutes at 325°.

PINEAPPLE NUT BREAD

This moist, rich bread has lots of flavor.
1. Sift together
    2 c. flour
    3 ts. baking powder
    ⅓ c. sugar
2. Add
    1 beaten egg
    3 tbs. melted margarine
    1 tbs. lemon juice
    ½ ts. grated lemon rind
    ½ c. chopped nuts
    1 small can crushed pineapple
3. Mix altogether to a stiff batter and bake in a loaf tin
    for one hour at 350°.

APPLE BANANA BREAD

1. Cream together
    ½ c. shortening
    ¾ c. sugar
2. Add
    2 beaten eggs
    3 tbs. buttermilk
    1 small mashed banana
    1 c. applesauce
3. Sift in and mix well
    2 c. flour
    1 ts. soda and 1 ts. salt
    Bake in greased loaf tin for 45 minutes at 350°.

CARAWAY SEED CHEESE TWISTS

1. Sift together
    2 c. flour
    2½ ts. baking powder
    1 ts. salt
    ½ ts. caraway seeds
2. Cut into the flour mixture
    ¼ c. shortening and add
    ¾ c. milk and
    ½ c. grated cheese
3. Mix to a soft dough; knead several times and roll out
    to ¼-inch thickness. Cut in narrow strips, 3 inches long
    and ½ inch wide. Twist two strips together and form a
    twirl. Place on a greased baking sheet, brush with
    melted butter, and sprinkle with caraway seeds. Bake
    10 minutes at 450°.
    Garlic salt or flavoring may be added for some occasions.

CINDIE'S SESAME CRISPS

1. Toast until light brown in a 350° oven
    1 c. sesame seeds
    ½ c. coconut
2. Cream together
    ¾ c. butter
    1 c. brown sugar
    1 egg
    1 ts. vanilla
3. To the creamed mixture, add
    2 c. flour, sifted with
    1 ts. baking powder
    ½ ts. soda
    ½ ts. salt
4. Mix altogether and form into little balls. Flatten them
    with a floured spatula or glass to ⅛-inch thickness.
    Place on greased cookie sheet. Bake at 350° for 10
    minutes.

FRUIT AND NUT BREADS

Tasty breads are just the right touch to finish off a meal
or for a snack between meals. They are especially good for
luncheons and buffet suppers. They are an all-occasion
healthful food.

ORANGE BREAD

1. Place through a chopper
   3 orange rinds, cover with cold water and place on
   stove. Cook until tender. Drain and rinse in cold
   water. Then add
   1 c. sugar and cook slowly to a thick syrup.
2. Beat until light
   3 eggs and add
   1 c. milk, the cooled orange rinds, and the juice from
   the oranges.
3. Sift in and mix well
   3½ c. flour
   1 ts. salt
   3 ts. baking powder
4. Pour into 2 greased loaf pans and bake for 45 minutes
   at 350°.

BANANA BREAD

1. Cream together
   ½ c. butter or margarine
   1 c. sugar
   1 egg (beaten)
2. Add
   3 large ripe bananas (mashed)
3. Sift in and mix until smooth
   2 c. flour
   1 ts. soda
   ½ ts. salt
4. Pour into greased loaf pans and bake at 350° for 1 hour.

HELEN B.'S COFFEE CAKE, FIRST METHOD

Helen is a dear. This recipe is very choice and was given
to her by a friend. She in turn gave it to me. You, too,
will like this very much.

1. Cream in mixing bowl
   3 tbs. shortening
   1 c. sugar
   1 egg

2. Add
    1 c. milk
    1 ts. flavoring (I like cardamon)
    1 tbs. melted butter
3. Fold in
    2 c. sifted flour
    2 ts. baking powder
    1 ts. salt
    ½ c. chopped nuts and mix until smooth
4. Top with the following topping before baking
    Mix: 2 tbs. flour
    2 ts. cinnamon
    ½ c. brown sugar
    1 tbs. butter
    Bake in a shallow greased pan at 350° for 1 hour.

SECOND METHOD

1. Pour half of the batter in the prepared pan and sprinkle with part of the topping. Then pour the rest of the batter on top and sprinkle with the balance of topping. This method makes the cake richer. May be baked as in method one. This cake retains its lusciousness when warmed over.

BASIC DOUGH FOR COFFEE CAKE

This never-fail recipe may be made into many interesting types.
1. Soak in mixing bowl
    ¾ c. warm water
    ¼ c. sugar
    1 pkg. dry yeast or 2 cakes of moist yeast
2. Add the following and mix until partially smooth
    2 beaten eggs
    1¼ c. flour
    1 ts. salt
    ¼ c. melted and cooled shortening and then add
    1 more c. flour. Mix again until all blended.
3. Drop by spoonfuls onto the bottom of a buttered pan. Cover and let rise until double in bulk.
    Try the following toppings for variation and choose your favorite.

TOPPING 1, TUTTI-FRUTTI

1. Into one batch of basic dough add
    ¼ c. candied fruits
    ¼ c. chopped nuts
2. Spoon into prepared pan or mold.
3. Bake at 375° for 20 to 25 minutes. While still warm,
    frost with a soft white frosting and garnish with can-
    died fruits.

TOPPING 2, CRUMB CINNAMON

1. Mix together
    2 tbs. butter or margarine
    ½ c. brown sugar
    1 tbs. flour
    2 ts. cinnamon
    1 c. cookie or cake crumbs
    1 tbs. cream or canned milk
    ½ c. nuts, if desired
2. Spread over top of spooned-out dough and let rise till
    double. Bake for 20 minutes at 375°.

TOPPING 3, CARAMEL NUT

1. Melt in a frying pan
    ⅓ c. butter
    ½ c. brown sugar
    1 tbs. dark syrup (maple)
    1 ts. vanilla. Cool.
2. Pour the cooled syrup into a well-buttered ring mold
    or pan. Arrange whole pecan halves, face down, on the
    bottom of the mold.
3. Use 1 batch of basic dough. Drop by spoonfuls on top
    of the syrup. Cover and let rise until dough is double
    in bulk. Bake in oven 375° for 20 minutes. Turn out on
    plate as soon as possible after removing from oven,
    because the rich syrup will have a tendency to stick
    to the pan. Serve warm. To reheat, cover with alumi-
    num foil and warm slowly.

TOPPING 4, CHERRY BUTTERSCOTCH

1. Melt in a pan
    ⅓ c. butter

½ c. brown sugar
2 tbs. maple syrup
2 ts. butterscotch flavoring

2. Pour into buttered, ring-mold pan. On top, arrange bits of pineapple, whole maraschino cherries and walnut halves, placing them face down.
3. Then arrange the dough over the top and let it rise until double in bulk. Bake for 20 minutes at 375°.

TOPPING 5, COCONUT FLUFF

1. Use a well buttered baking dish. Cover the bottom with fresh currant jelly or raspberry jam. Sprinkle generously with coconut and arrange dough in mounds over the top. Cover and let rise until double in bulk.
2. Bake for 20 minutes at 375°. Turn out on rack and serve warm.

TOPPING 6, ALMOND ROKA

1. Melt in a pan
    ½ c. butter or margarine
    1 c. brown sugar
    1 ts. almond flavoring. Pour into a buttered baking pan and sprinkle with
    1 c. ground or chopped almonds
    1 c. crushed almond brittle (peanut brittle may be used)
2. Pour batch of dough over the top. Let rise, then bake for 20 minutes at 375°. When baked turn out on serving plate and break gently in pieces—serve warm.

TOPPING 7, JELLIED ORANGE

1. In a buttered baking dish gently sprinkle a little powdered sugar. Pour over the top.
    1 can fresh-frozen orange juice. Arrange jellied orange slices in a pattern and dip one batch of basic dough in spoonfuls over the top.
2. Let rise and bake 25 minutes at 375°.

LILLIAN'S ORANGE COFFEE CAKE

Lillian is my beloved sister. She is happy to have you enjoy this recipe with her.

1. Beat
   1 egg and add
   1/2 ts. salt, then add
   1/2 c. cooking oil
2. Slowly add
   1/2 c. milk
   2 tbs. grated orange rind
   1/2 c. sugar
   1/2 c. flour
   1/2 c. orange juice
3. Mix until smooth, then fold in the following
   1 1/2 c. flour sifted with
   3 ts. baking powder
   Mix until flour is blended, then pour into well-greased, 10-inch loaf pan.
4. Before baking, sprinkle the top with the following mixture:
   2 tbs. butter
   1 c. brown sugar
   1 ts. nutmeg
   1 ts. cinnamon
   1/2 c. finely chopped walnuts
5. Bake for 30 minutes at 375°. Serve hot.

GINGERBREAD

1. Cream
   1 c. butter or shortening
   1 c. sugar
   2 eggs
2. Sift in
   5 c. all-purpose flour
   3 ts. soda
   2 ts. cinnamon
   2 ts. ginger
   1 ts. cloves
   1 ts. salt
3. Mix until well blended with
   2 c. molasses mixed in
   2 c. hot water
4. Pour into greased pan and bake at 350° for 45 minutes. Serve hot with whipped cream or pudding sauce.

GINGERBREAD WAFFLES

1. Sift together in mixing bowl
    2¾ c. flour
    ¼ ts. cloves
    1½ ts. soda
    1 ts. salt
    1 ts. cinnamon
    1 ts. ginger
2. Mix the following together and stir in slowly
    1 c. molasses
    ⅔ c. boiling water
    1 beaten egg
3. Bake in waffle iron until done. Serve with hot apple-
    sauce, warm honey, or your choice of topping.

Pies

PIE CRUST

How often do you hear someone say, "I would love to make a pie but I make a poor pie crust."

The secret of good pie crust is in the handling of the dough; it must be mixed lightly and quickly. Good pastry it flaky, tender, and delicate. It is not crumbly but, when broken, shows layers of flakes with air spaces between.

During baking each fat particle melts to form a delicate flake. Rough handling may cause the flakes to form a solid, tough dough, producing a poor pie crust. All ingredients should be cold—cold fat, cold water or milk; hands should be washed and rinsed in cold water before beginning.

A knife, fork, or pastry blender may be used to mix the fat, flour, and moisture.

The flour, salt, and sugar, if recipe calls for it, are sifted together. Add the cold fat and work it into the flour mixture allowing the fat particles to remain the size of a pea. Quickly add the cold liquid, beginning in the center of the mixture. Gently form the dough. Move the moistened part to the edge of the mixing bowl and repeat being sure to mix the dough from the bottom. Do not become alarmed if portions of the flour do not appear to be moist enough. It will adhere to the moistened dough when you begin rolling. Use a pastry cloth, canvas, or marble, on which to roll the pastry. Gently pick up just enough dough at a time to make one layer of crust. Rerolling doesn't improve the crust, so use only the right amount. Keep the unrolled pastry covered while working. Begin by rolling carefully from the center to the edges. Do not press too hard with the rolling pin, as this will cause the dough to stick to the canvas. With the finger tips gently raise the rolled dough to prevent it from sticking, or turn it over if necessary and add a sprinkling of flour. Roll the dough as nearly as possible in a round circle and as thin as desired. To place the rolled dough on the pie tin, gently fold the dough, then cover the tin and proceed to form the edges for the type of pie you are making.

To protect the crust from shrinking away from the edges, press the unbaked pastry lightly against the edge of the pie pan, then with the palm gently press the dough from the outer edge instead of cutting it off with a knife. This leaves a firm, full edge that is neat appearing when baked. To make a fluted edge, press the first and middle finger of the left hand one inch apart into the dough and with the first finger on the right hand press forward between the other two. This will make a nice edging and also hold the dough tightly on the tin.

When baking shells for one-crust pies, make several indentations with the prongs of a fork across the bottom before placing in the oven. This will prevent the crust from rising in bubbles during baking.

Bake single crusts in a hot oven, 400° to 450°, for 10 to 15 minutes.

To bake double-crust pies, arrange the dough as for single crusts. Before filling with fruits, fillings, etc., brush over the top of the bottom crust with melted butter or the white of an egg. This will prevent it from absorbing the moisture from the fillings and becoming soggy. Do not fill the crusts so full that the juice will ooze out while baking.

To insure the edges of the top and bottom crust remaining together, moisten the edge of the bottom crust with a little water or milk before putting on the top crust. Flute the edges firmly together either with the fingers, a pastry blender, or the back of a fork. To make a luscious appearance to the tops, brush them lightly just before putting them in the oven with one of the following:

    Beaten whole egg
    Evaporated milk
    Thick cream
    Milk and sugar mixed

Double-crust pies should be placed on the lower rack of the oven for the first 15 minutes and then placed on the center rack to finish baking. This will assure the proper baking of the bottom crust. The oven should be preheated. Bake at 450° to 475° for the first 15 minutes, then reduce to 350° to finish baking. Pies should be placed directly on a rack when removed from the oven to allow air to cool the bottoms; this will also prevent sogginess.

Pie doughs may be chilled before rolling if you desire. This will not be necessary if you work quickly while mixing and rolling.

On the top crusts of fruit pies you may make designs with the sharp point of a small knife to determine the flavor of pie. This also allows the steam to escape while pie is baking. Each cook has her own method of designing the top.

Suggestions for designing:

Capital C for cherry
Capital A for apple
Capital M for mince, etc.

BUTTER PASTRY FOR FRUIT PIES

1. Sift together
   1 c. flour
   1/8 ts. salt
   1 tbs. sugar
2. Blend in
   1/4 c. butter and
   1 egg yolk (beaten)
3. Press into pie plate to 1/4 in. thickness.
4. Brush bottom crust with egg white and pour in filling.

CRUMB PIE PASTRY

1. Mix together
   1 1/2 c. fine cookie crumbs
   1/4 c. brown sugar
   1/2 c. melted butter
2. Press in pie tins and bake 6 minutes in 400° oven and chill, or bake in 350° oven for 10 to 15 minutes. Use crumbs from the following:
   chocolate cookies
   graham crackers
   zwiebacks
   cereal flakes
   vanilla wafers
   macaroon wafers

FLAKY PIE CRUST (Rich)

1. Sift together
    2 c. flour (pastry or all-purpose)
    ⅔ ts. salt
    1 tbs. sugar
    1 tbs. cornstarch
2. Work in lightly
    ⅔ to 1 c. shortening
3. Add a few drops at a time
    ¼ c. ice water, or just enough ice water to hold the dough together. Don't overmix. Roll carefully and place in tins.

SWEET MILK CRUST

1. Sift together
    2½ c. flour
    1 ts. salt
    1 tbs. sugar
2. Gently work in
    1 c. cold lard
3. Add, a small amount at a time,
    ½ c. cold milk. Mix only until dough holds together. Roll quickly, or if desired chill before rolling.

PLAIN PASTRY

1. Sift together
    2 c. sifted flour
    ¾ ts. salt
2. Cut in
    ⅔ c. shortening
3. Add
    4 to 6 tbs. cold water
4. Mix carefully and roll. Use caution not to pull or stretch pastry while lining the pans.

SOUTHERN PASTRY

This is nice for pecan pies.
1. Sift
    2 c. flour

½ ts. salt
¼ ts. baking powder
2. Cut in carefully
1 c. shortening (vegetable)
3. Mix lightly adding
6 tbs. ice water
This pastry is rich and must be handled carefully.

CHEESE PASTRY

This is especially good for apple pies.
1. Cut together
1 c. flour
½ c. butter
2. Add and mix to a smooth dough
¼ lb. cottage or cream cheese
3. Roll carefully on floured board and line tin. Bake at 450° for 12 minutes.

CHEESE STICKS

1. These may be made by using a recipe of pastry. Roll out and sprinkle with grated cheese, fold twice, roll out and repeat.
2. Cut into thin strips and bake on a cookie sheet for 12 minutes at 425°.

CHOCOLATE COCONUT CRUST

1. In a double boiler melt
2 squares of bitter chocolate and
2 tbs. butter, then remove from hot water and
2. Add and beat well
2 tbs. hot milk
⅔ c. powdered sugar
3. Add
1½ c. fine shredded coconut and mix well.
4. Spread on bottom and sides of greased pie tin.
5. Chill in refrigerator until firm and fill with chiffon filling, pudding, or ice cream.

CHIFFON FILLING

1. Cook in double boiler until smooth
       1½ c. milk
       ½ c. sugar
       1 pkg. vanilla pudding mix
2. Cool and add
       1 ts. vanilla and
       2 beaten egg whites
3. Chill before putting into crusts and add just before serving.
4. Whip ½ pt. cream and garnish the top in twirls.

ORANGE CHIFFON PIE

1. Soak for 5 minutes
       1 tbs. gelatin
       ¼ c. cold water
2. Beat real well
       4 egg yolks and add
       ½ c. sugar
       1 c. orange juice
       ½ ts. salt
       2 tbs. lemon juice
3. Place in top of double boiler over boiling water and cook until of custard consistency, then add the softened gelatin and
       1 ts. grated orange rind. Remove from heat and partially cool.
4. Gradually add
       4 egg whites, beaten stiff with
       ½ c. sugar
5. Pour into baked crust and chill. Can be served with whipped cream.

EGG WHITE PASTRY

1. Blend together
       1½ c. flour
       ½ ts. salt
       ½ c. shortening
2. Whip
       1 egg white and add
       4 tbs. cold water. Add this a little at a time to flour mixture blending until dough holds together.

FRENCH PASTRY

1. Crush
   1½ c. graham crackers or zwiebacks
2. Add
   1 c. sugar
3. Mix in
   ⅓ c. soft butter and
   1 egg white
4. Press gently in pie pan to form the shell.
   Bake at 400° for 10 minutes.

PUFF PASTE

1. Wash in cold water to remove salt from
   1 lb. butter. Allow ⅔ of the butter to become soft.
2. Cut the
   ⅓ lb. butter into
   2 c. cake flour using a blender
3. Add
   ½ c. ice water, using just enough to hold the pastry together
4. Roll out on a slightly floured board, making a square layer, then spread ¼ of the soft butter over ⅔ of the dough. Fold the unbuttered part over the center. Repeat folding and spreading the butter until you have used ½ lb. butter and you have 3 layers of buttered pastry. Chill and reroll. Spread with the remaining butter and chill again. Roll again and form into patty shells or shapes desired and bake at 450° for 10 minutes, then reduce heat and bake at 400° for 5 minutes, then for 15 minutes at 350°.
   Cool before filling.

PASTRY FLAKE

This makes an especially good crust for lemon pies.
1. Cream
   ¼ c. butter
2. Spread a thin layer of soft butter on rolled pastry (use recipe of your choice), fold over, and reroll.
3. Arrange pastry on pie tins and bake at 450° for 10 minutes.

MERINGUE SHELLS

These are dainty little pie shells, nice for parties and special occasions. The baking is the secret of their success so follow the rules closely.

1. Have at room temperature
     4 egg whites
2. Mix together
     1⅓ c. sugar and
     2 tbs. cornstarch
3. Beat egg whites till they stand up in soft peaks. Add the sugar and cornstarch 2 tbs. at a time, beating all the time. After the third addition add
     2 tbs. vinegar and before the last addition beat in
     ¾ ts. flavoring, any flavor desired.
4. Pour into pastry bag and squeeze the meringue in the shape of cup—first make a round, flat base, then follow the edge and squeeze rows on top of each other to resemble a cup of the size desired.
5. Bake in a 325° oven for 1 hour without opening the oven door; the shell will collapse if you do. Turn off oven and leave the shells in the oven to completely dry before removing.
6. When cool fill with ice cream, sherbet, custard, or whipped cream.
     If you prefer making individual pie shells smooth the meringue with a rubber spatula across the tin up to the edges. Bake as directed. Another procedure is to pre-heat the oven to 450°, place the shells in, and turn the oven completely off. Allow the shells to remain in oven for 3 hours.

GRAHAM CRACKER CRUST

1. In a bowl mix altogether
     1½ c. graham cracker crumbs
     ⅓ c. powdered sugar
     ½ c. butter or margarine
     1 egg white
     Mix until smooth and pat with the fingers in a pie tin. Press the mixture up to the edges firmly and bake in a 400° oven for 8 to 10 minutes.

ORANGE PASTRY PIE CRUST

1. Sift
     1 c. all-purpose flour
     ¼ ts. salt and mix in grated rind of
     1 large orange
2. Cut in lightly
     ⅓ c. shortening with pastry blender or tips of fingers.
3. Stir in
     4 tbs. chilled orange juice and mix gently. Pat in a
   ball ready for rolling.
4. Roll as for pie crust. Cover tins, flute the edges, and
   gently press a fork into the crust across the bottom to
   prevent it from forming raised pockets when baking.
   Bake at 425° until golden brown (about 12 to 15 minutes).
   This pastry is especially nice for fruit chiffon pies such
   as lemon, orange, pineapple, etc.

HOT-WATER CRUST

1. Sift together
     3 c. flour
     1 ts. salt
     1 ts. baking powder
2. In a bowl place
     1 full c. lard and
     ½ c. boiling water
3. Sift the flour mixture into the hot water and lard. Stir
   just enough to combine the dough.
4. Mold in floured hands for 1 minute.
5. Chill in refrigerator and then roll as desired. Makes two
   two-crust pies.

MERINGUES AND TOPPINGS FOR PIES

1. Beat until frothy
     2 egg whites and add gradually
     4 tbs. sugar. Continue beating until it holds in peaks.
2. Add
     ½ ts. flavoring (your choice)
     Immediately pile on pie and spread to the edges with a

spatula. Arrange fluffy peaks with the point of spatula.

Bake in a slow oven 325° for 15 to 20 minutes.

PUFF PASTE (PATTY SHELLS)

Puff Paste requires more careful handling but is lighter and more flaky than other paste. In making it, it is necessary to work rapidly and with a light touch. Make in a cold room. Use a cotton cloth cover for both the board and rolling pin. A glass rolling pin filled with ice is desirable.

1. Wash and work under cold water, to remove salt and buttermilk,

    1 lb. butter. Pat and fold until all the water is gone.

2. Work ¼ of the lb. of butter into

    1 lb. (2 c.) flour, with the finger tips or pastry blender.

3. Moisten the flour and butter with cold water to form a dough. Turn out on a lightly floured board and knead one minute. Cover with a towel and put in a cool place for 5 minutes.

4. Roll out ¼-inch thick, place the remaining ¾ lb. of butter on the center of the lower half of the rolled dough, fold the upper half of dough over the butter, press the edges firmly together. The sides are then turned one under the other. Turn the dough halfway around, cover, and let stand five minutes. Roll out again ¼-inch thick, lifting often to prevent paste from sticking. Dust the board with flour if necessary. Fold the ends forward to the center 4 times and reroll. Repeat, rolling twice. Turn paste halfway around each time before rolling. Chill thoroughly.

5. Form into patties and bake in a hot oven 400° for 20 minutes, then turn heat to 350° and continue baking until golden brown.

    Cool before filling.

6. Fill with creamed chicken, creamed turkey, creamed peas and carrots, mushrooms and crab, or any choice of fillings you desire.

Patty shells are easily made by cutting the rolled dough in circles to make the bottoms of the shells. Then cut rings the size of the circles with the outer edges about ½-inch wide. Stack in layers to the height desired and bake as instructed above. When baked, the shells should have a cup like appearance. Fill when cool.

EGYPTIAN PASTRY (MILLEFEUILL)

This recipe was given to me by our dear Moonie—an Egyptian boy who lived in our home for years.
1. Mix together
    2 egg whites
    1 lb. flour
    Knead lightly and roll on board or paper until ½-inch thickness, then
2. Spread on
    1 lb. soft butter. Fold edges of pastry to the center. Roll dough just once and chill in refrigerator.
3. Reroll and chill again, repeat 4 times. This process perfects the pastry.
4. Cut into 3 pieces and roll very thin. Bake until light brown, at 350°, for 10 minutes or more.
5. Spread each piece with strawberry jam, and arrange in layers. Cover with whipped cream and nuts.

FRENCH PASTRY (Cake Type)

1. Over a pan of hot water, place in a bowl
    3 eggs and
    ¼ lb. powdered sugar
    Whip briskly about 20 minutes. When mixture is nicely warmed, remove from water and beat until quite stiff.
2. Pour into a mold lined with paper. Bake 30 minutes at 350°.

MAIDS OF HONOR (By Augusta)

This recipe was given to me by Augusta, one of my dear friends.
1. Roll out one batch of rich pastry, cut with round biscuit cutter and line a muffin tin, pressing pastry firmly to the edges of the tin.
2. Place
    1 ts. of firm jelly or jam in the center of the pastry. Add a spoonful of cake batter on top of the jelly or jam. Bake at 375° until light brown, about 15 minutes.

3. When cool, spread a layer of your choice of frosting on the top of each Maid of Honor. The frosting may be applied with a pastry tube in fancy patterns, if desired.

MERINGUE

1. Beat until frothy
      4 egg whites
2. Add a small amount at a time
      8 tbs. sugar and
      1/2 ts. cream of tartar
      Continue beating until meringue holds firm, high peaks.
3. Arrange on top of pie and brown in 350° oven without opening oven door for 15 or 20 minutes.

MARSHMALLOW MERINGUE

1. In top of double boiler heat together
      1/2 lb. marshmallows
      1 tbs. milk
2. Fold over and over until marshmallows are partially melted. Remove from heat and beat until smooth.
3. Beat stiff
      2 egg whites and add
      1/4 c. sugar
      1/4 ts. salt. Continue beating, then add
      1/2 ts. vanilla
4. Blend into marshmallow mixture, spread over pie, and bake in 450° oven for 1 to 2 minutes.

BROWN SUGAR MERINGUE

1. Beat until frothy
      2 egg whites and add gradually
      4 tbs. brown sugar and
      1/2 ts. vanilla
2. Beat until stiff and cover filled pie shell.
      Bake 15 to 20 minutes at 325°.

MERINGUE TOPPING FOR PIES (Large Recipe)

1. Place in beater bowl
   1 qt. cold water and
   5 oz. of meringue powder
2. Beat on low speed for three minutes, then raise the speed to high and add 3 lbs. of sugar (granulated). Beat until stiff.
3. Spread in folds over pies, spreading near the edges, so meringue won't pull from the sides while baking.

ICEBOX PASTRY

This is an unusual pastry, but it is delicious. You will be thrilled when you see the finished product, and you will be proud to offer it to anyone as an outstanding treat. It must be made the day before you expect to serve it.

1. Cream together
   ½ lb. butter
   2 tbs. sugar
   3 egg yolks
2. Dissolve
   1 yeast cake in
   ½ c. lukewarm milk and add slowly to the first mixture.
3. Then sift and add a little at a time
   2 c. flour
   ½ ts. salt. Mix until smooth and free from lumps.
4. Place in a buttered bowl, cover, and store in refrigerator overnight.
5. Cut the dough into pieces and roll on a wax paper to ½-inch thickness.
6. Beat
   3 egg whites until stiff and add
   ¾ c. sugar gradually, beating all the while until it is meringue. Spread quickly over each piece of dough. Add a layer of cooked crushed pineapple and finely crushed nuts on top. Immediately roll like jelly roll and slide from the wax paper with a large spatula onto a buttered cookie sheet. Bake in a preheated 350° oven for ½ hour. Serve while hot.
   Raspberry jam may be used in place of pineapple, if you prefer.

FRENCH PIE PASTRY

1. Sift together
     2 c. flour
     ¼ ts. salt
     1½ ts. sugar
2. Add
     1 ts. grated lemon rind
3. Cut into the flour mixture and stir in lightly
     ⅔ c. shortening
4. Mix together
     1 egg yolk beaten
     3 tbs. cold water
     2 tbs. lemon juice. Blend into the above mixture.
5. Roll very thin in a pastry cloth and fit into pie pan.
   Trim off ½ inch beyond the pan edge and fold the pastry
   back over the edge. Bake at 425° for 12 to 15 minutes.

PUMPKIN PIE (Flossie)

Flossie is a very good cook. This is her recipe.
1. In a bowl mix
     1 large can pumpkin and
     1 large can milk
     ⅔ c. fresh milk
2. Add
     3 beaten eggs
     2 ts. vanilla
3. Mix together
     2 tbs. flour
     1 ts. ginger
     1 ts. cinnamon
     ½ ts. nutmeg
     ½ ts. salt
     1½ c. sugar
4. Stir altogether until well mixed and pour into unbaked
   pie shells. Bake in hot oven (450°) for 10 minutes, then
   reduce heat to 300° and continue baking for 25 or 30
   minutes. Serve plain or with whipped cream.

MOLASSES PUMPKIN PIE

1. Mix together
     1 tbs. flour

        1 c. sugar
        ½ ts. ginger
        ½ ts. nutmeg
        1 ts. cinnamon
2. Melt
        1 tbs. butter
3. Beat
        2 egg yolks and add
        1 c. canned pumpkin
        1 tbs. molasses
        2 c. hot milk
4. Add the sugar, flour, spices, and melted butter to the pumpkin mixture and stir well.
5. Pour into unbaked pie shells and bake in a 450° oven for 10 minutes, then reduce heat to 300° and continue baking until firm.

PUMPKIN CHIFFON PIE (Gladys)

1. Soak
        1 envelope of gelatin in
        ¼ c. water
2. Mix altogether
        1¾ c. pumpkin
        1 c. brown sugar
        2 ts. cinnamon
        1 ts. nutmeg
        ¼ ts. cloves
        5 tbs. flour
        2 c. milk
        1 tbs. butter
        3 egg yolks
3. When well mixed, pour into double boiler and cook over boiling water until mixture thickens to a firm custard. Add the soaked gelatin and cook a few minutes more.
4. Remove from hot water and cool for 10 minutes or more. Add
        3 egg whites beaten stiff with
        ⅓ c. sugar
5. Pour into baked pie shells and store in refrigerator until time to serve. Top with whipped cream, if desired.

PUMPKIN PIE GARNISHES

1. Nut glaze topping:
   Mix
   > 1 tbs. butter
   > 2 tbs. brown sugar
   > ½ ts. orange extract
   > ½ c. pecan halves, arranged on top.
   > Sprinkle over pie 10 minutes before baking time is completed, return to oven for 10 minutes.
2. Mapleine topping:
   To whipped cream, add
   > 1 ts. maple flavor and
   > ¼ c. sugar
   > Spread over pie and sprinkle with finely chopped walnuts.
3. Cheese Pumpkins Topping:
   > Roll spoonfuls of cheese and shape to resemble pumpkins. Mark ridges with a fork and insert whole cloves (bud ends down) for the stems. Place 1 cheese pumpkin in the center of each serving of pumpkin pie.

CUSTARD PUMPKIN PIE

Everyone likes pumpkin pie. This custard-like pie is very good, a little smoother than the conventional type. Try it, you will like this one.

1. Mix in large bowl, stirring after each addition,
   > 1 c. canned pumpkin (strained and not too moist)
   > ¾ c. sugar
   > 1¼ ts. pumpkin pie spice
   > ¼ ts. salt
   > 3 slightly beaten eggs
   > 1 c. evaporated milk
   > 1 c. top milk
2. Have the pie shells ready, brush over the crusts lightly with melted butter. Pour the filling into the crusts up to the edges of the shells.
3. Bake in 450° oven for 10 minutes. Be sure the bottom crust is quickly baked to avoid a soggy crust. Then turn the oven to 300° and continue baking for 30 minutes or until custard is firm. Cool on a rack and serve with whipped cream.

PECAN PIE

1. Beat until light
      6 eggs and
      1½ c. sugar
2. Add
      1 tbs. melted butter
      ⅛ ts. salt
      1 c. dark syrup
      1 ts. vanilla
3. Stir until mixed and add
      1½ c. pecan pieces
4. Pour into pie shells and bake at 300° for 1 hour. Serve plain or with cream.

SOUTHERN PECAN PIE

1. Beat together
      1 c. brown sugar
      3 eggs and add
      ¾ c. dark syrup
      ¼ c. melted butter
      ¼ ts. salt. Stir and add
      1 c. pecan pieces
2. Pour into unbaked pie shells and bake at 350° for 45 minutes. Serve with whipped cream.

PUMPKIN PIE (By Cinda)

1. Mix together
      1½ c. pumpkin
      ¾ c. brown sugar
      ½ ts. salt
      2½ ts. pumpkin pie spice
      1 ts. maple flavor
2. Add
      2 eggs slightly beaten
      1 c. hot milk
      ½ c. hot cream (may use evaporated milk)
3. Pour into unbaked pie shells and bake in a 450° oven for 10 minutes, then reduce heat and bake at 325° for 30 minutes. Serve with sweetened whipped cream with maple flavoring.

CUSTARD PUDDING PIE

1. Make a rich pastry and fill pie tins. Then brush over the bottoms with egg whites.
2. Beat until light
    4 eggs and slowly add
    ½ c. sugar
3. Warm
    2 c. milk and add
    ½ ts. vanilla
    ½ ts. lemon
    ¼ ts. salt
4. Pour the warm milk over the eggs and sugar. Stir until mixed and fill the crusts to the top of the shells.
5. Bake slowly at 325° for 40 minutes. Do not cook custard pies too fast in hot ovens because custard will become watery.

BROWN SUGAR CUSTARD PIE

1. Cream together
    1 c. brown sugar and
    4 eggs and
    1 ts. vanilla
    ¼ ts. salt
2. Pour over eggs and sugar
    2½ c. warm milk and stir
3. Then pour into unbaked pie crusts and bake slowly at 325° for 40 to 50 minutes.

CHERRY RASPBERRY PIE

1. Mix altogether and let stand for 1 hour
    2 c. raspberries
    1 c. stoned cherries, fresh or canned
    3 tbs. minute tapioca
    1½ c. sugar
    1 ts. lemon juice
2. Pour into unbaked pie shells. Cut pastry in long, thin strips and braid over the top by beginning in the center and continuing to the edges. Then braid in the opposite direction over the top of the first strips. Press gently all around the edge with the back of a fork. This gives

the pie a pretty edge and also seals the braiding. Brush lightly over the top of the braiding with cream or canned milk.
3. Bake at 450° for 10 minutes and at 325° for 35 minutes. Serve hot or cold.

CHERRY PIE

1. In a bowl combine and let stand for several minutes
    2 c. pie cherries
    ⅓ c. cherry juice
    ⅓ ts. almond extract
    ⅓ c. sugar
    ⅓ c. brown sugar
    3 tbs. minute tapioca or prepared pie thickener
    1 tbs. butter
2. Pour into pastry shell. Cut pastry into strips to make a latticework top. Press edges firmly and brush over latticework with a beaten egg, then sprinkle with sugar. Bake in a hot oven 450° for 15 minutes, then turn oven to 325° and continue baking for 20 to 30 minutes.

HEAVENLY LEMON CHIFFON PIE (Makes 5 Pies)

1. In a large double boiler cook, stirring all the time,
    3 c. water
    1 c. lemon juice
    1 c. orange juice
    2 c. sugar
    ½ ts. salt
    1½ tbs. lemon rind
    1½ tbs. orange rind
    ¾ c. cornstarch, moistened in a little water.
2. Separate enough eggs to make
    2 c. egg whites
3. Beat the yolks and add to the cooking custard. Continue cooking until it thickens and will drop from a spoon.
4. Remove from heat and fold in the egg whites which have been beaten until stiff with
    2 c. sugar
5. Pour quickly into baked pie crusts and place in refrigerator until well chilled. Serve with whipped cream, sweetened and flavored with lemon.

LEMON MERINGUE PIE (Four Pies)

This is an old favorite.

1. In a double boiler, over boiling water, place
   4¾ c. sugar
   1⅓ c. cornstarch
   ¼ ts. salt
2. Add
   7 c. boiling water and cook until thick.
3. Add
   1⅓ c. melted butter
   juice of 7 lemons and
   grated rind from 4 lemons
4. Add
   10 well-beaten egg yolks. Continue cooking, stirring constantly, until mixture thickens and forms a custard.
5. Remove from heat and cool slightly. Pour into baked pie shells, cover with meringue. Bake at 325° for 20 to 25 minutes.

LIME CHIFFON PIE

1. Soak until soft
   1 tbs. gelatin
   ¼ c. cold water
2. Beat until light
   4 egg yolks and
   ½ c. sugar
3. Add
   ½ c. fresh lime juice
   1 ts. grated lime rind
4. Place in double boiler over hot water, stirring often, until mixture thickens.
5. Add softened gelatin, stir, and cool.
6. When mixture begins to set, fold in
   4 beaten egg whites whipped with
   ½ c. sugar
7. Pour into baked pie shells and chill. Decorate with whipped cream and serve.

LEMON SPONGE PIE

1. Cook in a double boiler over hot water
    8 egg yolks
    1½ c. sugar
    2 lemons, the juice and grated rind
    Stir continuously until mixture will drop from a spoon.
    Remove from heat.
2. Beat until very stiff and fold into the cooked mixture
    4 egg whites beaten with
    ¼ c. sugar
3. Pour into baked pie shells and cover with meringue made
    from the remaining
    4 egg whites beaten until stiff with
    ¼ c. sugar
    Spread in peaks over the filled pie shell and bake at
    350° until golden brown (about 20 minutes), without
    opening the oven door.

CREAM PECAN PIE

1. In a bowl mix
    2 beaten eggs
    ½ c. sugar
    1 c. white syrup
    2 tbs. butter
    1 ts. vanilla
    1 tbs. flour
2. Stir in
    1 c. pecan pieces
3. Pour into unbaked pie crusts and bake at 350° for 45
    minutes.

LEMON EGG PIE

1. In a double boiler cook, stirring constantly, until thick
    4 egg yolks
    1 c. sugar
    grated rind of 1 lemon
    4 tbs. lemon juice
    ⅛ ts. salt
2. Remove from hot water and add the following meringue:
3. Beat until foamy
    4 egg whites and

¼ ts. salt, then add

½ c. sugar very slowly, beating until mixture is glossy and stiff. Fold into the lemon mixture and fill the baked pie shells.

4. Place in a 325° oven and bake until delicately browned for about 20 minutes.

SWEET MILK CHOCOLATE PIE

This recipe will become a popular one in your home. It is quickly made and very sure of success.

1. Place in double boiler over hot water and cook until mixture drops from spoon

    1 can of sweetened condensed milk

    2 squares of unsweetened chocolate and

    ¼ ts. salt

2. Stir in

    ½ c. hot water and continue cooking for 3 minutes.

3. Remove from heat and add

    1 ts. vanilla

4. Pour into cookie crumb crust and chill at room temperature for ½ hour, then chill in refrigerator for 3 hours or longer.

5. Serve with whipped cream or vanilla ice cream.

ORANGE CHIFFON PIE

1. Soak for 5 minutes

    1 tbs. gelatin

    ¼ c. cold water

2. Beat until light

    4 egg yolks, then add to them

    ½ c. sugar

    1 c. orange juice and a little orange rind

    2 tbs. lemon juice

    ½ ts. salt. Place in double boiler over boiling water and cook until of custard consistency and then add the softened gelatin.

3. Remove from heat and cool.

4. When filling begins to thicken add

    4 egg whites stiffly beaten with

    1 c. sugar. Pour into baked shells.

5. Garnish with Mandarin orange slices and decorate with whipped cream flavored with orange extract and sugar.

RHUBARB CREAM PIE

1. Blend together until smooth
   3 tbs. flour
   1½ c. sugar
   1 tbs. butter
   2 beaten eggs
   ½ ts. nutmeg
2. Have pastry arranged on pie tins.
3. Put
   3 c. finely cut rhubarb in the pastry and pour the above mixture over the top.
4. Make a fancy top from rolled pastry and seal over the filling.
5. Bake in 450° oven for 10 minutes, then at 350° for 30 minutes.

OLD-FASHIONED CHERRY PIE

1. Arrange two pie plates with your favorite pastry. Sprinkle them generously with the following mixture.
   4 tbs. cornstarch
   ½ ts. salt
   ¼ c. sugar
2. Mix together
   1¼ c. sugar
   3 c. drained cherries (fresh, frozen, or canned)
   ¼ c. cherry juice (maraschino preferred)
   ½ ts. almond extract
   12 drops of red food coloring
   2 tbs. melted butter
3. Fill pastry shells in layers, first with the cornstarch-sugar mixture, then a large layer of the cherry mixture. Repeat, until shells are filled.
4. Cover with a layer of pastry, either in latticework or fancy cut design. Seal the edges and flute them firmly. Brush over the top with cream. Bake in a hot oven at 425° for 10 minutes and then at 350° for 40 minutes. Each pie makes six nice servings.

BUTTERSCOTCH PIE

1. In the top of a double boiler, place
   ¾ c. flour

1¼ c. brown sugar
½ ts. salt
¼ c. milk. Stir and cook to a creamy paste.
2. Add
2½ c. scalded milk and cook until mixture thickens.
3. Then add
3 beaten egg yolks. Stir rapidly and cook for 5 minutes more.
4. Remove from heat and add
1 ts. vanilla
1 ts. butterscotch flavoring
3 tbs. butter
5. Stir until well mixed, cool, and pour into baked pie shells. Cover with marshmallow meringue.

CHOCOLATE CUSTARD PIE

1. Beat slightly
3 eggs and add
¾ c. sugar
½ ts. salt
1 ts. vanilla
2½ c. milk
2. Melt over hot water
1 square of chocolate and
¼ c. milk
3. Mix altogether and pour into unbaked pie shell. Bake in 450° oven for 20 minutes, then bake at 325° until custard is set.

RHUBARB PIE

1. Prepare pie tins with your favorite pastry.
2. Wash and cut in very small pieces, enough rhubarb to make
3 c.
3. Add, mix well, and pour into unbaked crust
1 c. sugar
½ ts. lemon rind (grated)
3 tbs. flour
⅛ ts. salt
4. Dot over top
2 tbs. soft butter

5. Arrange pastry in braided form over the top. Seal edges
    well and bake at 450° for 10 minutes, then continue
    baking at 350° for 30 minutes.

BANANA CREAM PIE (1 9-Inch Pie)

1. Scald in double boiler
    2 c. milk
    12 marshmallows
    ¼ c. light syrup
    ¼ c. sugar
2. Blend
    4 tbs. cornstarch with
    ¼ c. milk
    ¼ ts. salt
3. Stir into hot milk mixture and cook until smooth.
4. Add
    3 beaten egg yolks and cook for 5 minutes more.
5. Remove from heat and add
    1 ts. vanilla
    ½ ts. banana flavoring
    Then cool slightly before adding to baked crusts
    which have been lined with sliced bananas. When
    filling has set in the crusts, slice a generous layer of
    bananas over the top and cover with mounds of
    whipped cream.

CRUMBLY CRUST APPLE PIE

1. Blend together to a fine crumbly mixture
    ¼ c. butter or margarine
    ½ c. flour
    ⅔ c. brown sugar
2. Butter a casserole and fill ⅔ full of thin slices of apples.
3. Sprinkle with cinnamon and sugar, then cover with
    crumb mixture. Bake for 45 minutes at 375°.

PINEAPPLE SPONGE PIE

1. Sift together
    1 c. sugar
    3 tbs. flour
    ½ ts. salt

2. Beat well
      3 egg yolks
      3 tbs. lemon juice
      1 ts. grated lemon rind
3. Heat
      1 c. milk
4. Add to the hot milk
      1½ c. pineapple tidbits
5. Combine all together quickly and fold in the
      3 egg whites, stiffly beaten.
6. Pour into unbaked crust and bake in a 450° oven for 10
    minutes, then reduce heat and bake at 350° for 35
    minutes.

TASTY LEMON PIE

1. In a saucepan mix together
      4 tbs. cornstarch
      1 c. sugar
2. Pour
      1¼ c. boiling water over the starch and sugar. Stir
      quickly and cook for 5 minutes, stirring constantly.
3. Add
      ½ tbs. butter and the juice of
      2 lemons and
      1 tbs. grated lemon rind
4. Beat until light
      4 egg yolks and fold into the hot mixture. Quickly
      pour into baked pie crust and cover with meringue.
      Bake until golden brown.

LEMON CHIFFON PIE

1. Soak for 5 minutes
      1 tbs. gelatin in
      ¼ c. cold water
2. Mix together, place in double boiler, and cook until it
    forms a custard
      ½ c. sugar
      ½ ts. salt
      ½ c. lemon juice
      4 beaten egg yolks

3. Add and stir thoroughly
        1 tbs. grated lemon rind and the softened gelatin
4. When mixture begins to thicken and is slightly cool,
    fold in
        4 beaten egg whites, whipped with
        ½ c. sugar
5. Fill baked pie shells and chill. Serve with whipped cream
    or seven-minute frosting.

    Variations:
1. Orange Chiffon
        Orange juice and rind and lemon juice
2. Strawberry Chiffon
        1 c. strawberries
        1 tbs. lemon juice and red coloring
3. Chocolate Chiffon
        6 tbs. cocoa or 2 squares melted chocolate
4. Peach Chiffon
        1 c. mashed fresh peaches and
        1 tbs. lemon juice

Danish Recipes

Being of Danish descent, I cherish the recipes I have of real Danish food. As a child, I remember the luscious rolls, sweet breads, pastries, cookies, etc., that my mother and my dear, little, old grandmother used to make. The smell of the hot Pebernodder (pepper nuts), AEbleskivers, and Klejnor comes back to me in memories.

Danish pastries are rich and tasty and are of world renown. The delicious fillings for the coffee cakes and rich rolls are enticing made from almond pastes, chopped dates, raisins, prunes, and other fruits.

Will you join me in making a wonderful Danish, almond sweet roll?

ALMOND FILLED SWEET ROLLS

This is a large recipe. Reduce, if smaller amount is desired.

1. Sift together
     2 qts. flour
     1 ts. salt
2. Cream well
     1 c. sugar
     ½ c. shortening
     2 eggs
3. Dissolve
     2 yeast cakes in
     ½ c. lukewarm milk
4. Mix altogether and add enough scalded and cooled milk to make a soft dough. The amount of milk varies with the quality of flour used. Cover and let rise for 1 hour.
5. Roll out on floured board and spread lightly with soft butter. Fold each end to the center. Roll again to ½-inch thickness. Then spread with the following Danish Paste:

Danish Paste:
1. Mix together

        1 c. almond paste
        2 c. sugar
        ½ c. egg whites
        2 c. bread crumbs
        1 tbs. cinnamon

2. Spread over rolled dough and roll like a jelly roll. Cut in 1-inch strips. Place in well-buttered pans, 1 inch apart, and let rise until light.
3. Before baking, top with the following topping:

Cardamon Topping
1. Mix with finger tips or blender
        1 c. brown sugar
        1 c. butter or margarine
        1 egg
        1 ts. cardamon or 5 cardamon seeds crushed
        1 c. cake crumbs
        1 c. cake flour
        1 tbs. cinnamon
2. Sprinkle over top of each roll.
3. Place in center of each roll, being careful not to cause roll to collapse,
        ½ ts. apricot marmalade
4. Bake in 375° oven for 20 minutes or until glossy brown.

DANISH FILLING (For Sweet Rolls)

This filling is adapted for any type of sweet roll.
1. Mix until smooth
        1 lb. almond paste
        1 lb. toasted cake crumbs
        1 pt. egg whites
        ½ ts. salt
        2 c. sugar
        1 lb. shortening (part butter)
        1 pt. milk
2. If thinner paste is desired, add milk to make of the right consistency.

DANISH FRY CAKES

These little cakes are very well liked and are quickly made.
1. Beat until light
        2 eggs

    6 tbs. sugar

    ¾ ts. salt

2. Add

    ¼ ts. nutmeg

    2 tbs. melted shortening

    6 tbs. milk or cream

3. Sift in and mix well

    2 c. flour

    3 ts. baking powder

4. Drop by teaspoonfuls into deep fat (375°) and fry until brown, gently turn and brown other side.

5. Drain on an unglazed brown paper and roll in powdered sugar. Makes 3 dozen cakes.

DANISH COFFEECAKE (A Large Recipe)

1. Sift together

    3 c. cake flour

    9 c. all-purpose flour

    2 ts. salt

2. Cream

    ¾ lb. shortening

    1 c. sugar

3. Add

    6 beaten eggs and

    4 yeast cakes that have been soaked in

    ½ c. warm milk

4. Add all mixtures together with enough scalded and cooled milk to make a soft dough.

5. Cover and let rise until light.

6. Roll out on a floured board. Chill in a cool place and then roll again. Spread with soft butter or margarine, fold ends to the center, and roll again. Then spread with the following filling:

Filling

1. Break in pieces

    ½ c. almond paste

2. Add

    1 c. cake crumbs

    1 ts. cinnamon

    2 egg whites

3. Add enough milk to make a soft paste.

4. Spread evenly over the top of rolled dough, then roll up like a jelly roll. Top with the following topping:

Topping
1. With the finger tips mix like pie dough
      ½ c. margarine
      ½ c. brown sugar
      1 c. cake flour
      1 ts. cinnamon and moisten with
      2 eggs
2. Sprinkle over the roll before baking or, if you desire, you may cut roll in strips, as for cinnamon rolls, and sprinkle individually with topping. Bake in 350° oven for 25 to 35 minutes.
3. While warm, top with frosting and decorate with candied fruits.

DANISH PASTRY

Danish pastry is known the world over, but it requires skill to produce a perfect product. You will, however, enjoy making this recipe. Follow the instructions closely and be patient. The finished product will pay in dividends and your efforts will be rewarded.
1. Scald and cool
      1 c. milk
2. Soak
      4 yeast cakes and
      1 tbs. sugar in
      1 c. warm water. Add to the milk.
3. Stir in
      3 c. flour and beat until smooth.
4. Cream thoroughly
      6 tbs. shortening
      ½ c. sugar
5. Beat until light and add to the creamed mixture separately
      2 egg whites
      3 egg yolks
6. Add
      ½ ts. vanilla
      ½ ts. lemon
      ½ ts. salt
7. Mix all ingredients together and stir until well blended.

8. Add
>4 c. flour. This makes a moderately stiff dough. Knead lightly on a floured board, place in a greased bowl, and let rise one fourth in bulk.

9. Roll out on a floured board into an oblong piece ½-inch thick. Place in small pieces in the center of the dough.
>¾ c. soft butter
>Fold one side over to cover the butter, then place ¾ c. butter on top and fold the other third of the dough over to completely cover this layer of butter. Press the edges down well, turn the dough one-fourth way around and roll again to ½-inch thickness. Fold one fourth of the dough at each end into the center, then fold again and chill in the refrigerator for ½ hour. Roll out again, fold as before, and chill again for ½ hour. Roll out again and the dough is now ready to mold. Shape as desired into crescents, pin wheels, braided rings, figure eights, etc. Place 1 inch apart on a buttered baking pan and let rise in a warm place, free from draft, until light, about 45 minutes.

10. Beat together and brush lightly over the top of each pastry
>1 egg white and
>1 tbs. cold water

11. Bake in a 475° oven for 5 minutes. Reduce heat to 400° and bake until light brown, from 10 to 25 minutes depending on the size. Remove from oven and when cool top with the following frosting and toppings:
>Frosting

1. Mix together
>2 c. powdered sugar
>1 tbs. butter
>1 tbs. shortening
>4 tbs. top milk or evaporated milk
>⅛ ts. salt
>1 ts. lemon flavoring

2. Beat until smooth and satiny and spread over the top of each pastry.

Topping
1. Spread quickly on the soft frosting your choice of the following:
>chopped raisins, nuts, or dates
>assorted candied fruits

cracker or cake crumbs
toasted coconut
Brazil chips
Danish Pastry may be rewarmed as follows: Sprinkle
a few drops of water over the top and place an aluminum foil cover over it. Put in a warm oven for a few
minutes. This method will make it fresh and moist.

FILLED DANISH COFFEE CAKE

1. Soak
   1 yeast cake in
   ¼ c. warm water and
   3 tbs. sugar
2. Add
   2 beaten eggs
   ½ c. melted and cooled butter
3. Sift in
   4 c. all-purpose flour and enough scalded and cooled
   milk to make a soft dough.
4. Beat well and let rise for
   1 hour or longer
5. Roll out on floured pastry board and spread with a thin
   layer of soft butter or margarine. Fold dough over from
   both sides to the center and reroll. Then spread with the
   following paste:
   Paste
1. Mix altogether
   2 egg whites
   1 c. cake crumbs
   1 ts. cinnamon
   1 ts. cardamon or lemon extract
   1 c. chopped raisins
   1 c. chopped dates
   Spread evenly over dough.
6. Roll up like a jelly roll. With a scissors or knife cut two
   thirds of the way through the roll, 2 inches apart. Place
   on a buttered pan, forming the roll into a large ring.
   With the fingers gently turn each cut piece over so filling
   will show through.
7. Brush lightly over the top with
   1 beaten egg mixed with
   ¼ c. canned milk

Sprinkle with finely chopped crumbs, and let rise until light.

Bake for ½ hour at 375°.

8. When cool, frost with butter cream frosting and decorate with candied cherries. Serve on any occasion.

DANISH KLEJNOR

This is a Danish doughnut and is a favorite treat by the lovers of Danish foods.

1. Cream well
    4 eggs
    1 cube margarine
    2 c. sugar
2. Add
    2 ts. lemon rind (grated)
    1 ts. lemon extract
3. Then sift in
    4 c. flour alternately with
    2 tbs. cream
4. Mix and knead lightly. This will be a stiff dough.
5. Roll on a floured board or pastry cloth to ½-inch thickness. Cut in strips 1 inch wide and 3 inches long. Cut a slit in the center of each piece, then pull one end of the strip of dough through the slit, thus making a twisted effect. Pick up carefully and drop into 400° fat or cooking oil. Brown, turn, and brown on the other side. Place on rack or paper to cool. Roll in sugar if desired.

DANISH BRAID ROLL

To make this tempting roll:

1. You will need
    1¼ c. scalded and cooled milk
    1 yeast cake, dissolved in the milk when just warm
    1 ts. lemon flavoring or cardamon, if desired
    ½ c. sugar
    ½ ts. salt
    ⅓ c. melted butter or margarine
    4 c. flour
2. Mix altogether, then let stand for 10 minutes.
3. Scrape onto a floured board and knead for a few minutes. Place in a greased bowl and let rise until light. Punch down and let rise again until light.

4. Put out on floured board again and roll out. Cut into two pieces, divide each piece in 3 parts. Cut in 3 long strips and braid in the customary way.
5. Place on a buttered baking pan, brush lightly with melted butter and beaten egg. Sprinkle with sugar, then let rise until light. Bake at 375° until golden brown, about 30 minutes.

DANISH "JULEKAKE"

This rich, little, yeast-type cake is enjoyed so much at holiday time.
1. Begin by scalding
       1 c. milk
2. Add
       ½ c. sugar
       ½ ts. salt
       ½ ts. cardamon flavoring or 4 mashed cardamon seeds
3. Add to the warm milk
       2 yeast cakes
       ⅔ c. rolled oats. Let stand 5 minutes.
4. Stir in
       2 tbs. melted shortening
       1 beaten egg
5. Sift in
       2¾ c. flour and mix to a soft dough.
6. Mix in
       1½ c. chopped candied fruit
       ½ c. raisins
7. Sprinkle a little flour over the fruit and knead the dough lightly.
8. Turn out on a floured board and knead until satiny. Place in a greased bowl, spread with butter, and let stand in a warm place with a cover until double in size. Punch down and let rise again, then form into loaves. Brush the tops with butter and beaten egg. Bake at 350° from 40 to 45 minutes.

LIEBESKRAENZE "DANISH CHRISTMAS COOKIE"
(German Origin)

This all-season cockie is enjoyed by children and grownups alike.

1. Cream together
     1 c. butter
     ⅔ c. sugar
2. Add to the butter and sugar
     4 hard cooked egg yolks (grated) and
     1 raw egg yolk
     Beat until smooth and creamy.
3. Add and beat until mixed, then place in refrigerator overnight
     1 ts. vanilla
     ½ ts. salt
     3 c. cake flour
4. Roll out on pastry board until very thin, cut in favorite shapes, and spread tops with
     1 egg yolk beaten
     1 ts. brandy flavoring
5. Place on greased baking sheets. Bake for 10 to 12 minutes in a 375° oven. When cool store in a cookie jar until serving time.

DANISH BUTTER COOKIES

1. Cream until light
     1 lb. butter
     2 c. sugar
2. Add
     4 egg yolks, and beat again, then add
     1 ts. vanilla
3. Sift in, mix to a stiff dough, and knead thoroughly
     2 c. flour and
     2 c. tapioca flour
4. Put through a cookie press onto baking trays. Sprinkle with decorative cookie candies.
5. Bake 5 or 10 minutes at 350°.

AEBLESKIVERS

AEbleskivers are wonderful little Danish cakes, fried in a special pan adapted for them. The pan is composed of six or eight little cup compartments and is made of heavy metals to hold the heat well. Each little cake is fried separately, first on one side, then turned and fried on the other. The name, AEbleskivers, means apple cakes in English. They may be served on any occasion, for meals or lunches. The pans may be purchased from your retailer by special order, if you are unable to buy one locally.

You will delight in making these cakes because they will please everyone.

The pan should be heated in advance and buttered well, then reheated. This tempers the pan so that the cakes will not stick to it.

(AEbleskivers) APPLE CAKES
(Grandma's Method)

1. To make the batter you scald and cool
  1⅓ c. milk
  2 tbs. butter
2. Dissolve
  1 yeast cake in
  ¼ c. warm water and
  1 tbs. sugar
3. Beat lightly
  2 eggs and add to the milk
4. Sift in, mix, and beat well
  2 c. flour
5. Have ready some thin slices of sweetened, cooked apples
6. Put one spoonful of batter in each hot buttered compartment and place a slice of apple in the center.
7. Cover with one more spoonful of batter and fry.
8. When brown on one side, slip a knitting needle or thin wire in the side of the cake and turn gently. Fry until brown, then remove from pan with a wire.
9. Place in warm bowl, sprinkle with sugar, or serve with honey or jam.

AEbleskivers (By Mrs. Rasmussen)

1. Separate
  8 eggs and beat the yolks until thick and lemon colored
2. To the yolks add
  3 c. flour sifted with
  2 tbs. sugar
  2 ts. baking powder
  1 ts. salt

3. Mix with enough milk to make a pancake-consistency batter.
4. Fold in the stiffly beaten egg whites and fry immediately. This batter should not be allowed to stand too long. Serve hot with jelly or honey.

AEbleskiver (By Esther)
(Yeast Method)

Many times we enjoyed this recipe, made by Esther's mother when we were youngsters.
1. Scald and cool
   1½ c. milk and cream (mixed)
2. Soak and then add to the milk
   1 yeast cake in
   ¼ c. warm water
3. Melt
   2 tbs. butter and add to the mixture
4. Sift together
   2 c. flour
   2 tbs. sugar
   1 ts. salt
   ½ ts. cardamon spice. Stir until well mixed.
5. Add
   3 beaten egg yolks and stir again.
6. Fold in last very carefully
   3 stiffly beaten egg whites. Cover and let rise until light.
7. Heat AEbleskiver pan and butter it generously, using half shortening and butter mixed.
8. Drop dough by spoonfuls into each little cup of the pan. Brown until cakes show bubbles on top. Turn carefully with a wire or knitting needle and fry on other side. Lift each cake out with the wire and place in warm bowl. Cover and keep warm until ready to serve.
   Serve with jam, jelly, or honey.

AEbleskiver
(Buttermilk Method)

1. To
   1 pt. buttermilk add
   1 ts. soda

        1 ts. salt
        2 tbs. sugar

2. Stir in and beat until smooth
        6 beaten egg yolks and
        2 c. flour
3. Fold in
        6 beaten egg whites
4. Drop by spoonfuls in hot buttered pans. Fry as directed in previous recipes. Serve with choice of toppings.

EVERYDAY AEbleskiver

1. Sift together in mixing bowl
        2 c. flour
        1 ts. baking powder
        1 ts. soda
        ½ ts. salt
        2 tbs. sugar
2. Beat lightly and add
        3 egg yolks
3. Add
        2 c. buttermilk
4. Add
        1 ts. cardamon flavoring (Spice or crushed cardamon seeds may be used)
5. Fold in last
        3 egg whites beaten stiff
6. Fry in buttered pan and turn. Serve hot with sugar or honey.

WHOLE-WHEAT AEbleskivers

1. Beat
        2 eggs and
2. Add to
        1½ c. milk
        4 tbs. butter
        1 ts. molasses
3. Sift into the first mixture, mix well, and beat until smooth
        1½ c. whole-wheat flour
        2 ts. baking powder
        ½ ts. salt

4. Drop by spoonfuls into hot AEbleskiver pans which have been buttered well. Brown first on one side, then the other. Serve hot with honey or syrup.

JULEKAGE

Julekage in Danish means Christmas cake. The Danish people always serve this luscious loaf at holiday seasons.

1. Soak
   1 yeast cake (or pkg. yeast) in ¼ c. lukewarm water
2. Mix as for pie crust
   4 c. flour
   1 ts. salt
3. Add
   1 lb. shortening and
   8 cardamon seeds, that have been husked and mashed
4. Add
   ½ c. sugar and
   ½ pt. lukewarm water, also the yeast liquid
5. Mix altogether and knead lightly.
6. Add
   ½ c. raisins
   1 c. citron
   Knead again, place in buttered loaf pans, and let rise for 1½ hours.
7. Bake at 350° for 1 hour. Slice in thin slices and serve.

DANISH KAFFA (Coffeecake)

This is delightful for afternoon snacks.

1. Sift together
   2 c. flour
   2 ts. baking powder
   ¾ ts. salt
2. Cream
   5 tbs. butter
   6 tbs. sugar
3. Add
   ⅓ c. milk
   1 egg beaten
   1 ts. lemon extract

4. Add altogether and mix until smooth. Then pour into a greased pan and cover with the following topping:

Topping
1. Mix together and sprinkle over the top of the batter
    1½ tbs. melted butter
    4 tbs. sugar
    1 tbs. flour
    ½ ts. cinnamon
2. Bake 25 minutes at 350°.

PEBERNODDER (Pepper Nuts)

This is a Danish confection loved by all, young and old.
1. Mix in a bowl
    ⅔ c. shortening
    ¾ c. molasses
    3 c. flour
    1 ts. ginger
    1 ts. salt
    1½ ts. soda
2. Mix to a soft dough and chill for several hours. Instead of rolling as in Grandma's Ginger Cookies, roll in small balls and place on a greased cookie sheet and bake 15 minutes at 375° or until brown. They may also be cut with a tiny round cutter the size of a quarter. I prefer to roll them. They may be stored in jars for some time.

Desserts

DATE DELIGHT

This recipe is a luscious rich dessert. It may be served on any occasion and is one that will please the men folks. It was a favorite among the Army officers, for whom I made pastries at the hospital during World War II.

1. Sift together
   - 1 c. flour
   - 1 c. sugar
   - 1 ts. baking powder
   - ¼ ts. salt
2. Beat until light and fold into the flour
   - 3 egg whites
3. Add
   - 1 c. moist chopped dates
   - 1 c. chopped walnuts
   - 1 ts. vanilla
4. Pour into individual custard or baking cups and set in a pan of warm water. Place in oven and bake at 375° for ½ hour without opening oven door.
   Serve warm or cold with whipped cream.

DATE AND NUT ROLL

1. Cut into small pieces
   - 1 lb. dates
   - 20 marshmallows
   - 1 c. walnuts
2. Whip
   - 1 c. whipping cream and add
   - ¼ c. sugar
3. Mix altogether and stir in
   - ½ c. chopped maraschino cherries
4. Crush 20 graham crackers and place the crumbs on a wax paper. Form the date mixture into a large roll and roll it in the crumbs. Then wrap the paper around it and chill in the refrigerator.

PINEAPPLE ICEBOX DESSERT

1. Cover bottom of flat greased pan with cracker crumbs or leftover cake crumbs.
2. Beat
    4 egg yolks
3. Cream
    ½ c. butter
    2½ c. powdered sugar and add to the egg yolks. Then add
    1 ts. almond flavoring
4. Beat until stiff
    4 egg whites and fold into first mixture.
5. Pour into the cake crumbs and cover with 1 pt. of whipped cream mixed with
    1 c. cooked, sweetened, crushed pineapple
6. Cover the top with more cracker or cake crumbs. Cover and put in icebox overnight. Cut in slices and serve.

ALMOND ICEBOX CAKE

1. Cook over low heat until thick
    1 c. sugar
    ⅓ c. water
    ⅛ ts. salt
    1 tbs. butter
    8 egg yolks
2. Remove from stove and add slowly
    8 beaten egg whites
    1 c. whipped cream
    1 ts. almond flavoring
3. Butter a flat dish and cover with crushed almond wafers. Pour on a layer of the filling, then a layer of wafer crumbs, another layer of filling, etc., until the pan is full.
4. Place in refrigerator overnight. Cut in squares and serve.

RICE ALMOND DESSERT

A perfectly luscious dessert, rich and creamy, is this number-one favorite among the Danish folk.
1. Wash in several washings of cold water
    1 c. white rice

2. Cook rice in double boiler with
    5 c. milk, until tender and soft. Stir very little, to
    preserve the whole grain of rice.
3. When cool, mix with
    1 c. sugar
    1 ts. almond flavoring
    2 tbs. white wine
    1 c. finely chopped blanched almonds
4. Soak
    1 envelope gelatin in
    ¼ c. warm water
5. Then fold softened gelatin into rice mixture with
    1 c. of whipped cream. Chill. Serve with the following
    fruit sauce:

Fruit Sauce

1. Mix together
    3 tbs. tapioca flour and enough water to make a thin
    paste
2. Heat to boiling
    2 c. raspberry or cherry juice
3. Add
    ¼ c. sugar
4. Thicken with the flour paste
5. Add
    1 ts. almond extract
    1 c. cherry preserves or jam
6. Cool and serve as a garnish over the rice.

LEMON SOUFFLE

1. Beat until thick
    5 egg yolks
    3 tbs. sugar
2. Add
    ¼ ts. salt
    3 tbs. lemon juice
    1 tbs. grated lemon rind
3. Beat until stiff, then fold into the first mixture
    5 egg whites
4. Bake in a 375° oven until firm (30 minutes or more).
    Serve at once.

APPLE CAKE PUDDING

1. Beat well
    - 4 tbs. butter
    - 1 c. sugar
    - 1 egg
2. Sift in
    - 1 c. flour
    - 1 ts. baking powder
3. Add and stir in
    - 1 c. milk
4. Pare and slice
    - 2 c. apples. Cook 2 minutes in
    - ½ c. water. Place in bottom of baking dish.
5. Sprinkle with
    - cinnamon to taste
    - ⅓ c. melted butter
    - ½ c. sugar, mixed together
6. Pour the batter over the apples and bake for 40 minutes at 350°.

ECONOMICAL CHRISTMAS PUDDING (Mama)

No matter how we tried we could never make this pudding as well as Mama could.

1. Mix together
    - 1 c. bread crumbs
    - 1 c. currants
    - 1 c. raisins
    - 1 c. suet
    - 1 c. mashed potatoes
    - 1 c. grated carrots
    - 1 c. molasses
    - ½ c. sugar
    - 1 c. flour
    - 1 ts. baking powder
    - ¼ ts. salt
    - 1 ts. nutmeg
    - 1 ts. ginger
2. Put in steamer pans and steam for 3 hours. Serve hot with sauce.

CHOICE PLUM PUDDING

1. In a large bowl mix together
    1 c. grated carrots
    1 c. grated potatoes
    1 c. sugar
    1 c. flour
    ½ ts. nutmeg
    ½ ts. cloves
    ½ ts. allspice
    1 c. raisins
    1 c. currants
    ½ c. citron peel
    1 ts. soda
    ½ ts. salt
    5 tbs. melted butter
    1 ts. vanilla
    1 ts. victorine or rum extract
2. When well blended, pour into steamer pans or cookers
    and steam for 2 hours or more. Serve hot with choice of
    sauce.

HELEN'S PLUM PUDDING WITH KENTUCKY SAUCE

My friend Helen is from Kentucky. She is noted for her
cooking and hospitality. This is her recipe.
1. Sift together
    2 c. flour
    1 ts. soda
2. Mix together
    ¾ c. molasses
    1 c. brown sugar
    1 c. chopped suet
    1 c. milk
3. Mix the two mixtures together and blend well.
4. Add
    1½ c. mixed raisins, citron, currants, and figs. Add
    ½ c. chopped nuts if desired.
5. Mix in
    3 c. bread crumbs (fine)
6. Wet a tea towel, sprinkle it with flour, and put the pud-
    ding mixture in the center. Tie the towel ends securely
    together, leaving space for the pudding to rise. Place

in a kettle of boiling water, fastening the towel to the sides to prevent the pudding from touching the bottom of the kettle. Boil slowly for 3 hours. Serve hot with the following sauce:

Kentucky Sauce

1. Mix together and cream well
    2 c. brown sugar
    ½ c. butter
2. Add
    2 eggs, beaten and
    ½ c. milk. Cook until it thickens and remove from heat.
3. Add
    2 tbs. brandy extract
    ¼ ts. nutmeg

ORANGE PLUM PUDDING

This is a very large amount and can be placed in jars or cans and stored until needed.

1. Mix together
    ½ lb. orange peel (diced)
    3 pkgs. seedless raisins
    1 pkg. currants
    2 pkgs. seeded raisins
    6 c. grated carrots
    6 c. grated potatoes
    12 c. chopped apples
    3 c. ground suet
    12 c. bread crumbs and graham cracker crumbs mixed
    5 c. brown sugar
    1 c. white sugar
    2 tbs. soda
    1 tbs. cloves
    1 tbs. allspice
    1 tbs. nutmeg
    2 tbs. cinnamon
    1 c. molasses
2. Place in jars or cans and steam for 1 hour.
    Serve with pudding sauce.

PUDDING SAUCE

1. Melt in frying pan
   1 c. sugar
2. Add and mix well
   1½ c. water
   1 tbs. butter
   2 tbs. flour (moistened in water)
   1 ts. rum flavoring
   1 ts. vanilla
3. Serve hot on top of pudding.

PUDDING SAUCE

1. Mix
   2 tbs. flour
   4 tbs. milk. Stir into
   2 c. hot milk and add
   2 tbs. butter or margarine
   1 ts. vanilla
   ½ ts. ground cloves
   1 c. sugar
2. Serve hot over pudding.

CUSTARD RICE PUDDING

1. Make a custard by adding
   2 c. scalded milk to
   2 beaten eggs
   ½ ts. salt
   ½ ts. vanilla
   1 ts. lemon
   ¼ c. sugar
2. Cook in double boiler until it thickens. Remove from stove and beat hard for about 2 minutes. Chill rapidly.
3. Bring to a boil and cook until tender without stirring, then cool
   ½ c. rice
   1 c. water
   1 ts. shortening
   ¼ ts. salt
4. Just before serving, combine the custard and rice and dip into serving dishes.

YUMMY PLUM PUDDING

This is ideal for holiday occasions.

1. Sift together
      1 c. flour
      1 ts. soda
      ½ ts. salt
      1 ts. cinnamon
      1 ts. nutmeg
2. Beat
      6 eggs
3. Add altogether to the flour and eggs
      1 c. brown sugar
      ¾ c. ground suet
      1 c. bread crumbs
      2 c. seedless raisins
      2 c. currants
      ¼ c. orange peel
      ½ c. pecan pieces
      2 c. apple cider
      Stir well and place in greased pans. Cover with foil
      to keep moisture in.
4. Steam for 3 hours. Serve hot or cold.
5. For Christmas serve with brandy sauce or hard sauce
   and garnish with holly.

LEMON PUDDING

1. Cream together
      4 tbs. butter
      2 c. sugar
      4 egg yolks
2. Mix well
      6 tbs. flour and
      ½ c. milk
3. Add
      1½ c. milk
      3 lemons, juice and grated rind
4. Fold in
      4 stiffly beaten egg whites
5. Pour into baking pan and bake at 325° for 1 hour.

DATE CARROT PUDDING

1. Mix in large bowl
     2 c. bread crumbs
     1 c. flour
     1½ c. suet
     1 ts. cinnamon
     ½ ts. nutmeg
     1 ts. salt
2. Add
     1 c. grated carrots
     3 eggs beaten
     ½ c. chopped citron
     2 c. cut dates
3. Stir
     ½ ts. soda into
     ½ c. molasses and add to all the other ingredients and mix well.
4. Steam in steamer for 2½ hours. Serve with hot pudding sauce.

STEAMED DATE PUDDING

1. Pour
     1 c. hot water over
     1 lb. cut dates, then add
     1 ts. soda. Cool.
2. Add
     2 beaten eggs
     1 tbs. melted butter
     1 c. sugar
     1½ c. flour
     ½ c. nuts, if you desire them.
3. Mix well and steam for 3 hours. Serve with cream while hot.

MILK CHOCOLATE PUDDING

This is a very nice dessert for the chocolate lovers.
1. Sift into a bowl
     ½ c. flour
     ⅓ c. sugar
     2 tbs. cocoa
     ¾ ts. baking powder

2. Stir in
    2 tbs. canned milk
    2 tbs. water
    4 tbs. melted shortening
    ½ ts. vanilla
3. Add
    ½ c. broken nuts, if desired
4. Mix quickly and pour into flat greased pan.
5. Have ready in advance
    ¼ c. sugar
    2 tbs. cocoa
    ⅓ c. boiling water
6. Pour this over the batter before putting in preheated oven.
7. Bake for 20 minutes at 350° or until the pudding is firm to touch.
8. The cake portion of the pudding will be on top when baked and the rich chocolate syrup will be on the bottom.
9. Serve warm with cream, if desired.

VIOLA'S PUDDING

1. Mix together
    1 c. sugar
    ½ c. butter and add
    1 c. crushed pineapple
    ½ c. pecans
2. Line flat dish with sweet-cracker crumbs, pour in mixture, then cover with crumbs.
3. Chill overnight. Serve with whipped cream.

OLD-TIME CHERRY PUDDING

Use this especially during the month of February when cherries are so popular.
1. Measure in bowl and cream until light
    ¼ c. margarine
    ½ c. sugar
    1 ts. almond flavoring or maraschino cherry juice
2. Add
    2 well-beaten eggs

3. Sift
    1 c. flour
    1 ts. baking powder
    ¼ ts. salt
4. Add altogether with
    ⅓ c. milk
    After mixing well, pour into greased and floured pan.
    Cover with 2 c. sweetened red cherries and sprinkle
    with the following crumb mixture:
1. Mix like pie dough
    ⅓ c. flour
    ½ c. sugar
    ½ ts. cinnamon
    ¼ c. margarine
2. Bake at 375° for ½ hour or longer, until firm. Serve with
    cream or cherry sauce.

LODGE FUDGE PUDDING

1. Cream together
    ⅛ c. shortening
    ⅞ c. sugar
    2 squares chocolate (melted)
    1 ts. vanilla
2. Add and stir in
    ½ c. milk
3. Sift in
    1¼ c. flour
    1 ts. baking powder
    ½ ts. salt
4. Mix well and add
    ½ c. nut pieces
5. Spread evenly in baking pan and sprinkle with the fol-
    lowing topping:
    Topping
1. Mix together
    ½ c. brown sugar
    ½ c. white sugar
    ⅛ c. cocoa
    ¼ ts. salt
    1¼ c. boiling water
2. Pour quickly over the top of pudding. Bake in 375° oven
    for 1 hour. Serve plain or with cream.

FROZEN LEMON DESSERT

1. Beat until light
      3 egg yolks
      1 c. sugar
2. Add
      4 tbs. lemon juice
      2 ts. lemon rind
3. Place in double boiler and cook over hot water for about 10 minutes until thick.
4. When cool add
      1 c. whipped cream and
      3 stiffly beaten egg whites
5. Pour into refrigerator tray and freeze until mushy. Beat up quickly and refreeze.

BUTTERSCOTCH ICE CREAM

1. Place in a pan and melt slowly
      ¾ c. brown sugar
      3 tbs. butter, and add
      6 tbs. water. Cook until smooth.
2. Pour the syrup over
      3 well-beaten egg yolks, and add
      ⅛ ts. salt and cook in double boiler over hot water until mixture forms a custard. Cool.
3. Fold in
      1½ c. cream
      1 ts. vanilla or butterscotch flavoring
4. Freeze until firm.

FROZEN LEMON DESSERT

1. Cook in double boiler for 10 minutes
      3 egg yolks
      ½ c. sugar
      4 tbs. lemon juice
      2 ts. lemon rind
2. Remove from heat and cool.
3. Beat
      3 egg whites until stiff and add
      1 c. whipped cream
4. Freeze in refrigerator tray.

PINEAPPLE SMOOTHER (Large Freezer)

1. In freezer can place
   2 qts. milk
   1 pt. cream
   2 tall cans milk (evaporated)
   3 c. sugar
   ¼ ts. salt
   Mix well. Then freeze for 5 minutes or until slightly frozen.
2. Remove cover and add
   4 lemons (juice) and a little grated rind
   1 large can crushed pineapple. Begin freezing again and turn freezer until sherbet is firm.

PINEAPPLE SHERBET

Many times we at home have made our freezer full of this sherbet and the family has gathered together and devoured the entire contents of a six-quart freezer. I hope you enjoy this recipe too.

1. In a large container, mix together until sugar is dissolved
   2½ qts. milk
   3 full c. sugar
2. Pour into freezer can and freeze until it begins to thicken. Remove cover and add
3. Juice of
   2 lemons
   1 No. 2 can crushed pineapple
   Freeze again until fruit is well mixed with milk and slightly frozen. Remove cover again and add
4. 1 pint of whipped cream
   Freeze again, turning handle quickly until sherbet is all frozen and firm.

   To freeze ice cream in a hand or electric freezer, use finely chopped ice and 1 c. coarse salt to each full layer of ice. Turn steadily and continue turning until the contents are firm and it becomes difficult to turn. Pour off water and re-ice. Cover until ready to serve or place in trays in freezer compartment.

FROZEN PEPPERMINT DESSERT

1. Mash
   ½ lb. peppermint stick candy and add to
   ½ c. thin cream
2. Cook over hot water until candy dissolves
3. Dissolve
   1½ tbs. gelatin in
   1 tbs. cold water, then add to hot mixture.
4. Cool in refrigerator until thick and then fold in
   1½ c. whipped cream.
5. Crush
   12 lady fingers and arrange on flat dish, then pour the
   mixture over them, cover the top with lady finger
   crumbs and chill or freeze overnight.

LIME SHERBET

1. Dissolve
   1 pkg. of lime gelatin in
   1 c. hot water. Chill.
2. Add
   1½ c. sugar
   2 lemons, juice and a little rind
   1 qt. milk
   2 limes (juice)
3. Beat in beater bowl for 2 minutes. Pour into freezing
   trays and freeze, stirring occasionally.

ORANGE SHERBET

1. Boil together to make a syrup
   1 c. sugar and
   ½ c. water
2. Cool and add
   1 can fresh frozen orange juice
3. Freeze until the mushy stage and then add
   1 c. light cream. Freeze until firm.

ICE CREAM (VANILLA) 6-Quart Freezer

1. Stir together until mixed
   3 c. sugar
   3½ c. powdered milk

2. Add a small amount at a time and beat well
    4 c. cream
    8 c. milk
    2 ts. vanilla
    1 ts. lemon
3. Dissolve in a little milk
    4 ts. gelatin, then add to
    1 c. hot milk and stir until dissolved. Strain and add
    to the other mixture.
4. Fold in
    6 beaten egg yolks. Pour into freezer can. Cover and
    pack with crushed ice and salt. Use 1 c. of salt alter-
    nately with the ice in three layers. Freeze until firm,
    turning as rapidly as possible.

CHOCOLATE TRAY ICE CREAM

1. Soak
    $\frac{1}{2}$ ts. gelatin in a little milk and add to
    1 c. scalded milk
    $\frac{1}{3}$ c. sugar
    1 ts. lemon juice
    $\frac{1}{4}$ ts. salt
2. When cool fold in
    1 c. whipped cream
    1 ts. vanilla. Freeze until firm in refrigerator tray.
3. Mix together
    $\frac{1}{2}$ c. butter
    3 c. sweet-cracker crumbs (chocolate preferred)
    $\frac{1}{2}$ c. sugar
4. Spread on bottom of large dish and spoon frozen ice
    cream over crumbs. Cover with more crumbs and return
    to freezer tray until frozen firm.

MILK CHOCOLATE ICE CREAM

1. Melt over low heat until thick
    1 lb. sweet chocolate, then add
    1 qt. milk
2. Beat until light
    4 eggs
    $\frac{1}{4}$ ts. salt
    2 c. sugar

3. Add gradually
   1 pt. table cream
   2 ts. vanilla and fold in
   1 pt. whipping cream
4. Combine mixtures and freeze either by hand freezer or in refrigerator.

BANANA LEMON SHERBET

1. In the beater bowl place the following and beat on low until well mashed
   5 large ripe bananas
2. Add and beat until blended
   1/3 c. lemon juice
   1/2 c. sugar
   1/8 ts. salt
3. Gradually add
   2 c. milk
4. Pour into freezing trays and partially freeze at coldest point.
5. Meanwhile beat until stiff
   2 egg whites and add
   1/3 c. white syrup
6. Remove partially frozen sherbet from trays and beat all together carefully. Return to freezing trays and freeze.

SAUCES FOR TOPPINGS

CARAMEL

1. Melt in pan
   2 tbs. butter and add
   1 1/4 c. brown sugar
   2 tbs. dark syrup
   Cook slowly for one minute.
2. Remove from heat and add
   1/4 c. light cream
   1/2 ts. vanilla
3. Cool and dilute with cream.

HOT FUDGE SAUCE

1. Melt in pan
   2 squares chocolate and add
   2 c. boiling water

2. Mix together, then stir into the water and chocolate and cook slowly

    1¼ c. sugar
    4 tbs. flour
    ⅛ ts. salt

3. Add

    3 tbs. dark syrup
    1 ts. vanilla

4. Stir until thick before serving.

MARSHMALLOW CUSTARD

1. Scald

    4 c. milk and
    12 marshmallows

2. Beat

    6 eggs
    ½ c. sugar
    ¼ ts. salt
    ¼ ts. nutmeg

3. Pour slowly into scalded milk. Add flavoring if desired.

4. Bake with bowl in a pan of water in a 325° oven for 30 minutes or until firm.

Candies

HOMEMADE CANDY

The art of candymaking, both the homemade type and all professional candies, may be acquired by following the rules and methods given in this chapter. Everyone, young and old, enjoys homemade candy, and it is such a pleasant pastime to make it with good results.

The first rules of candymaking are: using proper measurements; washing the sides of the kettles used while cooking candies; knowing the proper temperatures of cooking in the locality in which you live; having the correct knowledge of stirring while candy is cooking; also, knowing when to stir candy and when not to, and the correct way to cool and beat candies after they are cooked.

The advantages of making homemade candies are:

First, you may choose the best materials obtainable.

Second, you may flavor the candy to your taste.

Third, you may have fresh candy when desired.

Fourth, you may be proud and happy with the results.

Equipment needed for candymaking is:

Heavy cooking kettle with lid

Wooden stirring paddles—flat on the ends. These may be whittled from pieces of hard wood.

Marble slab. (Platters or trays may be used.)

A wall scraper or putty knife to be used in beating

A good small brush—pastry or bottle brush

Thermometer

Materials needed are:

Sugar

Glucose (corn syrup)

Dipping chocolate

Nuts

Cocoanut

Flavorings of all types

Maraschino cherries

Raisins

Pineapple (candied)
Cream
Milk (canned and fresh)
Butter
Margarine
Cocoa butter
Eggs
Gelatin

Candies made with milk or cream should be stirred constantly while cooking; those made with water should be stirred only before putting on the heat.

All candy mixtures should be stirred until all sugar is dissolved before the cooking begins. When the candy begins to boil, wash the sides of the kettle with a small brush dipped in tepid water, then place the lid on the kettle for a few seconds, thus making sure all sugar particles are removed from around the pan. This procedure is very important so that the candy will be free of a sugary texture and grainy tendency. Fine, creamy, soft candies are more desirable. If, by chance, a batch of candy is overcooked, it may be revived by adding a small amount of milk or glucose and recooking it.

Most candies should be cool before beating begins and should be beaten in a back and forward motion. Marble slabs should be damp or greased, whichever the recipe states, before you pour candies out to cool. Beating the candy while it is still warm will cause it to set up and become firm sooner, but it will cause the candy to have a coarse grain. It will not be soft and creamy.

If you are making candies to be chocolate dipped and wish to do the dipping at a later date, the candy for the centers may be made and then stored in covered crocks or jars until you are ready for it. Also, batches which are to be spread and cut in squares, etc., may be placed on tins and covered with plastic covers until ready for use.

The method of preparing the centers for chocolate dipping is as follows:

1. Sprinkle a portion of powdered sugar on a board, marble, tin, etc., and knead the beaten batch of candy with the fingers. You will find that the candy (fondant, mazzeta, fudge, etc.) will soften as you knead it.

2. Cut in portions and roll in a long roll about ¾ of an inch thick. With a sharp knife, cut small pieces the size of

the chocolate you desire. Prepare a cookie sheet by covering it with wax paper and spreading a small amount of powdered sugar over it to prevent the centers from sticking. Next, roll each piece in the palm of the hand (which has been dipped in powdered sugar) into round or oblong rolls, as desired. Place rolls on the cookie sheet so they do not touch. Allow them to set at room temperature for a while before dipping them in chocolate.

While you are in the kneading process you may divide the batches, if you care to, and flavor them differently. Also, you may add nuts, cocoanut, etc., as you desire.

To roll oblong pieces, you begin by rolling each piece round first and then along the palm in the opposite motion to make them long. Different shapes are needed to make your packed box appear pretty.

Have trays of centers ready before you begin to dip them in chocolate, thus saving time in having to wash the chocolate from your hand to prepare more centers.

Rules for chocolate dipping may be found on page 289.

Fudges, nougats, caramels, etc., should be poured out on marbles or trays to set. Small iron bars are convenient to hold the candy in place and may be scraped and washed and used for several types of candy. They may be purchased at the iron works, foundry, etc. Bars should be 1 inch wide and 1 inch thick and 24 or more inches long.

Try your luck at candymaking.

TESTING CANDY

The safest and surest way to test candy is by using a thermometer while cooking the batch. To test the boiling point of your area, place the thermometer in cold water, then put the water on to boil and watch the exact time of boiling and note at what degree the water boils. Boil for several minutes to be accurate. At sea level, water boils at 212°; in our mountain altitude, water boils at 204°. I have written all of my candy recipes for this altitude. You may adjust the cooking time of every recipe by adding or subtracting the point of boil in your vicinity from 204°. For instance, if water boils at 206°, add 2° cooking time to all of these recipes.

If you prefer to test by the cold water method, test by dropping a few drops of the candy being cooked into a little cold water. The following schedule may help. When hot candy will drop a thread it is 230° to 234°.

a soft ball is ....234° to 238°
a firm ball is ....244° to 248°
a hard ball is ....248° to 254°
a very hard ball is ....254° to 256°
a light crack is ....270° to 285°
a hard crack is ....290° to 300°

FONDANT

Fondant is more or less what a candymaker would call the king of candies, because of its many uses and the variety of candies that may be made of it. Fondant is easily made and may be stored for weeks in readiness. It may be used for chocolate centers, bonbons, *petits fours,* dipped creams, nuts, fruits, etc., and may be made into mazzeta for the higher grades of chocolate creams.

To make perfect fondant, the rules for mixing, boiling and beating must all be followed closely. When you have accomplished this, the making of all other candy is much easier.

Rules for Fondant Making:
1. Measure sugar, glucose and water carefully; stir until sugar is dissolved before putting on to cook.
2. To obtain soft, creamy fondant, you must remove all sugar crystals from the sides of the kettle while boiling. You do this by dipping a small nylon or other soft brush of some kind in warm water and quickly brushing all around the inside of the kettle, one or more times during the first processes of the cooking. If you haven't a brush, use a spoon with a piece of gauze or cloth tied on it. The drop or two of water falling into the cooking batch of candy will do no harm, because the water will have to boil away before the candy reaches the proper temperature. Dip the brush well down into the boiling candy while washing the sides.
3. Place the lid on the kettle for a few moments. This tends to steam away any sugar particles that remain on the kettle.
4. Use a thermometer in testing candies. This is the surest and most perfect method. If you do not have one, I have made a chart to follow, giving the test instruc-

tions, by the dropping of some of the cooked candy in water, to test for a soft ball, hard ball, crack test, etc.

5. Cooling the fondant after you have poured it on a damp slab is very important. Allow the batch to remain, undisturbed, until it cools sufficiently to be past the warm stage but not too cold. Test by gently touching with the fingers to feel the coolness, then you begin the beating process. Further instructions are given under the recipe for fondant.

FONDANT

1. In a kettle place
   4 c. sugar
   ½ c. glucose or corn syrup, stirring until completely dissolved with
   1 c. water

2. Place on high heat and bring to a boil. Wet a soft brush and wash the sides of the kettle to remove the sugar particles. Place the lid on the kettle for a few moments to allow the steam to break the sugar crystals, then boil to 232° without stirring.

   Pour out on cool, damp marble slab and allow the fondant to cool. Test by gently touching with the tips of fingers. When the candy feels moderately cool, begin beating by using a large spatula or a firm putty knife. Slide the candy forward and back. This process will take some time, so do not become discouraged. Continue beating until the fondant begins to turn light in color. Slide the spatula under the fondant and push it away from you, then turn spatula over and bring it back across the top of the batch. Do not stop beating until the fondant sets up because the candy will grain if beating is stopped. When the fondant turns creamy white and becomes firm, it is finished.

3. Place fondant in a crock or jar, cover with a damp cloth and lid. Store until time to use. Several batches may be made in advance and stored until needed.

   Fondant is the king of candies, so to speak, and is the foundation of several types of choice candies.

FONDANT FOR BONBONS (Large Batch)

1. Soak square of (sheet) gelatin in
    ¼ c. cold water
2. Mix together and stir well
    10 c. sugar
    ½ c. glucose
    enough water to dissolve the sugar
3. Bring to a boil, without stirring, wash the sides of the
    kettle, and place the lid on for a few seconds. Cook to
    233°.
4. Remove from heat and add the soaked gelatin.
5. Pour out on a damp slab and sprinkle very lightly with
    cold water. When cool, begin beating with a spatula.
    (Refer to instructions on fondants.)
    Store in covered crocks until time to melt to dip the
    bonbons.
    Instructions for dipping bonbons (See Orange bonbons
    on page 254):
1. Place the quantity of bonbon fondant needed in the top
    of the double boiler over hot water. Stir occasionally
    until the fondant melts just enough to cling to the
    centers. Flavor with favorite flavoring and color as de-
    sired. Prepare the centers by rolling a piece of the
    fondant in a long thin roll and cutting in small pieces.
    Roll in round balls.
2. Have centers prepared in advance by rolling a portion
    of the fondant in small balls, first adding flavoring and
    crushed nuts and coconut, or almond paste.

BONBONS

Bonbons are such fun to make and are the last word in
fine candies for parties, teas, weddings, and all special
occasions.

Instructions for making:
The base centers for bonbons are made primarily from
fondant; the outer coating should be made from a richer
grade of fondant melted over warm water. The centers are
made by taking a batch of fondant as soon as it is creamed
and preparing it for the centers of the bonbons. There are
several varieties.

ORANGE BONBONS

1. When the batch of fondant is creamed, divide it in half.
   To one half add
   ½ ts. grated orange rind and
   ½ ts. fruit acid
   Knead and mix well, then roll into a long roll. Cut
   in very small pieces and roll round in the palm of the
   hand. Place on a waxed-paper-lined tray, sprinkled
   lightly with powdered sugar. The remaining half
   may be used to make another type of bonbon or, if
   you prefer, use it for dipping the bonbons in rather
   than make a separate batch of dipping fondant. In
   making big quantities it is wise to make seperate
   batches of fondant.

2. Place the other half of fondant in the top of the double
   boiler over warm water, stir with a wooden paddle, and
   melt slowly. Reduce heat and

3. Add
   ½ ts. orange flavoring or emulsion
   2 or 3 drops of orange coloring
   Stir, but do not let the fondant become too hot as this
   tends to harden the finished bonbon and makes the
   coating so thin that it will spread on the bottoms.
   Keep the water under the fondant nearly the same
   temperature, raise the top of the double boiler from
   the water and tilt it slightly to one side to help cool
   the fondant. Now place one of the little round rolled
   centers on the tip of a bonbon fork or dipping wire,
   dip it down in the warm fondant, raise it out, shake
   the fork a little to shake away the surplus fondant,
   gently tap the fork on the edge of the pan, and then
   drop the bonbon on a waxed paper. Carefully raise
   the tip of the fork up so the fondant will cling to it
   and make a swirl over the top of the bonbon to give
   it a finished look. While the bonbon is still moist,
   place a dainty piece of candied orange peel on the top.
   Allow to cool. It will take practice to judge just the
   right thickness and temperature to have the fondant
   while dipping. If the fondant is not hot enough, the
   bonbon will not set up. It will remain sticky. If
   the fondant is heated too hot the bonbons will be hard
   and void of shine. So it is necessary to learn the ideal

temperature for the dipping. Do not melt too much at one time and wash the pan after each dipping.

COCONUT BONBONS

These are the most popular of bonbons.

1. To one-half batch of fondant, while it is being beaten and reaching the creamed stage, add enough macaroon coconut to suit the taste.
   1 c. or more coconut
   1 ts. vanilla. Knead and mix well and roll on a sugared board into a long, thin roll. Cut in small pieces and roll round in the palms of the hands.
2. Dip in hot fondant colored any color with choice of flavoring added. Place on waxed paper to harden.

FRENCH BONBONS

This is a choice bonbon. I am sure you will enjoy trying this recipe.

1. Mix together and stir well
   1 c. honey
   1 c. glucose
2. Bring to a boil, then turn off heat and add
   1 ts. vanilla
   ¼ ts. salt, then add
   1 lb. macaroon coconut
3. Stir until the syrup is completely absorbed.
4. Roll into small balls and place on waxed-paper-lined trays.

   To dip:

1. Make a batch of bonbon fondant.
2. Melt part of it in the top of the double boiler, over hot water. Follow instructions given on bonbon dipping.
3. Top each bonbon with a dainty flower and leaf.
   This recipe may also be spread on a buttered marble or platter, cooled, and cut in squares for a (macaroon center) chocolate dipped confection.

CHOCOLATE COCONUT BONBONS

1. To a batch of coconut bonbons add
   1 square of melted chocolate. Mix and roll as directed.

2. Plain coconut centers may be dipped in chocolate fondant. Simply add
    1 or 2 squares of bitter baking chocolate to the melting fondant and stir. If fondant thickens slightly, thin with a spoonful of light syrup.

JOLLY BACHELORS

A choice caramel center, fondant dipped candy.
1. Make a batch of Helen B's caramel, with
    1 c. chopped nuts added. When cool and firm cut in ½-inch squares.
2. Melt a portion of fondant in the top of the double boiler over hot water.
    (Avoid letting fondant become too hot.)
    Flavor with
    1 ts. maple flavoring
3. With a dipping fork, quickly dip caramel squares in the melted fondant and turn out on a pan of finely chopped nuts. Allow them to remain until cool. The nuts will cling to the fondant making tempting pieces of candy. The fork may be swirled when releasing the dipped caramel, making a large C on the back of each piece.

MERRY WIDOWS

These lovely candies are made by the same procedure as used for Jolly Bachelors except the fondant is flavored with vanilla in place of maple. These candies do not stay fresh more than a few days, as the fondant becomes hard.

FONDANT DOCTOR

The following is a mixture which may be added to fondant while it is melting to cause it to soften allowing the juices of cherries, pineapple, etc., to form the luscious liquid we admire in those chocolates. Just a few drops are necessary in a pan of fondant. Ingredients may be purchased in the drug stores.
    ½ oz. acetic acid (8%)
    ½ oz. glycerine
    1 oz. distilled water
    ½ oz. grain alcohol

FONDANT MAZZETA

Mazzeta is the secret of good chocolate centers. It is a preparation added to the beaten fondant which makes a soft, delicate, creamy mixture. From it many different chocolate centers may be made.

1. Method

   In a small kettle place

   ½ c. glucose and heat to boiling, then pour it quickly over

   1 egg white, beaten stiff. Beat for a few minutes.

2. Make a batch of fondant (refer to the recipe) and cook 3° higher. Cool and beat as instructed. When the batch begins to turn white and a little firm, quickly add the egg and syrup mixture and continue beating in the same method, pushing with a scraper forward, over, and back, until the mazzeta begins to turn white and become firm. You may add any flavoring you desire while beating and add the other ingredients such as nuts, coconut, candied fruits, etc. Continue beating until the batch holds its shape. You may now proceed to roll the centers for chocolate dipping, or you may place the mazzeta in a bowl, cover with a damp cloth or foil, and roll later.

   The following recipes are variations of chocolate centers made from batches of mazzeta.

CENTERS

1. For Almond Paste Centers

   To a batch of Fondant Mazzeta add

   1 c. almond paste, broken in small pieces

   1 ts. almond flavoring

   1 c. chopped almonds

2. For Peanut Butter Centers

   1 c. fresh peanut butter

3. For Coconut Pecan Centers

   1 ts. butterscotch flavoring

   1 macaroon coconut

   ½ c. chopped pecans

4. For Black Walnut Centers

   1 ts. black walnut flavoring

   1 c. chopped black walnuts

MILK FONDANT (Follow Fondant Instructions)

No. 1

1. Mix together
   5 c. sugar
   2 c. milk
   4 tbs. butter
   ⅛ ts. cream of tartar
   (Stir while cooking)

No. 2

1. Mix together
   4 c. sugar
   2 c. milk and cream
   1 c. glucose
   1 c. butter
   ¼ ts. cream of tartar

VANILLA CENTERS

1. Proceed as before, adding
   1 ts. vanilla just before the mazzeta starts to set.
2. Ground nuts may be added, also coconut.
   Follow instructions for rolling the centers.

PLAIN FRUIT CENTERS

1. Orange:
   To a batch of mazzeta add
   4 or 5 drops of fruit acid (may be obtained at any drug store)
   ½ ts. orange extract or emulsion
   several drops of orange coloring

2. Lemon:
   To a batch of mazzeta add
   ½ ts. lemon juice or extract
   3 drops of yellow coloring
   3 drops of fruit acid

3. Pineapple:
   To a batch of mazzeta add
   ½ ts. pineapple flavoring
   3 tbs. candied pineapple (tiny pieces)
   3 drops of fruit acid

4. Strawberry:
   To a batch of mazzeta add
   1 ts. strawberry flavoring
   2 or 3 drops of red coloring

OTHER CENTERS

1. Maple Walnut
     1 ts. maple flavoring
     ½ c. finely chopped walnuts
2. Coconut
     1 c. finely shredded coconut or macaroon
     1 ts. vanilla or almond
3. Butterscotch Nut
     1 ts. butterscotch flavoring
     ½ c. chopped pecans

BUTTER RUM CENTERS

1. Mix together and stir until sugar is dissolved
     4 c. sugar
     ½ c. glucose
     1 c. water
2. Bring to a boil and wash the sides of the kettle. Cook to 232°, then add ½ cube of butter. Cook without stirring to 235°, then pour out on a damp marble slab to cool.
3. When cool, beat like fondant until smooth and creamy.
4. When the batch begins to set up, add a batch of mazzeta and
     ½ ts. rum flavoring
     1 ts. vanilla
     ½ ts. salt
5. Continue beating until stiff. Roll and cut, then form into centers for chocolate dipping.

VICTORIA CENTERS

1. Make a batch of butter rum centers, instead of adding rum flavoring and vanilla, add
     1 ts. victorine flavoring
     1 ts. brandy flavoring
2. Roll into centers for chocolate dipping.

PINEAPPLE CREAMS

1. Bring to a boil and cook to 228°
     1 c. sugar
     1 small can of crushed pineapple

2. Make a batch of fondant mazzeta and when it has been beaten to the creamy stage, add the above cooked pineapple and
    1 ts. pineapple flavoring
    1 ts. fruit acid. Continue beating until it sets.
3. Roll into round balls for chocolate dipping.

PEPPERMINT CENTERS

1. Make a batch of mazzeta. Beat. When it is almost ready to set, add
    3 or 4 drops of oil of peppermint
    2 or 3 drops of green coloring, if desired
2. Continue beating until the batch is firm. Roll as instructed.

VANILLA NUT ROLLS

1. Make a batch of vanilla fudge or fondant. Roll in round rolls and dip in chocolate mixed with ground nuts. (Refer to chocolate dipping instructions.)

BUTTER RUM ROLLS

1. Make a batch of butter rum centers. Make into small, round rolls, dip in milk chocolate, and roll in chopped pecans or almonds.

COCONUT TOPS

1. Make a batch of fondant mazzeta. When it is in the creaming stage, add
    2 c. macaroon coconut
    1 ts. vanilla
2. Roll in small balls, roll each ball lengthwise, then dip in cooled vanilla chocolate. Place in a pan of shredded coconut, and set aside to dry. When you pick up the chocolates the coconut will cling to the tops. The leftover coconut may be reused for coconut rolls.

COCONUT ROLLS

1. Make small balls of coconut centers, dip them in cooled chocolate, and roll in coconut.

CHOCOLATE CENTERS

Coconut Squares:
1. Into 1 lb. of warm fondant fold
   ½ lb. of macaroon coconut
   1 c. chopped walnuts
2. In the top of the double boiler over hot water, melt
   1 lb. additional fondant
3. Make a batch of mazzeta (refer to recipe)
   (½ c. hot glucose and 1 beaten egg white)
4. Heat in a pan
   ½ lb. coconut butter. Add this to the fondant alternately with the mazzeta, a little at a time. At this point the batch may be divided in portions and colored and flavored in many ways.
5. Spread out on a paper and cover with coconut or nuts. Press them with the tips of the fingers.
6. When cold, turn the batch over, wet the paper and remove it. Turn the batch back and cut in squares with a sharp knife. These also may be dipped in cooled chocolate.

LAURALEEN'S

This is one of my latest recipes, obtained by experimenting. It is a choice maple flavored, coconut center. I named it after my neighbor girl Laura Lee, who has been my pal since childhood and who loves being with me and helping me while I am making candy.
1. Mix together and stir until sugar is dissolved
   2 c. white sugar
   2 c. brown sugar
   ½ c. glucose
   1 can condensed milk. Place on heat and bring to boil. Wash the sides of kettle. Cook to 232°, then pour out on marble slab or platter to cool.
2. Beat with a scraper. Even though this candy seems sticky like caramel, it will beat up nicely.
3. Flavor with
   1 ts. maple flavoring
   1 ts. butterscotch flavoring. Then add 1½ c. macaroon coconut.
4. Cut and roll for chocolate centers.

PARTY MINTS (Fondant)

The ever-popular candy mint is made of fondant by melting a batch of fondant in the top of the double boiler over hot water, stirring occasionally, adding flavoring and coloring as desired. Avoid getting the fondant too hot; this tends to make the mints hard instead of creamy.

1. Pour the melted fondant into a parchment paper cone or canvas bag using a No. 8 or 10 decorating tube. Squeeze the fondant out on a ribbed rubber mat to the size of the mint desired, leaving enough space between pieces to prevent them from touching. Make them all the same size for appearance.

2. Let them cool on the mat until firm, then remove and store in waxed-paper-covered trays.
   The ribbed rubber mat may be obtained by buying a small piece of matting from the hardware stores; scrub and wash well and dry before using.

3. Flavorings popular are:
   Peppermint .... (white)
   Wintergreen colored .... (pink)
   Lemon colored .... (yellow)
   Mint colored .... (green)

4. These mints may be decorated with frosting flowers and birds for weddings, receptions, and teas.

COCONUT MACAROON

1. Bring to a boil in a kettle, stirring first,
   1⅓ c. glucose
   1 c. sugar
   ½ c. water

2. Wash the sides of the kettle and cook to 226°. Remove from the heat and add
   2 tbs. flour, stir in well. Add
   1 ts. vanilla or almond flavoring

3. Then stir in enough macaroon coconut to make the candy hold its shape. It may be cut in squares or rolled into round balls. This candy also may be dipped in chocolate.

COCONUT KINGS

1. Mix together and stir well
    1 c. sugar
    ½ c. water
    1 c. glucose
2. Bring to a boil, wash the sides of the kettle, and cook
   to 222°. Remove from heat and add
    1 tbs. dry flour. Stir well.
3. Add
    1 ts. almond or vanilla extract
    ½ lb. macaroon coconut
    ¼ lb. shredded coconut
    Mix well and let cool, then roll in bars or centers for
    chocolate dipping.

CRYSTAL SYRUP

This is a syrup used to dip bonbons and plain creams. It
gives them a crystal coating which protects them from
drying out, thus lengthening their period of freshness.
1. In a large kettle, place
    6 c. sugar
    2 c. water. Cook to 220°.
2. Place the kettle in a pan of cold water.
3. Sprinkle a little cold water over the top of the syrup
   if it begins to crystal on top. Cool to 85°.
4. Then place the candies to be crystallized in a wire basket,
   dip the basket into the syrup and submerge the candies.
   It is well to have a cover on the basket. Allow them
   to remain in the syrup for 2 hours or more. Then raise
   the basket and drain the syrup from the candies. Spread
   them on a waxed paper to dry.

FONDANT DIPPED NUTS

1. Melt a portion of fondant in the top of the double boiler
   and add your choice of flavoring and coloring. Then dip
   the nuts in the hot fondant and place them on a waxed
   paper to harden.

Varieties:
Maple Brazils
    Maple flavoring

Brazil nuts
Vanilla Walnuts
   Vanilla flavoring
   Walnut halves
Fruit Filberts
   Fruit flavoring
   Filbert nuts (whole)

Nut pieces also may be made in cluster. Brazil nuts are nice dipped in vanilla fondant and, when cool, dipped in chocolate.

FONDANT FILLED DATES

1. Cut and remove stones from fresh dates.
2. Fill the inside with a small piece of fondant and press the date closely to it. Then dip in chocolate or roll in sugar.

STUFFED DATES

1. Cut and remove stones from dates and fill the centers with nut pieces. Press together and roll in sugar or chocolate dip them.

FONDANT DIPPED FRESH FRUIT

1. Strawberries and cherries may be held by the stems and dipped in hot fondant. Other fruits such as pineapple chunks, peaches, etc., also may be dipped in fondant, but they must be eaten the same day they are dipped, because the acid in the fruit will cause the fondant to leak.

PETITS FOURS (Fondant Dipped)

A dainty, decorated little cake, fondant dipped, is a party fantasy.

1. Bake in advance tiny cakes of angel food or sponge cake for round *petits fours* or a sheet cake of the same to be cut in small squares.
2. Heat previously made fondant in the top of the double boiler over hot water, color and flavor as desired.

3. With a bonbon fork dip each small cake into the fondant. Work quickly and drop each from the fork onto a waxed paper to harden. Place sugar flowers or decorations desired on top while fondant is still warm, or decorate later with decorative frostings or whipped cream, using a decorating tube and bag, when the dipped cake has cooled sufficiently.
4. Nut-covered *petits fours* may be made by rolling the cake in finely chopped nuts immediately after dipping in hot fondant.
5. Coconut covered *petits fours* may be made as above using shredded coconut in place of nuts.

FILLED PETITS FOURS

1. Cut each little cake through the center, spread a layer of frosting filling such as mint, pineapple, cherry, caramel, etc., over the bottom half and replace the top piece. Then fondant dip and proceed as directed.

PETITS FOURS

These also may be made by frosting the sides and tops of the cakes with butter-cream frosting, then pressing finely ground nuts or coconut to the sides. Decorate the tops in designs or with flowers and leaves.

Warmed fondant may be poured over the cakes if you have difficulty in dipping with a fork. Place on a rack to harden.

ALMOND PASTE BONBONS

1. Into a portion of fondant knead enough almond paste to suit taste. Mix well.
2. Add
        1 ts. almond flavoring and mix again.
3. Roll and dip as directed.
4. Split a blanched almond and place smooth side up on top, for decoration, while bonbon is still soft.

DECORATED BONBONS

1. Have ready a selection of daintily colored small rosebuds

and tiny green leaves made of frosting. Place on top of dipped bonbons while they are still warm and soft.
2. Candied fruits, such as cherries and pineapple, also make pretty toppings for bonbons.
3. Nuts of all varieties are appealing as toppings.
4. Tiny birds, such as bluebirds, canaries, love birds, etc., made of royal or meringue frosting, are very nice to have for toppings.

PLAIN MARSHMALLOWS

1. In a kettle, place
     2 c. sugar
     $2/3$ c. glucose
     $2/3$ c. water
     Mix well and place on heat to boil, wash the sides of the kettle, and cook to 232° without stirring.
2. While the batch is cooking, dissolve
     $1\frac{2}{3}$ tbs. gelatin in
     $2/3$ c. hot water. Stir well.
3. Remove batch from the heat and pour into a large mixing bowl. Add the dissolved gelatin slowly, beating all the while on high speed for 10 minutes.
4. Add
     1 ts. vanilla
     $1/8$ ts. salt
     Continue beating for 10 minutes more or until a spoon dropped on top of the batch will not submerge.
5. Line a flat pan with brown paper, then pour the marshmallow on the paper. Spread evenly and allow to set 12 hours or more.
6. Sprinkle powdered sugar over a marble or pan and turn the set marshmallow over the sugar. Wet the paper a little and peel it off the bottom. Dust the marshmallow with powdered sugar and cut in squares.

MY RECIPE FOR CREAM MINTS

1. In a kettle place and let soak for several minutes, stirring several times,
     1 c. thick cream
     3 c. sugar

2. Bring to a slow boil and add
   2 tbs. glucose, stirring constantly. Wash the sides of the kettle several times while boiling to be sure of no grains. Cook to 226°.
3. Pour out on a damp slab to cool.
4. Place
   1 tbs. butter in the center of the batch
5. When well cooled, begin beating with a scraper forward, over, and back, until mixture turns creamy and firm.
6. Add
   4 drops of oil of peppermint while beating
7. Roll into a long roll, 1 inch thick, on a board sprinkled with powdered sugar. Cut with a knife into small pieces and roll round in the palms. Place on tray, sprinkled with powdered sugar, to cool for chocolate dipping.

STRAWBERRY MARSHMALLOWS

1. Make a batch of marshmallow using
   ⅔ c. strawberry jam and
   1 ts. strawberry extract in place of the glucose in the recipe.

MARSHMALLOW DRESSING

1. Mix together and stir well
   2 c. sugar
   1⅓ c. glucose
   ½ c. water
2. Bring to a boil, wash the sides of the kettle, and cook to 228°. Slowly add to the stiffly beaten whites of
   2 eggs
3. Continue beating until the marshmallow is of the right consistency.
4. Add
   1 ts. vanilla

TOASTED MARSHMALLOWS

1. Place in a flat baking dish and put in a 325° oven, stirring occasionally until it toasts a golden brown,
   ½ lb. macaroon coconut

2. Soak in the beater bowl
   1½ oz. gelatin and
   ¾ c. cold water
3. Mix to a creamed paste in a large kettle
   3 heaping tbs. cornstarch
   1¼ c. cold water. Cook over low heat, stirring constantly, until it thickens, then add
   2 c. sugar. When it begins to boil, remove from the stove and add 2⅔ c. melted glucose. Stir well and pour over soaked gelatin. Stir until gelatin is dissolved.
4. Beat until marshmallow is very stiff and then add
   1 ts. vanilla
5. Pour out on a piece of wrapping paper. Use some 1-inch iron bars, 2 feet long, to space the candy and to prevent it from spreading out too thin. These bars may be used in several different types of candy.
6. Sprinkle the top of marshmallow with toasted coconut. When the batch is completely set, turn it over, dampen the paper with a wet cloth, then pull the paper away. Sprinkle this side with toasted coconut.
7. Cut in 1-inch squares and roll all sides in the coconut. Dry before packing.

MARSHMALLOW

Marshmallow may be used in so many different ways in candymaking. It may be made into bars, Easter eggs, little animals, molds, etc., or it may be chocolate dipped.

EASTER EGGS

1. Obtain some plastic molds for Easter eggs from a variety store. Choose the size you wish to make.
2. Grease the insides with mineral oil or vegetable shortening.
3. Make a batch of plain marshmallow, pour the finished batch in the molds, and allow to set.
4. When entirely set up, release eggs and frost them with decorative frosting. These may be decorated or chocolate dipped.
5. Place on wax paper and allow to dry.

6. Then decorate with frosting in pretty designs, such as flower arrangements, birds and butterflies, tiny white lilies, orange blossoms, forget-me-nots, small rosebuds, etc., or decorate with tiny bunnies, chickens, etc. Also in fancy writing, add the names of the little ones for whom you are making the eggs, or make Happy Easter scrolls for older members.

7. Use only dainty pastel colors of pink, yellow, blue, green, etc.

8. Make little nests from frosting, cover them in green-tinted coconut, make an indentation in the center, and fill with tiny candy eggs. Then place a small chicken on the edge of the nest. Use your own creative ideas in decorating Easter eggs. You will delight in the results. Candy Easter eggs may be made from other types of candy, such as divinity, fudge, fondant, or solid chocolate.

In decorating, make pretty edges around the egg in pastel colors, using different decorating tubes to make an assortment of edges. Lacing with frosting may be applied to the outer edge.

PLAIN CARAMELS (Cream Method)

This recipe is recommended for pecan rolls, turtles, caramel covered nuts, etc. It has a smooth texture and very nice flavor.

1. With a pastry brush, butter the sides of a large kettle.

2. In it mix together and stir until dissolved

   2 c. sugar

   1 pt. cream. Bring to a boil. Wash the sugar grains from the sides of the kettle. Boil for 3 minutes, stirring slowly, so the boil will not stop and cause the candy to curdle.

3. Add very slowly

   1 more pt. cream or 1 large can of milk

4. Add and continue stirring slowly

   2 oz. coconut butter

   ½ ts. salt

5. Add

   1⅓ c. hot glucose. Stir and cook until a hard ball is formed in a test of tepid water. Remove from heat and add

1 ts. vanilla. Stir carefully and pour out on a cool oiled marble or platter.

When cool, proceed, depending upon what type of candy you are making.

CHOCOLATE CARAMELS

1. To a batch of plain caramel, just before removing from heat, add
   2 squares melted baking chocolate.

CARAMEL SYRUP FOR TOPPINGS

1. Slowly bring to a boil
   1 qt. good maple syrup
2. Add
   1 pt. cream, stirring constantly. Then add
   1 c. boiling glucose and cook to 220°. Remove from heat and add
   1 ts. vanilla
   Chill and serve. May be kept in refrigerator for several days.

CARAMEL PECAN ROLL

This is a fascinating recipe and such fun to make. You begin by making the centers you prefer, such as fudge, fondant or divinity. My favorite is the following:

1. Mix together and stir until dissolved and smooth
   2 c. sugar
   1 c. brown sugar
   ½ c. glucose or syrup
   1 c. evaporated milk
2. Bring to a boil; wash the sides of the kettle to prevent graining. Cook to 228° stirring carefully to prevent burning.
3. Pour out on a marble and cool, then beat until creamy.
4. Add the following, knead lightly, and form in long 1½-inch rolls
   1 ts. rum flavoring
5. Set aside until caramel is prepared.
6. Cook a batch of plain caramel and, when it is slightly

cool, cut pieces to cover the rolls. Work quickly with buttered fingers and roll the caramel around each roll. Place pecans face up all around the roll, press lightly, and set on a waxed paper until ready to cut in slices.

CARAMEL CENTERS FOR DIPPING

To prepare caramels for chocolate dipping, make several batches of different recipes of caramel. Add a variety of chopped nuts and coconut to some of the batches, and leave some plain. When the caramel is cold, which usually requires standing overnight, place large pieces on a wooden board, butter the fingers lightly and, using a very sharp knife, slide through the caramel making shapes desired. Caramel should be cut quickly. Do not press down too firmly; sliding the knife usually helps. Scrape the knife often with another knife so the caramel will not stick. Caramels should be kept in a cool room (not cold) and should be chocolate dipped soon after cutting so they will maintain their shape. Arrange the dipping table and marble in a cool room—68° is best.

CARAMELS (Helen B.)

This is a firm, choice caramel. It cuts evenly and holds its shape well. It is recommended for chocolate-dipped caramels.
1. In a large kettle, place
     2 c. sugar
     1 large can evaporated milk. Bring to a boil.
2. Add
     ½ lb. butter
     1 c. hot glucose
3. Stir constantly back and forth with a wooden paddle. Boil slowly and keep at an even boil. Wash the sides of the kettle with a small brush or cloth softened in warm water, to prevent graining. Continue boiling slowly and stirring until it forms a hard ball in cold water. It usually takes 1 hour cooking time.
4. Just before removing from heat add
     2 pieces of pure paraffin wax the size of a pea. Stir very gently. Add flavoring, also nuts, if desired. Pour out on a buttered platter and set aside. Cut into

shapes desired (square or long). To cut caramels, use a sharp, thin knife and slide it quickly through the cooled caramel (do not press).

CARAMEL FONDANT

1. To one batch of finished fondant, add
   ¼ batch of cooled caramel
   ½ ts. vanilla. Cream on marble with a scraper or spatula until smooth and firm.
2. This candy may be cut in squares when it sets up or may be rolled into balls to be chocolate dipped.

EASY CARAMELS

1. Combine and stir well, then let stand for a few minutes
   2 c. sugar
   1 c. dark syrup
   1 c. cream
2. Bring to a slow, steady boil, stirring all the time.
3. Wash the sides of the kettle with a small brush dipped in warm water.
4. While boiling, slowly add
   1 more c. cream. Do not stop the boil. Continue stirring and cook to a hard-ball stage, testing often by dropping a few drops of candy into cold water. Pour out on a buttered platter and cool, then cut.

CARAMELETTES

1. Make a batch of penuche or creamed fudge. Cut in small squares and allow to dry a little.
2. Make a batch of Log Roll Caramels and pour it in the top of a double boiler over hot water.
3. With a bonbon fork or cream dipping fork, dip pieces in the hot caramel. Drop them in a pan of finely chopped pecans or walnuts.
4. Butter the fingers lightly and roll each caramelette round. Place on waxed paper to cool.

BLACK WALNUT CARAMELS

1. Place in a kettle, mix until smooth and sugar is dissolved
   1 c. sugar

¾ c. dark syrup
½ c. butter or margarine
½ c. cream

2. Place on to boil. Wash the sides of the kettle well. Stir continually while boiling slowly to 252° or to a very hard-ball stage when tested in cold water.
3. Remove from heat and add
    ½ ts. black walnut flavoring
    1 c. broken black walnuts
4. Pour out on a buttered or oiled pan to cool. Then with the back of a knife mark gently into squares.
5. When set, cut in strips. Wrap in paper or dip in chocolate.

CARAMEL NOUGAT

1. After you have made a batch of nougat, spread it evenly on the marble slab between the bars. Then make a batch of caramel, spread it over the top of the nougat, and allow them to cool.

    The nougat may be colored pink and the caramel made with chocolate for a variety.

LOG ROLL CARAMEL

1. Mix together and stir until dissolved
    2 c. sugar
    1 c. cream
2. Bring to a boil, wash the sides of the kettle, then add
    1⅓ c. hot glucose
    2 tbs. coconut butter
    ½ cube of butter
3. Cook to 232°, remove from heat, and add
    1 ts. vanilla. Color red, if desired.
4. Pour out on an oiled slab to cool.
    While the batch is cooling, make the following centers for the rolls:

Log Roll Centers
1. Mix together and stir well
    3 c. sugar
    1 c. cream (or ½ c. cream and ½ c. canned milk)

2. Bring to a boil and add
    1 c. hot glucose. Cook to 230°, remove from heat, and
    add
    1 tbs. butter. Begin creaming the batch by beating
    in the kettle.
    Beat until thick, then add
    1 ts. vanilla
    ½ ts. salt
    1 ts. custard flavoring or
    1 ts. rum flavoring
3. Place on marble slab and knead until it will form a roll.
    Place rolls in the center of the caramel. Press the edges
    and cut into pieces 10 inches long. Place on waxed
    paper to cool.
4. When cool cut in slices.
    Log Rolls also may be made like a jelly roll. Spread
    the creamed centers on top of the caramel and begin
    rolling from one side to the other in one long roll,
    cinnamon-bun fashion. Cut in pieces for the size of
    roll desired. Wrap in wax paper until served.

MARSHMALLOW CARAMEL KISSES

1. Make a batch of Log Roll Caramels. Spread it ¼ inch
    thick on an oiled slab. Cover one half of the caramel,
    while it is hot, with marshmallows cut in pieces. Pull
    the other half of the caramel over to cover the marsh-
    mallows. When cool, cut in squares or roll into round
    centers for chocolate dipping.

FIRM CARAMEL (By Nancy)

This is a never-fail recipe for firm caramel. It cuts
nicely, holds its shape, and is delicious. I call this recipe
Nancy after my little friend whom I adore.

1. Mix together and stir until dissolved
    2 c. sugar
    2 c. glucose
    ½ ts. salt. Boil to 245° after washing sides of kettle.
2. Add slowly
    ½ c. butter
    2 c. canned milk

If you desire to use thick cream instead of canned milk, use only ¼ c. butter, or use
1 c. cream and 1 c. canned milk.
3. Cook slowly, stirring all the while, to 238° for a real firm caramel, or to 235° for a soft caramel.
4. Just after removing from the heat add 1 ts. vanilla and nuts, if desired.
5. Pour into buttered pans. Cut when firm.

BROWN SUGAR CARAMELS

1. In a kettle place and bring to a boil
      ¾ c. syrup
      ½ c. butter
      ¼ ts. salt
2. Add to the hot syrup
      2½ c. brown sugar (1 pkg.)
3. Remove from heat and add
      1 c. sweetened condensed milk
      1 ts. vanilla
4. Boil again, stirring constantly, to a hard-ball test. Pour on buttered platter or tin and cool.

NOUGAT

This is a chewy type of candy and makes a delicious chocolate center.
1. Cook
      1 c. glucose to 260°.
2. Beat
      3 egg whites until stiff. Pour the hot glucose slowly over the beaten egg whites, and beat for 5 minutes.
3. Combine in a kettle and stir well
      2 c. glucose
      1½ c. sugar
      ¼ c. water
4. Boil and wash the sides of the kettle. Continue boiling to a soft crack, 272°, then pour slowly over the egg-white mixture, beating over and over.
5. Add
      3 tbs. butter
      1 ts. vanilla

6. Beat until the nougat leaves the sticky stage and begins to look firm. Pour on a large platter and let set for several hours.

NUT NOUGAT

If you desire the nut nougat, add the following to the nougat recipe.

1. Add
    1 c. shredded blanched almonds
    ½ c. pistachio nuts
    1 c. chopped pecans

TOFFEE

1. In a candy kettle place
    4 c. sugar
    ¼ c. glucose
    1 c. water. Stir until sugar is completely dissolved.
2. Place on heat and bring to a boil. Wash the sides of kettle, then stir while you add
    4 ozs. of hard coconut butter. Cook until it reaches 272°.
3. Add
    ⅔ lb. butter. Continue stirring and cook to 307°.
4. Add
    ⅔ ts. salt
    ½ c. ground raw almonds
5. Continue stirring and cook to 312°. Remove from heat and add
    1 ts. vanilla. Pour out on oiled slab. Spread out with spatula. While still warm, mark in squares with a dull knife and, when cool, break, dip in cooled, melted chocolate, and roll in chopped almonds or walnuts.

BOSTON CREAMS

1. In a large frying pan, place
    1 c. sugar. On medium heat caramelize until golden brown, by just shaking the pan to move the sugar. Do not have heat too high. Avoid using a spoon; just shake the pan while sugar is melting and browning.

2. To the browned sugar add
   ½ of a tall can of evaporated milk. The sugar will bubble a great deal, but just stir quickly with a wooden spoon or paddle.
3. When candy has reached a full boil, add
   1 more c. sugar and the other
   ½ can of milk
4. Continue stirring back and forth, cooking slowly, until it makes a firm ball when tested.
5. Remove from heat and beat in the same pan until candy sets.
6. Add
   Nuts or coconut, then pour on buttered plate and cut in squares.

DIVINITY

Divinity is a candy, quite common to homemakers and young people. It is a lovely candy, when it is moist, creamy, and free from any sugar grain. In this candy the boiling process is very important, as is also the correct degree of cooking temperature.

1. Begin by placing in kettle
   2½ c. sugar
   ½ c. glucose
   ⅔ c. water. Stir until sugar is completely dissolved. Place on to cook.
2. Wash the sides of the kettle twice to be sure no crystals remain, also cover the kettle for one minute. Then boil to 232° without stirring.
3. While candy is boiling, whip in a warm bowl until stiff, but not too dry, the whites of
   2 eggs
4. When the candy has cooked to 232°, add
   ⅓ of the batch slowly to the beaten egg whites.
   Turn beater on medium speed and continue beating.
5. Place candy back on the heat and cook to 244°, then add to the beaten portion very slowly. This allows the egg and syrup to fluff and become light. Continue beating slowly until the candy becomes firm in the bowl. At this point you add any of the following: nut meats, coconut, candied fruits, chocolate chips, gumdrops, etc.

6.   Gently spoon the candy in mounds on a wax paper, using
     2 spoons or the tip of the finger to release each mound.
7.   You may add
         2 tbs. of melted coconut butter just before the candy
         is to be spooned out, if you intend to keep the
         divinity for some time. This will keep it moist.

AFTER-DINNER MINTS

1.   Mix together in candy kettle
         4 c. sugar
         ¼ ts. cream of tartar
         1 c. water
         Stir until dissolved, place on heat, and boil without
         stirring. Wash the sides of the kettle to prevent
         graining. Cook to 252°.
2.   Pour out on oiled marble or platter and let cool.
3.   Pick up in fingers like taffy and begin stretching, pull-
     ing forward and back with the tips of the fingers.
4.   Add
         10 drops of oil of peppermint while pulling. Keep
         pulling the candy until it is quite firm. Stretch into
         a long roll and snip off small pieces with the scissors.
         Drop them in a bowl of powdered sugar and allow
         them to crystallize in a covered tin or jar.

BUTTER CREAM MINTS

1.   To a batch of after-dinner mints, add 2 ozs. of butter,
     just before the final cooking. Follow the instructions
     as above. Coloring may be added.
     Other flavoring may also be used such as:
     Wintergreen colored pink
     Spearmint colored green
     Violet colored violet
     Mint colored green
     Lemon colored yellow
     In butter cream mints the powdered sugar may be
     omitted.

OPERA CREAMS

This is a good recipe for candy pulls.

1. Mix together
    4½ c. sugar
    ¼ ts. salt
    ½ pt. coffee cream
    4 tbs. hot water. Stir until sugar is thoroughly dissolved.
    Put on heat to boil. Do not stir.
2. Cut in small pieces
    ⅛ lb. butter and add to the candy while it is boiling.
3. Cook slowly until mixture is slightly browned, then test in cold water. If the test separates in tiny flakes, remove from heat and pour out on a buttered marble to cool.
4. When cool, add
    ½ ts. vanilla.
    Pick up with fingers and begin stretching like taffy, pulling each end with tips of fingers, lapping out and back. Just before candy begins to set, lay out on the marble and pull in strips. Clip with scissors in small pieces.

DATE NUT CANDY ROLL

1. Stir together well
    4 c. sugar
    1 large can milk
2. Cook slowly, stirring continually, wash the sides of the kettle, and cook to 232°.
3. Remove from heat and add
    1 lb. chopped dates. Cook again until the dates dissolve slightly.
4. Pour out on marble to cool.
5. When cool beat until candy starts to set, then add
    2 c. chopped walnuts
    1 ts. vanilla
    1 tbs. butter. Continue beating until firm.
6. Shape into roll and place on a damp towel. Cool before slicing.

GELATIN CANDY (Mom Spurrier)

This is a choice gelatin candy. The recipe was given to me by a wonderful lady doctor, Mom Spurrier.

1. Dissolve
   4 tbs. gelatin in
   1 c. cold water
2. Place in a kettle
   4 c. sugar
   1½ c. boiling water. Stir until dissolved.
3. Add gelatin to the sugar and water.
4. Boil slowly without stirring for 25 minutes, remove from heat, and divide into bowls.
   Color 1 part yellow and flavor with lemon.
   Color 1 part red and flavor with oil of wintergreen.
   Color the other part green and flavor with mint or peppermint.
   Pour into flat tins and let stand overnight.
5. Cut in pieces or squares and roll in sugar. This gelatin candy may be used in many ways. It may be poured, when cooled, over a batch of set white fudge, cut in strips and chocolate dipped, or rolled in sugar. It may also be chocolate dipped for jelly centers, or stacked in tiers with a layer of fondant between, then cut in squares and rolled in sugar.

PECAN FUDGE (Large Recipe)

This recipe is a mixture of fudge and fondant and is a very nice candy to serve in squares or to chocolate dip.
1. Make a batch of fondant (refer to recipe).
2. Mix together in a kettle and stir well
   4 c. sugar
   ½ c. glucose
   1 c. cream
   ½ cube butter
3. Place on to cook. Wash the sides of the kettle at least twice and cook to 234°, stirring constantly while cooking to prevent candy from burning.
4. Remove from heat and add
   1 batch of fondant, stirring with a wooden spoon until mixed, then add
   1 ts. vanilla
   ½ ts. salt and continue beating until fudge becomes creamy.

5. Pour into buttered pans, spread evenly with a spatula, and cover top with pecan halves. Press nuts down so they will stick in the fudge. Cool and cut in squares.

This recipe may be divided into portions and flavored chocolate, maple, butterscotch, etc.

BROWN SUGAR FUDGE

1. Mix together and let stand in the kettle for several minutes
    3 c. sugar
    1 c. brown sugar
    1 c. cream
    ½ c. milk
    ¼ ts. salt
2. Stir for 2 or 3 minutes before starting to cook.
3. Cook slowly, stirring constantly. Wash the sides of the kettle and continue cooking to 226°.
4. Pour out on marble and cool.
5. When cool, beat until creamy. Flavor with your choice of flavoring.
6. Prepare for centers, if the fudge is to be dipped, or cut in squares when thoroughly set.

MAPLE FUDGE

1. Mix together and stir thoroughly
    1 c. sugar
    1 c. brown sugar
    2 ts. vinegar
    ½ c. maple syrup
    ½ c. water
2. Place on heat, boil slowly, wash the sides of the kettle, cover with the lid for 1 minute, and cook to 236°.
3. This candy may be cooled in the pan. When cool beat until fudge begins to set. Add maple flavoring and nuts. Beat until set.

CHERRY ORANGE FUDGE

This is a decorative as well as luscious fudge.
1. Melt in a kettle
    1⅓ tbs. butter. Remove from heat and add
    2 ts. orange rind (grated)

2. Add
    1 c. thin cream
    3 c. sugar
    ⅜ ts. cream of tartar
    3 tbs. orange juice
3. Stir well, place on to cook over low heat, wash the sides
    of the kettle, and cover kettle for a few seconds, to
    prevent candy from crystallizing. Cook to a firm, soft
    ball, when tested in cold water, or about 242°.
4. Pour out to cool. When cool add
    1 ts. lemon juice. Beat until thick, add
    1 c. candied cherries, cool, and cut in squares.

PENUCHE (Plain)

This soft, creamy-textured candy has a good flavor.

1. Mix together in a kettle and stir well until sugar is
    dissolved
    2 c. sugar
    1 c. brown sugar
    ⅔ c. glucose
    1 c. cream or canned milk
2. Place on to cook, wash the sides of the kettle. Cover the
    kettle for a few seconds to steam the sugar crystals
    from the sides of the pan. Stir continually to keep
    candy from burning. Cook to 232°.
3. Remove candy from the heat and add
    1 tbs. of melted sweet chocolate
    ½ ts. vanilla
    1 tbs. butter. Beat until penuche is creamed and firm.
    Add chopped nuts if desired.
4. Turn out on a buttered plate and allow to stand awhile
    before cutting.

PENUCHE CARAMELETTES

1. Make a batch of penuche (refer to recipe).
2. Cut in ¾-inch squares and spread them on a waxed
    paper.
3. Then make a batch of the following caramel:

Caramel
1. Mix together and stir until dissolved
     2 c. sugar
     1 c. cream
2. Bring to a boil and wash the sides of kettle.
3. Add, stirring slowly,
     1⅓ c. hot glucose
     2 ozs. of coconut butter
     ½ cube of butter or margarine
     Cook to 232°, remove from heat, and add
     1 ts. vanilla.
4. Pour the hot caramel into a double boiler and place over hot water to keep the caramel hot. With a dipping fork, place the penuche squares, one at a time, down in the hot caramel. Lift them out and drop them in a bowl of finely ground nuts.
5. Butter the fingers lightly, roll the pieces into round balls, and place them on waxed paper.

PLAIN NOUGAT CHEWS

1. Mix together and stir well
     2 c. sugar
     2 c. glucose
     ½ c. water
2. Place on to boil and, after washing the sides of the kettle, cook to 232°.
3. Beat until stiff
     3 egg whites and then add
     ⅓ of the hot candy syrup slowly to the beaten egg whites. Continue beating.
4. Cook the remaining ⅔ hot candy to 248° and then add it very slowly to the beaten egg mixture. Continue beating until batch is very stiff.
5. Add
     1 c. chopped nuts
     ½ c. candied fruits
6. Add alternately and do not stir too much while adding
     2 tbs. coconut butter
     2 ts. flour. Add
     2 ts. vanilla just before pouring the nougat out on buttered slab. Use the iron bars to keep the nougat in place.

7. Spread the top smoothly and allow candy to cool before cutting. May be eaten plain or chocolate dipped.

HONEY NOUGAT

This is a very good, chewy candy which also makes a choice chocolate center.

1. Mix together well
   1 c. sugar
   ⅓ c. glucose
   ⅓ c. honey
   ¼ c. water
2. Bring to a boil, wash the sides of the kettle, and cook to 252°.
3. Beat until stiff
   2 egg whites and
   ½ ts. salt
4. Pour the hot candy over the beaten egg whites and beat with a beater until creamy.
5. Add
   ½ ts. vanilla. Continue beating until thick.
6. Add
   1 c. chopped walnuts or almonds and pour on a buttered platter to set. Cut into squares. Use plain or dip in chocolate.

FUDGE

Fudge is probably the most common of all candy made in the home. It may prove one of the finest of candies and also may turn out grainy and coarse. The secret is entirely in the cooking process. By following just a few simple rules, one may become an expert in fudge making with never a failure.

The main reason for graining (sugaring) in fudge is that the sugar particles were allowed to cling to the sides of the kettle while the candy was cooking. Just the smallest crystals will turn the fudge to sugar again. To avoid this, the sugar and milk or cream must be thoroughly stirred before being put on to cook. The sides of the kettle must be thoroughly washed in the beginning of the cooking, by dipping a small brush or cloth on a spoon in tepid water and brushing around the sides of the utensil. Extend the brush down into the boiling candy. Shake the brush and dip again in the water and repeat. The lid of the kettle may be placed on the pan to steam away any crystals remaining.

Fudge candies should be cooked slowly and stirred continually while boiling to prevent burning on the bottom of pan and scorching the candy. All candies made with milk and cream and butter should be stirred while cooking. While all candies made with water should not be stirred during the cooking process. Most fudge must be allowed to cool before beating. Sometimes beating the batch when it is too warm will grain the candy.

There are many types of fudge. Try them all.

MY FUDGE

1. Mix altogether and stir well
       2 c. sugar
       2 squares of chocolate
       2 tbs. white syrup
       1/8 ts. salt
       3/4 c. canned milk
       4 tbs. cold water
2. When thoroughly stirred, put on to cook. Cover the kettle for 1 minute as it begins to boil, wash the sides of the kettle, and continue boiling, stirring slowly and evenly.
3. Cook to 232° and remove from heat. Pour out on a buttered slab or platter.
4. Place on top of cooling fudge
       1 tbs. butter
       1 ts. vanilla or a few drops of peppermint
5. When cool, beat until creamy and soft. When the fudge begins to look a little firm, add
       12 marshmallows, cut in pieces
       1 c. nuts. Continue beating until the fudge sets.
6. Spread on a buttered plate. The top of the candy should appear glossy and shiny. Allow to set a few minutes before cutting.

SWEET MILK FUDGE

1. Mix together
       1 can sweetened condensed milk

2 c. sugar
½ c. cold water
2. Cook slowly to 232°, stirring slowly.
3. Remove from heat and add
2 squares of bitter chocolate (melted)
1 tbs. butter
4. Beat until creamy and firm.

HELEN'S FUDGE (Million-Dollar Method, 5 Lbs.)

1. In a large container prepare the following:
4 squares of grated bitter chocolate or 2 pkgs. of chocolate morsels
1 lb. sweet chocolate, grated
1 pt. of marshmallow cream or 1 pkg. marshmallows cut in small pieces
2 tbs. butter
2 ts. vanilla
2. In another kettle place
4½ c. sugar
1 large can milk. Stir until sugar is completely dissolved.
3. Place on to cook. Wash the sides of the kettle and cover for a few moments. After a full rolling boil is reached, continue boiling for 6 minutes, stirring constantly.
4. Remove from heat and pour immediately over the prepared mixture. Stir rapidly to melt the chocolate and marshmallow. Beat for several minutes until fudge begins to set.
5. Add
2 c. broken nut meats
6. When thick, pour on a large, buttered sheet pan and allow to set until firm enough to cut. If you plan on chocolate dipping this fudge, make it the day before.
7. You may divide this batch of candy into 2 or 3 parts. Flavor each part differently, such as adding:
   a. to one part, ½ ts. powdered cloves
   1 ts. vanilla (nuts omitted)
   b. to one part, 1 ts. vanilla
   2 c. chopped pecans
   c. to one part, 3 or 4 drops of oil of peppermint

TAFFY

Many good times have been spent pulling taffy. Children delight in helping to make it.

1. In a kettle put
    3 c. sugar
    1⅓ c. glucose
    1 c. water. Stir well and bring to a boil. Wash the sides of the kettle and cover for a minute. Cook to 248° for a chewy taffy and 254° for a dry taffy.

2. Just before the desired temperature is reached, add
    ½ cube of butter

3. Pour candy on a cold, greased slab or platter and let cool. The edges will cool first, so gently pick them up and fold them over to the center of the candy. Repeat this process until the batch is cool enough to pick up.

4. Begin pulling the taffy by using just the tips of the fingers. Stretch the arms outward, pulling the taffy, then place the ends together. Do not squeeze because squeezing the taffy will make the air escape, and the taffy will be coarse. Light, pretty taffy depends on the pulling.

5. Pull until taffy holds its shape. Clip in pieces with a shears.

6. To make professional taffy, add
    ¼ of a sheet of gelatin
    2 ozs. of coconut butter
    Add the coconut butter just before adding the butter. Soak the gelatin in cold water. Take it out and add to the batch when the candy is removed from the stove. These ingredients are not necessary to make good taffy. Some candymakers use a small amount of paraffin in taffy, however, I have never used it.

7. Flavoring of your choice may be added to the taffy while you are pulling it. Also, the coloring may be added at this time. Nuts, too, may be added in very small pieces.
    Molasses may be added with mint flavoring using
    ¼ c. molasses, added just before removing the taffy from the heat.

OLD ENGLISH TOFFEE

English toffee is a favorite among so many. It is simple to make and takes only a few moments to prepare.

1. In a large, heavy frying pan, place

    ½ lb. butter or margarine, or 1 square of each

    5 tbs. water

    1 c. sugar. Cook, stirring constantly, to a light-brown color and until the cooked candy leaves the sides of the pan. If you prefer a caramel flavor, allow the toffee to become a dark brown by cooking a few minutes longer. Remove from heat and

2. Add

    1 ts. vanilla

    1 c. chopped almonds or other nuts (may be omitted). If you prefer the nuts to have a cooked taste put them in just before the last of cooking time. Pour immediately on cold, buttered marble slab or platter and spread evenly with a spatula. Just as soon as the toffee is cooled sufficiently to pick up without burning your fingers, turn the batch over to keep it from sticking to the marble.

3. Melt in top of double boiler over warm water enough dipping chocolate to spread over top and bottom. Sprinkle freshly chopped almonds over the moist chocolate, and set aside to harden. Break with a tiny candy hammer into generous pieces. Walnuts may be used in place of almonds if you prefer.

CHOCOLATE CHIPS

Chocolate chips candy is very fine, but it requires patience to make it.

You begin by preparing the board which is necessary for making the chips. You will need a ply board ½ inch thick, 12″ x 36″, covered with a piece of white canvas. Place the covered board under an electric light, a reflector, or a heat lamp to heat the canvas. Tilt the board as only half of it should be heated. Now prepare the candy by:

1. Mixing together well

    4 c. sugar

    ½ c. glucose

    1 c. water. Place on to cook, wash the sides of the kettle, and cook to 302°.

2. Add
    ¼ c. molasses and cook to 302° again. Remove from
    heat and pour on an oiled slab to cool. When cooling,
    turn the edges of the batch in to the center. Repeat
    until candy is firm enough to handle.
3. With gloves on, pick up the candy while it is still warm
    and pull like taffy until it's light, but still warm. Now
    fold it together and place on the hot canvas under the
    reflector. Pull the candy into thin strips, light and
    fluffy, until they are ¼ inch thick and ¾ inch wide in
    pieces the length of the canvas. Then mark with a
    knife in pieces 1½ inches long. Turn off the heat and let
    candy cool. When cool, break where it is marked and
    place on waxed paper. Serve plain or dipped in cool
    chocolate.

FILLED CHIP CANDY

1. Make a batch of chocolate chips. Follow the instructions
    closely. When stretching and pulling the batch, you
    may hurriedly place finely chopped nuts cooked in a
    small amount of hot glucose, on the candy. Cover with
    part of the batch and proceed as before.
2. Black walnuts are tasty in filled chips.

RULES FOR CHOCOLATE DIPPING

Items needed include:
1. A marble or slab, made of heavy material such as mica,
    glass, tile, etc. The marble is much preferred. Many
    people have marble-topped tables, antiques, dresser tops,
    etc., in their homes that may be converted into a marble
    for candymaking. A marble also may be secured from
    monument companies or contractors of building con-
    struction.
2. A double boiler and wooden spoons and paddles.
3. Several pieces of plywood to use as boards on which to
    place the dipped chocolates.
4. Roll of waxed paper to cover the boards.
5. Cookie or baking sheets to put candy centers on before
    dipping.

Instructions:

Chocolate dipping is a profession, but the skill may be acquired easily with practice. There are definite rules to be followed, and the success depends upon your determination to succeed. Hand-dipped chocolates are most desirable, but dipping may be accomplished by using a fork. Being a chocolate dipper by profession, I, of course, delight in teaching the hand-dipped method. You, no doubt, will hesitate to place your hand in the melted chocolate but, after a time or two, you will love the thrill you get in working the soft chocolate and trying your skill at dipping.

You may purchase a good grade of dipping chocolate from your neighborhood candy store. It may be obtained in grades (cheap, medium, and best) in light milk chocolate, dark vanilla, and bittersweet. I am partial to the very best grade, because it is pure chocolate and has no wax filler of any kind. It has a much better flavor and is easier to make into the decorative stripes on the tops of the chocolates.

You begin by breaking the chocolate in pieces with a small hammer or ice pick. Place several small pieces in the top part of the double boiler. Place it over hot water and turn the heat on medium until the water begins to boil; then turn the heat as low as possible to keep the chocolate barely warm. Stir the chocolate several times to help the unmelted portion to begin melting. Stirring also prevents it from sticking to the bottom and becoming too hot. Chocolate should never be heated higher than 120° which is much less heat than the hand can stand. Too high a heat may cause the chocolate to become grainy, lose its luster, and even become lumpy.

Rub a piece of cocoa butter across the surface of the marble before putting the melted chocolate on it. This will enable you to scrape the leftover chocolate off easily.

When lifting the top of the double boiler from the water to pour the melted chocolate on the marble, be sure to wipe away the drops of water clinging to it, because a small amount of water dropped in the chocolate may thicken it so much that you may not be able to use it for dipping.

Pour about 2 cups of the melted chocolate in the center of the marble. Allow it to cool slightly while you arrange a board on the right side of you on which to place the chocolates. Cover the board with a strip of waxed paper. Then place a tray of centers to be dipped on the left where you can reach them easily. Begin beating the chocolate by putting your hand in it. With a swirl of the finger form the chocolate into an oval ring on the marble. This will tend to form a surface for the chocolate to rest in and prevent you from spreading it all over the marble. Move the palm around the pile of chocolate, lifting some of it up occasionally to cool it evenly. Chocolate must be cool in order for candies to dry to a shiny, pretty color, and not turn grey and dull. Test the chocolate on the lip, if you are not sure of the coolness by your hand. Some chocolate is too thin for making the striping on the top. In order to thicken it slightly, add one or two drops of cold water. Use a dropper or just dip a finger in the water and let two drops fall in the chocolate. Beat it again for a few turns and then, with flat palm, push the chocolate to one side of the chocolate ring. Slide the fingers through the chocolate, picking up just enough to cover the prepared center. With the left hand, place the prepared center in your right palm and move the fingers gently, moving the center around it with the chocolate. With the thumb push the prepared center forward to the tips of the fingers, tap the back of the fingers lightly on the edge of the marble to remove surplus chocolate, then turn the hand over and with the middle finger place the dipped chocolate on the waxed paper. Gently tap the top to smooth the surface and raise the middle finger from the top, supported by the thumb, and pull a string of chocolate up carefully and make the marking desired to determine the kind of candy dipped, such as the following:

caramels	one plain line drawn up the center
square caramels	one plain line drawn from one corner across to the other
caramel brazils	five e's, starting at the bottom and following around the top to the beginning or one line across the chocolate with the zigzag back to the beginning

butterscotch	B
orange	O
lemon	L
mint	M
cream brazils	C
fudge	drop dip
cherries	a round C or @

There are no set rules of marking. You may use your own ideas if you desire. Usually the type of candy is distinguished by the shape of the pieces. Cream centers are usually round, fudges are square or oblong, etc.

Begin placing the dipped chocolates ½ inch apart at the top of the board nearest you. Continue in a straight line across the board, then follow with another row, until the board is filled. This may be difficult at first but eventually you will be able to do it nicely.

In moving the board to another place when filled, be careful to hold the board straight and not slide the wet chocolates. This will make what we call "feet" on the bottoms. You probably will have difficulty in covering the centers perfectly at first. Finger marks may show a little but, with practice, coating will become easy and you will learn the exact pressure to apply, just enough to cover and not mark the pieces. You may use a small plastic scraper to scrape the chocolate from the fingers and hand when finished. The chocolate also may be scraped from the marble, remelted, and used again. If just a small amount of chocolate is left over, you may make nut clusters by adding roasted peanuts or other nuts and swish them around in the chocolate then picking up small amounts and placing them on the waxed paper. After adding nuts to chocolate it must be all used at that time as the nuts interfere with dipping other candies. If you desire to place a nut or cherry on top of certain centers, place them on when chocolate is still moist. Also, for nut and coconut rolls, drop them in the pan of finely chopped nuts or coconut when chocolate is moist. Pick them up in the palm and roll them round, then place on waxed paper to dry.

Always be sure to have the room in which you are making chocolate centers, storing them for dipping, or dipping them at a temperature of 66° to 68°. Do not chill the centers before dipping as this will cause the chocolates to dry too suddenly, leaving them dull and grey. Keep the dipped chocolates at the same room temperature as they were when dipped as too cold a room will also turn them grey. A direct draft is bad too, so avoid that.

For those who may be able to dip the candies fast, it is well to place some additional melted chocolate on a small pan or pie tin to be cooling, thus time will not be wasted in cooling the chocolate by hand beating.

Chocolate coatings may be mixed together if desired, half milk and half vanilla, etc. It is well to mix them while melting or in the beating process.

If you choose to dip the centers with a fork, melt the chocolate as usual, dip them in the same method as for bonbons (refer to instructions), using a bonbon fork or wire dipper.

In either method arrange the centers to be dipped by placing the flat side down on the waxed paper and the rounded or smooth side up for the top of the chocolate. In some centers this isn't too important, but for such centers as cherry cordials, it is very important in order for the pieces to stand erect.

Allow the dipped chocolates to dry completely before packing them in boxes. When packing, pick each chocolate up with the fingers, touching only the sides of each piece. The candy tends to lose its shine if touched or scratched on the tops. In packing fancy or assorted boxes arrange a variety of different kinds of chocolates to make a tempting appearance. Pieces of the same kind may be placed in rows if preferred.

CHERRY CHOCOLATES (Cordials)

1. Secure firm, large maraschino cherries, drain the juice from them, and place the cherries on a paper towel for a few minutes before dipping them in warm, melted fondant.
2. Have a batch of fondant made in advance. Place a portion of it in the top of a double boiler over hot water. Melt the fondant to a creamy stage, stirring it often. If you prefer flavoring other than that from the cherry

you may add a little almond extract to the fondant while melting it. With a wire fork, or bonbon fork, dip each cherry in the melted fondant, shake the fork, tap it against the edge of the pan, and quickly lay it on a pan or board covered with waxed paper. Allow these to cool at room temperature before dipping them in cooled, melted chocolate.

Cherries must be chocolate dipped soon after dipping in fondant because the juice from the cherries will cause them to leak. This juice is what we want to preserve, because it is what makes the tasty, luscious liquid in good cherry cordials. The juice forms in two or three days after they have been dipped in chocolate. This process is called ripening—the natural juice from the cherry melts the fondant, thus forming the juice. Sometimes this juice will escape through small leaks in the chocolate after the chocolates are dry. To prevent this, spread a little cooled chocolate on the bottoms of the fondant-dipped cherries. Place them on waxed paper until they are dry and then dip them all over in chocolate, making a pretty twirl or a big C on the top of each piece.

VICTORINE CORDIALS

1. Place in a bowl
    1 c. maraschino cherries and add
    1 ts. of victorine flavoring to the juice and allow them to set overnight.
2. Just before dipping, drain off the juice and place the cherries on a paper towel for a few minutes. Dip them in melted fondant and let them cool before dipping in cooled, melted chocolate.
3. Rum flavoring or pure brandy may be used in place of victorine.
4. Use either milk or vanilla dipping chocolate.

HARD CANDIES

It is so much fun to try making hard candies, so try your luck. Follow the directions closely and have a pair of heavy canvas gloves to wear while handling the candy during the cooling and pulling process. A marble slab is as important in making hard candies as it is for every other type of candy.

The cooked batch of candy is poured out on the warm marble. (To warm the marble, wring a towel out of hot water and lay it over the slab. Repeat several times, and this will warm the marble sufficiently.)

As the batch cools, you turn the edges back to the center. When it is thick enough, run a spatula under the batch, lift it up with the spatula and allow the cooled side next to the slab to mix with the warm part. Put on the gloves and lift up the batch. Knead it lightly and fold in the cool side each time. When it holds its shape, cut a piece and roll it in a long roll. Clip it in pieces with a scissors. Work quickly so the balance of the batch won't become too hard before you are ready. After some practice you may attempt to stripe the roll with different colors and make the candy professional-looking. When the pieces are cold put them in a wire sieve, shake them over steaming, boiling water until they are sticky, then pour them quickly into a pan of sugar. Sieve the sugar away and then store them in a jar. This method is called sanding and will prevent the drops from sticking together. When making drop candies allow them to become cold, then store and pack.

Shall we begin by making a batch of:

LEMON DROPS

1. Mix together and stir until sugar is dissolved
     4 c. sugar
     1 c. water
     ½ c. glucose
2. Bring to a boil, wash the sides of the kettle, also cover the kettle for a few moments. Then boil to 302° without stirring.
3. Oil the marble slab with pure mineral oil and pour the candy on it to cool.
4. Follow the instructions above for handling the candy while cooling.
5. Mix into a paste and add to cooled candy
     2 ts. powdered tartaric acid (may be purchased at a drug store)
     ¼ ts. lemon emulsion

6. Do not add the acid while candy is too hot as it will make the batch taste bitter.
7. Roll, cut, and finish as instructed.

CANDY CANES

1. Combine and stir until sugar is dissolved
   2 c. sugar
   ½ c. glucose
   ½ c. water
   ¼ ts. cream of tartar
2. Cook slowly without stirring. Wash the sides of the kettle, and also cover the kettle with a lid for a few moments. Cook until the candy reaches 258°, then remove from heat and add flavor such as peppermint, wintergreen, annis, etc., to taste.
3. Divide the cooked syrup in two parts. Color one part red, using liquid color or paste. The other part may be left white or colored as desired.
4. Pour out on greased platters and, when cool enough to handle, pull each part separately. Roll in long ropes, twist the red batch around the other batch, pull until each color adheres to the other, then with a scissors, clip pieces the size of the canes desired. Form the handles of the canes at the top of one end. Hang on a stretched wire until needed.

BUTTERSCOTCH DROPS OR WAFERS

1. Combine and stir well
   ½ c. brown sugar
   ½ c. sugar
   3 tbs. glucose or white syrup
   3 tbs. heavy cream
   ¼ c. water
2. When well mixed, put on to cook.
3. Wash the sides of the kettle and cook to 252°, then add
   ¼ c. butter. Continue cooking to 262°, or to a light crack stage. Remove from heat and add
   ¼ ts. salt
   1½ ts. vanilla
4. Using a funnel, drop onto an oiled slab in round wafers, or pour on an oiled pan and break in pieces.

BRAZIL NUT BRITTLE

1. Caramelize in a large frying pan on low heat
     2 c. sugar
     ½ ts. salt
2. Shake the pan until the sugar is all dissolved and it reaches a brown color. Add and stir until all of the sugar is dissolved
     1 c. sugar
     2 c. Brazil nut pieces
3. Add
     2½ tbs. butter. Spread quickly on a greased platter or marble.
     Break into pieces when cool.

HOREHOUND DROPS

1. Mix together
     4 c. sugar
     ½ c. glucose
2. Steep
     ¼ oz. horehound tea (obtain at drug store) and
     1 c. water. Strain and add to the sugar. Mix well.
3. Cook, after washing the sides of the kettle and covering the kettle, to 307°, without stirring. Then pour on an oiled marble to cool.
4. Follow the instructions for handling hard candy.

MENTHOL DROPS

1. Make a batch of horehound drops and, while kneading, add
     ⅛ ts. menthol crystals (from the drug store)
2. Fold the batch over and over to work the crystals through the candy, then proceed as instructed.

MOLASSES-MINT DROPS

1. Make one batch of lemon drops and add
     ½ c. molasses in place of ½ c. glucose
     a few drops of oil of peppermint in place of lemon acid

CANDY SUCKERS

Make a treat for the young folk. Purchase some round steel rings from a hardware store. Wash them and place them on the oiled marble. Place a sucker stick (purchased from the candy factories) under each ring, or through an opening in the ring.

Make one batch of hard candy and pour it into the rings. Let set until hard.

1. Mix together
   - 4 c. sugar
   - ½ c. glucose
   - 1 c. water. Stir well. Cook without stirring to 302°. Wash the sides of the kettle at the beginning of the boiling.
2. Remove from heat and add the flavoring of your choice: 1 ts. of lemon, orange, a few drops of peppermint, or oil of cassia, etc. Color any color desired.
3. If you have no rings to use for the suckers, mold candy with gloves on hands until it is firm enough to roll in balls. Flatten balls with the palm of the hand, and insert the sticks while candy is still warm.

MOLASSES SUCKERS

1. Mix together
   - 3 c. sugar
   - ½ c. glucose
   - ¾ c. water. Mix well until sugar is dissolved.
2. Boil without stirring, wash the sides of the kettle, and cook to 272°. Add
   - ¼ c. molasses. Don't stir. Cook to 272° again.
3. Pour out on an oiled slab and follow the instructions given in the beginning of the chapter. Mold the candy into balls, place a stick in each, flatten with the palm of the hand, and set aside to cool.
4. These suckers may be chocolate coated, if desired, by dipping the cool suckers in cool chocolate. Place on a waxed paper to dry.

PEANUT BUTTER CHIPS

1. Place
   - 1 c. peanut butter in a small pan and heat slowly.

Then add enough dry flour to make a dough. Keep it hot until needed.

2. Make a batch of chips (refer to recipe for chocolate chips).
3. When it is cool enough on the slab, place gloves on hands, pull off a piece of candy the size of an orange, and place it on the hot, heavy cloth under a light. Turn it occasionally to prevent it from sticking to the cloth.
4. Pull and stretch the balance of the batch out to ½ inch thick and place it on the cloth under the heat. Put the hot peanut butter in the center of the batch, fold the sides over it, dampen the edges so they will stick together, and seal in the peanut butter. Now stretch it lengthwise again, folding the batch over 3 or 4 times or more. Then hurriedly stretch the small piece reserved under the heat in all directions until it is large enough to make a coating for the pulled part. Fold edges over and be sure the batch is all covered. Now stretch and spin the chips out thin enough to mark and break.
5. When cool, dip in cooled chocolate and place on waxed paper.

PRALINES

1. Mix together in a kettle
   2½ c. brown sugar
   1 c. water
   ⅛ ts. cream of tartar
   1½ ts. mapleine flavoring
2. Stir until sugar is dissolved, then place on to boil. Wash the sides of the kettle twice and cover with the lid for a few seconds. Cook to 228°. Do not stir while cooking.
3. Remove from heat and beat for 4 minutes.
4. Dip out on waxed paper. When making large quantities, use a bun pan with cup indentations rather than dip the pralines out on paper.

GLAZED NUTS

1. Have ready the nuts you wish to use, such as almonds, brazils, pecans, philberts, walnuts, etc.
   2 c. choice nuts. Place in oven for 5 to 10 minutes at 300° to become just warm.

2. In a kettle place
    3 c. sugar
    1 c. glucose
    1 c. water. Stir until sugar is dissolved.
3. Bring to a boil, wash the sugar from the sides of the
    kettle, place the lid on the kettle for 1 minute, and then
    boil to 302°. Add
    ½ of a square of butter and warmed nut meats.
    Continue cooking with heat turned down until the
    nuts are warmed through, about 2 minutes.
4. Remove from heat and spread quickly on an oiled slab
    or platter. When cool, break into pieces.

PEANUT BRITTLE

Peanut brittle is a favorite among candy lovers. It is
easy to make. Read through the recipe and arrange all material necessary in advance.
1. Measure out in kettle and stir well
    3 c. sugar
    1 c. glucose
    1 c. water
2. Bring to a boil, wash the sides of the kettle, and boil to
    232°. Add
    3 c. unroasted raw peanuts
3. When candy begins boiling, stir slowly with a wooden
    paddle. Avoid rubbing the paddle around the sides of
    pan. This causes a grain.
4. Have ready in a small dish, mixed together
    1 ts. vanilla
    ½ ts. salt
    1 ts. soda
5. Cook the sugar and peanuts to 305°, then add
    ¼ cube of butter. Remove candy from the stove,
    immediately add the soda and salt and vanilla, and
    stir briskly. Pour out on an oiled marble. Spread
    quickly with the back of the spoon.
6. When the brittle has cooled sufficiently to touch with
    the tips of the fingers, pick up the batch of brittle and
    turn it over. This is to force the peanuts to come to
    the surface on both sides. When hardened enough,
    break with a small hammer.

BROWN SUGAR POPCORN CRISP

Use the same method as for molasses popcorn crisp.
1. Mix together and cook as instructed at 282°
    1½ c. sugar
    1 c. brown sugar
    ½ c. glucose
    ¾ c. water
2. Add
    ½ cube butter
    1 ts. soda and
    1 ts. vanilla, mixed
    1 ts. salt (Refer to instructions on molasses popcorn crisp.)

NUT CHEWS

1. In a kettle put
    2 c. sugar
    1⅓ c. glucose
    ½ c. water. Boil to 292°.
2. Then add
    2 lbs. of assorted nuts. Just let the nuts warm through, then remove from heat.
3. Add
    1 ts. vanilla. Pour out on buttered slab.
    Fold the edges in to the center as soon as you can handle the candy. Fold the bottom part in and roll quickly to ½-inch thickness. Cut into squares while it is still hot.
4. Store in jars or waxed paper to keep the chews from becoming sticky.

SUGARED NUTS

1. Prepare nuts to be sugared and place them in a moderate oven to warm thoroughly.
2. Place in a kettle and stir well
    1 c. sugar
    ½ c. water
    1 ts. cinnamon or cloves
    1 ts. salt

3. Bring to a boil and cook to 228° without stirring. Remove from heat and add
     2½ c. warm nuts
     1½ ts. vanilla
4. Stir gently until mixture becomes creamy. Then turn out on waxed paper and separate each nut piece. These may be served warm or stored in a tin for days.

SUGARED NUTS

1. In a pan place
     1½ c. sugar
     ¼ c. honey
     ½ c. water. Cook to 242°.
2. Remove from heat and add
     1 ts. vanilla
3. Beat until syrup begins to thicken, then add enough whole nut pieces to use up all the syrup.
4. Dip out each nut and drop on waxed paper to harden. If nut pieces are used, dip them out in clusters.
     In place of vanilla you may add
     1 ts. cinnamon or
     1 tbs. grated orange rind

POPCORN BALLS

1. Pop a large panful of popcorn. Remove all unpopped kernels.
2. In a saucepan mix together
     1 c. sugar
     ½ c. syrup
     1 ts. cream of tartar
     Bring to a boil and cook without stirring to a hard cook test or 242°.
3. Remove from heat and add
     1 ts. butter
     ¼ ts. soda
     1 ts. flavoring (your choice)
     Color if desired.
4. Pour quickly over popped corn. Stir with a wooden spoon and then mold into large, firm balls in the palms of your hands. Place on waxed paper until served.

ORANGE GLAZED WALNUTS

1. Boil slowly to 232°
   1½ c. sugar
   ½ c. orange juice
2. Remove from heat and add
   1 ts. grated orange rind
   ½ lb. large walnut halves or pieces
3. Stir carefully until syrup looks cloudy and is creamy. Quickly drop from spoon on waxed paper. Separate if single pieces are desired, or drop in clusters.

HONEY SUGARED WALNUTS

1. Combine in a saucepan
   1½ c. sugar
   ¼ c. honey
   ½ c. water
   Mix until sugar is dissolved and cook slowly to 232°. Remove from heat and cool slightly.
2. Add and stir until thick enough to drop from a spoon on a wax paper
   1 ts. flavoring (your choice)
   3 c. walnuts or pecans
3. Cinnamon may be added if you prefer a spicy flavor.

QUICK METHOD SUGARED NUTS

1. Whip until light
   2 egg whites
   2 c. powdered sugar
   ½ ts. cream of tartar
   1 ts. vanilla
   ½ ts. ground cloves (may be omitted)
2. Mix altogether and pour assorted nut meats into mixture and stir until each nut is covered. Spoon out on wax paper to dry. Serve as desired.

SWEDISH COATED NUTS

1. Blanch and toast
   1 lb. of almonds
2. Toast
   1 lb. of pecans

3. Beat until stiff
    4 egg whites and add while beating
    2 c. sugar, a little at a time. Continue beating until it
    holds in peaks.
4. Add
    1 ts. of vanilla
    1/4 ts. salt
5. Pour in the roasted nuts and stir until they are well coated.
6. Melt in a large, shallow pan
    1/2 lb. butter or margarine. Pour the coated nuts in and mix them until the butter is absorbed.
7. Place in pan full of nuts in a 325° oven for 45 minutes. Stir them over every 10 or 15 minutes, until they are coated with a delicious, brown, sweet covering. Serve warm or when cooled. These are especially nice for holiday time.

SUGAR CORN

1. Sort
    4 qts. popped corn
2. In a saucepan melt
    2 tbs. butter. Add
    2 c. brown sugar
    1/2 c. water. Mix well and boil for 16 full minutes.
3. Pour over corn, mixing with a wooden paddle. Place in bowls ready to serve.

CRACKERJACK

1. Place in a large container
    2 qts. popped corn, just the large full kernels and
    1 c. roasted peanuts
2. Mix together
    1 c. sugar
    1/3 c. molasses
    1/3 c. water
    1 tbs. vinegar
    2 tbs. butter. Boil to a hard test in cold water
3. Remove from heat and add
    1/8 ts. soda
    1/2 ts. vanilla

4. Pour quickly over corn and peanuts and stir with a wooden spoon. Cool and serve.

MOLASSES POPCORN CRISP

1. Pop, pick out full kernels, put in a large pan, and keep warm in the oven at 225°
   ½ lb. popcorn
2. Mix together and stir well
   2 c. sugar
   1 c. glucose
   ½ c. water
3. Bring to a boil and cook without stirring, washing the sides, to 232°. Then add
   1 c. raw Spanish peanuts. Cook again to 282°, stirring slowly, then add
   ½ c. molasses
   1 ts. salt. Stir again and cook to 292°. Add
   ½ c. butter. When well mixed, remove from heat and add
   1 ts. vanilla and
   1 ts. soda mixed
4. Pour the hot syrup over the warm, popped corn and stir quickly. This may be made into balls by forming them in the palms of the hands and placing them on waxed paper.

PEANUT CRISPIES

1. In a flat baking tin arrange
   2 lbs. Spanish peanuts, and place them in a moderate oven to roast until they are light brown. Pour them on a board or paper and crush them with a rolling pin. The husks will release from the peanuts. Brush them away. Then place nuts back in the oven with 2 lbs. of coconut butter. Stir and keep them hot.
2. In a kettle mix and stir well
   2 c. sugar
   ¾ c. glucose
   ½ c. water. Cook to 293°. Be sure to wash the sides of kettle in the beginning of the boiling.

3. Add
   ¼ of a cube of butter. Remove from heat, then add the following mixed together
   ½ ts. salt
   1 ts. soda
   1 ts. vanilla
4. Quickly add the hot peanuts and pour on an oiled marble. Separate in pieces.

ALMOND COCONUT CRUNCH

1. In a kettle place
   3 c. sugar
   1½ c. glucose
   1 c. water. Mix well and place on to boil. Cook to 292°. Wash the sides of the kettle.
2. Then add and stir until dissolved
   ¼ lb. butter. Add
   ½ lb. roasted chopped almonds. Stir and cook 1 minute longer.
3. Remove from heat and add
   1 ts. soda
   ½ ts. salt
   1 ts. almond flavoring. Stir quickly and pour out on an oiled marble slab which has been covered with coconut. Spread out evenly and sprinkle the top with coconut, then roll the coconut in with a rolling pin.
4. When cool, break in pieces. Store in candy cans.

ROCKY ROAD

1. Melt slowly in top of double boiler over warm water
   2 lbs. dipping chocolate (light or dark)
2. Cut in small pieces and place on buttered cookie sheets
   40 marshmallows. Sprinkle over the marshmallow pieces
   1 c. chopped walnuts
3. Pour ½ of the melted chocolate over the top of marshmallows and nuts.
4. Repeat making two layers of each.
5. Put aside to set.
6. When cool and set, cut in pieces and serve.

TOFFEE CLUSTERS

1. Make a batch of Old English toffee and crush it with the rolling pin.
2. Add the crumbs to cooled melted chocolate. Place in clusters on waxed paper to cool.

PEANUT CLUSTERS

1. Pour fresh, roasted peanuts into a small amount of cooled melted chocolate. Use enough peanuts to take up the amount of chocolate used.
2. Place in small clusters on a waxed paper to set.

FILLED PEANUT CLUSTERS

1. Flavor to taste, a small amount of fondant or white fudge. Roll in a long roll and cut in small pieces. Place the pieces as the centers for each cluster. Cover with the peanut and chocolate mixture. Set aside to cool.

CHOCOLATE COATED BRAZILS

1. Use large Brazil nuts. Dip by hand in cooled chocolate and stripe with a straight line across each nut. Place on waxed paper to dry.

CHOCOLATE COATED ALMONDS

1. Dip almond nuts singly or in clusters of 3 in cooled chocolate. Drop on waxed paper to dry.

GROUND ALMOND CLUSTERS

1. Run almonds through a food chopper, then place the ground nuts in cooled chocolate and drop on waxed paper in clusters.

MARZIPAN

1. Beat in mixing bowl
      1 lb. of almond paste

2. Add
     4 egg whites
     1 oz. nulomoline. Beat for 3 minutes.
3. Then add
     2 lbs. powdered sugar. Beat for 5 minutes.
4. Flavor with your choice of flavoring:
     rose and vanilla
     rum and vanilla, or
     fruit flavor of any kind
5. By adding to or lessening the amount of powdered sugar, marzipan may be made heavier or softer.
6. Mold into shapes of every kind of fruit. For pears, use a yellow-shaded marzipan. Gently touch a drop of red coloring on one side, with the tip of the finger blend the coloring to shade the cheek of the pear, use a whole clove to represent the bottom, and roll a small stem of the marzipan. For peaches, roll round, tint as for pears, form a leaf from frosting to attach to the stem. For cherries, color red, make stems and leaves of frosting. For bananas, color yellow, make the brown stripes down the sides with marzipan flavored and colored with melted milk chocolate. Try to match all fruits to your liking.

HOLIDAY CANDIED ORANGE PEEL

1. Wash and peel
     6 large oranges
2. Mix together
     4 c. water
     1 tbs. salt. Pour this over the peels and let them stand overnight.
3. Drain and wash the peels thoroughly in several rinsings of cold water. Place on to cook in enough cold water to cover them. Bring to a boil, drain off the water, and boil again. Do this three times, changing the water each time.
4. Cut the peels in 1/4-inch strips with a scissors.
5. In a kettle place
     3 c. of the peels and add
     3 c. sugar and enough water to cover. Cook slowly until peels are clear and translucent.

6. Remove from heat, drain, then roll them quickly in sugar, and place on a rack to dry.

The syrup from the peels may be used in fruit cakes, to top orange rolls, etc.

SUMMER COATING

Summer Coating is a delightful tasting coating for a substitute for chocolate in dipping centers and Bon Bons, obtainable in white or pastels, or may be tinted in the shade you prefer by adding pure food coloring. It may be melted like chocolate over warm water and hand dipped just like chocolates. It is very nice for those who do not tolerate chocolate but like candy. It may be purchased at candy stores or at supply houses.

Hot and Cold Drinks

Many tasty drinks may be prepared at home for parties, afternoon snacks, dinner meals, etc.

HOT SPICY PUNCH

1. Tie in a cheesecloth or put in a large, metal tea ball
    ½ c. tea leaves
    4 sticks cinnamon
    6 whole cloves
    Submerge in
    2 qts. boiling water
    Remove from heat and steep 10 minutes, then remove tea bag.
2. Mix well and pour into hot tea
    ½ c. sugar
    1 c. lemon juice
    1 c. orange juice
    4 c. pineapple juice
    2 c. cranberry juice
    8 c. sweet cider
3. Just before serving add
    1 large bottle of ginger ale

HOT CRANBERRY PUNCH

1. Cook together until berries are tender
    1 qt. cranberries
    1 qt. water
    6 whole cloves
    Put them through a sieve.
2. Add to the juice
    1½ c. sugar
    ½ c. orange juice
    2 tbs. lemon juice
    Heat to boiling point and add
    2 c. water

HOT GRAPE CLARET

1. Bring to a boil
   - 1 qt. grape juice
   - ½ c. lemon juice
   - 1 stick cinnamon
   - 6 whole cloves
2. Just before serving add
   - 1 pt. bottle of claret

SPICED APPLE CIDER

1. Boil for 15 minutes
   - 2 qts. apple cider
   - 1 qt. tea—may substitute 1 qt. water
   - Juice from
   - 3 limes
   - 2 lemons
   - 3 oranges
   - ¼ ts. cinnamon
   - 3 whole cloves
   - ¼ ts. allspice
   - ¼ ts. mace
   - ½ c. brown sugar
2. Serve hot with orange slices.

HOT SPICED GRAPE JUICE

1. Bring to a boil
   - 2 c. grape juice
   - ½ c. sugar
   - 1 stick cinnamon
   - 1 ts. whole cloves
   - 1 ts. lemon juice
   - 1 can fresh-frozen orange juice
2. Strain and serve hot.

HOT CHOCOLATE (By Alta)

1. Combine in a saucepan and stir until sugar is dissolved
   - 5 squares bitter chocolate
   - 1 c. water
   - 1½ c. sugar

2. Cook, stirring often, for 4 minutes. Remove from heat and cool in refrigerator.
3. When cool, fold in
    ½ pt. whipped cream. Place in covered jar and keep in refrigerator until ready to use.
4. To serve, heat milk and add
    1 ts. chocolate mix to
    1 c. hot milk. Stir and serve.

COLD PUNCH AND DRINKS

CRANBERRY PUNCH

1. To make 5 qts., use
    2½ c. cranberry juice
    2 c. water
    3 c. orange juice
    1½ c. lemon juice
    2 c. grape juice
2. Keep chilled. When ready to serve, add enough sparkling water and sugar to suit taste.

RASPBERRY PUNCH

1. Dissolve
    3 pkgs. raspberry jello in
    4 c. boiling water
2. Add juice from
    9 oranges
    3 limes
    5 lemons
3. Add sugar to suit taste and
    4 c. cold water
    1 bottle of ginger ale
    1 pkg. frozen raspberries
4. Chill and serve.

MINT PUNCH

1. Squeeze the juice from
    2 limes
    2 lemons and add
    1 large can pineapple juice

2. Add sugar to suit taste and enough cold water to make the strength desired.

FRUIT COCKTAIL DRINK

1. Make a syrup from juice of
   6 lemons
   6 oranges
   2½ c. sugar
   2 sprigs mint
   Boil for a few minutes, then cool. Strain and pour over melon balls. Garnish with mint leaves dipped in powdered sugar.

FROZEN PINEAPPLE SLUSH

1. Mix together the juice from
   6 oranges
   6 lemons and add
   5 mashed bananas
2. Make a syrup of
   4 c. sugar
   7 c. water. Stir until dissolved and add to the juices.
3. Add
   1 qt. can crushed pineapple. Freeze until slushy.
4. When ready to serve, fill glasses ¾ full. Finish filling glasses with Seven-Up.

Sugar Ornaments

These are fun to make and decorate. Let the whole family join you in making these fascinating items, so easy and so new in cake decorating.

You will spend many happy hours in painting and decorating these ornaments and they will add a festive touch to cakes and will serve as banquet and special-occasion favors. They are very inexpensive to make.

When forming these ornaments it is advisable to drop them on a small cardboard the size of the mold instead of placing them on wax paper as in sugar bells. This will protect them from breaking. Proceed in making as many ornaments as desired.

If the molds become sticky, dust with a small pastry or other small brush dipped in cornstarch.

Use only a damp cloth to wipe the molds. Never use water to wash them.

Allow the ornaments to dry at room temperature.

Begin painting by using artist's small brushes, washing them after each color used.

Decorate them with decorative frosting using decorating tips and candy decors, dragees, colored sugar, and all frosting decorations.

Refer to page 108, Sugar Bells, for the recipe.

To paint begin by using

1. 1 egg white unbeaten and divided into small containers and 1 to 2 drops of liquid coloring mixed slightly.
    Paint each ornament according to your imagination.

2. Decorate them with frosting and while it it still damp add the decorative decors, candies, colored sugar, and frosting decorations which have been made in advance.

3. Each ornament, when painted and decorated, may be placed on a small cookie with a small amount of frosting to hold it in an upright position, when using it for a favor.

4. Crystal eggs or panorama eggs may be made in the same

way as sugar bells by making one half of the egg at a time and after grooving them out join them together with a little frosting and let them dry. It is wise to scrape a small amount of the sugar from one side of one of the halves of the molded egg to protect it from rolling. These eggs may be beautifully decorated and small frosting figures and flowers may be inserted inside of the sugar egg.

Index